Canadian Special Publication of Fisheries and Aquatic Scien

Salmonid Age at Maturity

Edited by

David J. Meerburg

Department of Fisheries and Oceans
Resource Research Branch
Ottawa, Ontario K1A 0E6

Department of Fisheries and Oceans
Ottawa 1986

Published by   Publié par

 Fisheries   Pêches
and Oceans   et Océans

Information and   Direction de l'information
Publications Branch   et des publications

Ottawa K1A 0E6

Canada: $10.00   Cat. No. Fs 41-31/89E
Other countries: $12.00   ISBN 0-660-12057-7
ISSN 0706-6481

Price subject to change without notice

Director and Editor-in-Chief: J. Watson, Ph.D.
Editorial and Publishing Services: G. J. Neville
Typesetter: K.G. Campbell Corporation, Ottawa, Ont.
Printer: K.G. Campbell Corporation, Ottawa, Ont.
Cover Design: André, Gordon and Laundreth Inc., Ottawa, Ontario

This publication has been peer reviewed.

Correct citation for this publication:

MEERBURG, D. J. [ed.]. 1986. Salmonid age at maturity.
Can. Spec. Publ. Fish. Aquat. Sci. 89: 118 p.

Contents

Abstract

MEERBURG, D. J. [ED.]. 1986. Salmonid age at maturity. Can. Spec. Publ. Fish. Aquat. Sci. 89: 118 p.

This publication contains the proceedings and contributed papers of an international workshop on salmonid age at maturity convened at the Biological Station in St. Andrew's, New Brunswick, September 25−28, 1984. The Anadromous and Catadromous Fish Subcommittee of the Canadian Atlantic Fisheries Scientific Advisory Committee (CAFSAC) organized this workshop to assess the biological, genetic and environmental factors which affect age and size at maturity of Atlantic salmon (*Salmo salar*), as well as other salmonid species (*Oncorhynchus* spp.). The workshop reviewed current knowledge on this topic and provided a forum for discussion and the development of synthesis papers which address the implications of varying sea-ages at maturity on yield to the fisheries and the effect of such fisheries on subsequent age at maturity.

Résumé

MEERBURG, D. J. [ED.]. 1986. Salmonid age at maturity. Can. Spec. Publ. Fish. Aquat. Sci. 89: 118 p.

La présente publication contient les actes et les documents présentés d'un atelier international sur l'âge des salmonidés à maturité qui s'est tenu à la station de biologie de St. Andrew's (Nouveau-Brunswick) du 25 au 28 septembre 1984. Le sous-comité des poissons anadromes, catadromes et dulçaquicoles du Comité scientifique consultatif des pêches du Canada dans l'Atlantique (CSCPCA) a organisé cet atelier pour évaluer les facteurs biologiques, génétiques et environnementaux qui influent sur l'âge et la taille à maturité du saumon de l'Atlantique (*Salmo salar*) et d'autres espèces de salmonidés (espèces *Oncorhynchus*). L'atelier en question a permis de faire le point des connaissances sur le sujet, de procéder à des échanges de vues et d'élaborer des documents de synthèse portant sur les répercussions de différents âges (en mer) à maturité sur le rendement de la pêche, et les effets subséquents de la pêche sur les âges à maturité.

Prologue and Acknowledgments

The Anadromous and Catadromous Subcommittee of the Canadian Atlantic Fisheries Scientific Advisory Committee (CAFSAC) is charged with the task of advising fishery managers as to appropriate levels of exploitation of Atlantic salmon stocks so as to provide acceptable numbers of spawners for major salmon-producing rivers in Atlantic Canada. This task is complicated by the remarkably plastic life cycle of *Salmo salar*; the progeny from a given spawning may be represented by diverse spawning types from mature male parr through 1-sea-winter (grilse) and multi-sea-winter (MSW) maiden spawners to grilse and MSW salmon spawning for their second or subsequent times (Saunders and Schom 1985). Of particular concern is the length of sea life before first spawning which varies from 1 to 3 and rarely as much as 5 years. Grilse are much smaller than MSW salmon and are less valuable to both anglers and commercial fishermen. Gardner's (1976) review of the extensive literature on factors which may influence the sea-age and maturation of *S. salar* shows both genetic and environmental influences on sea age at maturity. Effective management of the species demands a fuller understanding than we now have of these genetic and environmental influences. Assessment biologists and managers need a better appreciation of the grilse−MSW salmon phenomenon and the factors influencing sea age at maturity as a basis for deciding what mixture of grilse and MSW salmon should be available as spawners in order to maintain or augment populations sizes of salmon with appropriate sea age structure. These needs resulted in the Anadromous and Catadromous Subcommittee of CAFSAC organizing a workshop to assess the genetic and environmental factors which affect age and size at maturity of *S. salar* with the aim of providing a more enlightened management approach to the salmon resource in the Miramichi and other rivers in Atlantic Canada. The Steering committee of CAFSAC posed the specific questions: how does the proportion of total egg deposition contributed by MSW salmon influence the production of MSW salmon by the Miramichi stock(s); does age at maturity of male salmon (MSW vs. grilse vs. mature parr) influence the proportion of grilse and MSW salmon produced by Miramichi stocks and how should this be considered in establishing target numbers of spawners?

A Steering Committee comprised of Michael Chadwick, David Meerburg (Chairman), David Reddin, John Ritter, and Richard Saunders planned the workshop which was held at the St. Andrews Biological Station from September 25−28, 1984. We were fortunate in having the participation of Atlantic Salmon biologists from Scotland, Norway and the United States and Pacific Salmon biologists from British Columbia in addition to those in the Atlantic provinces who regularly or occasionally contribute during CAFSAC deliberations. I thank the authors of the 10 experience papers and four synthesis papers which appear in these Proceedings. The following participants, whose names do not appear among the authors of those papers, contributed significantly during discussions of the experience papers and work sessions to develop ideas for the synthesis papers: Terrance Beacham; Richard Cutting; Eugene Henderson; David Meerburg; Gunnar Naevdal; Randal Peterman and Arnold Sutterlin. I thank David Meerburg and Ann Luelo whose careful attention to organizational details allowed the meeting to run smoothly and for all participants to benefit from an open exchange of information and ideas which developed as a result of this meeting of salmon biologists. I thank both the participants in the Workshop and others who provided critical peer review of the manuscripts and the Scientific Information and Publication Branch of the Department of Fisheries and Oceans for publication of these Proceedings.

References

GARDNER, M. L. 1976. A review of factors which may influence the sea-age and maturation of Atlantic salmon, *Salmo salar* L. J. Fish. Biol. 9: 289−327.

SAUNDERS, R. L., AND C. B. SCHOM. 1985. Importance of the variation in life history parameters of Atlantic salmon (*Salmo salar*). Can. J. Fish. Aquat. Sci. 42: 615−618.

RICHARD L. SAUNDERS
Workshop Chairman

CHAIRMAN'S INTRODUCTION

The Scientific and Management Implications of Age and Size at Sexual Maturity in Atlantic Salmon (*Salmo salar*)

Richard L. Saunders

*Fisheries and Environmental Sciences, Fisheries Research Branch, Department of Fisheries and Oceans,
Biological Station, St. Andrews, N.B. E0G 2X0*

Abstract

SAUNDERS, R. L. 1986. The scientific and management implications of age and size at sexual maturity in Atlantic salmon (*Salmo salar*), p. 3–6. *In* D. J. Meerburg [ed.] Salmonid age at maturity. Can. Spec. Publ. Fish. Aquat. Sci. 89.

Stocks of Atlantic salmon (*Salmo salar*) are characterized as having one-sea-winter (grilse) or multiple-sea-winter (MSW) or a combination of these spawning types. Management of salmon is focused largely on the grilse–MSW salmon phenomenon because the MSW fish are larger and more valuable. Deliberate selection of larger salmon by commercial fisheries has resulted in reduced age and size of spawners. Management of salmon is concerned with possible genetic implications of such size-selective fisheries. The purpose of our workshop is to consider the question: to what extent do genetics and the environment determine age at maturity? It is clear that both genetics and the environment influence age at maturity. In our workshop we evaluate the relative contributions of and interactions between genotype and environment. Evidence is presented that maturation of parr and marine stages can be made earlier or later or prevented by manipulating the environment, i.e., by regulating time of first feeding and by thermal management. The "decision" to commence maturation appears to depend on physiological–biochemical conditions which appear to be determined genetically. The genetic influence appears, then, to be in the form of a capability with rather wide latitude, awaiting the appropriate environmental and physiological–biochemical conditions rather than a preset array of biochemical reactions and developments ordained to take place at a given time or age.

Résumé

SAUNDERS, R. L. 1986. The scientific and management implications of age and size at sexual maturity in Atlantic salmon (*Salmo salar*), p. 3–6. *In* D. J. Meerburg [ed.] Salmonid age at maturity. Can. Spec. Publ. Fish. Aquat. Sci. 89.

Les peuplements de saumons atlantiques (*Salmo salar*) sont caractérisés par leurs types de fraie : unibermarins (madeleineaux) ou polybermarins (PBM) ou une combinaison des deux. La gestion du saumon porte surtout sur le phénomène madeleineau–saumon PBM parce que les poissons PBM sont plus gros et possèdent une plus grande valeur. La sélection des plus gros saumons par les pêcheurs commerciaux a donné lieu à une réduction de l'âge et de la taille des géniteurs. En gestion du saumon, il est question des implications génétiques possibles des pêches sélectives suivant la taille. L'objet de notre atelier est de réfléchir à la question suivante : dans quelle mesure la génétique et l'environnement déterminent-ils l'âge à la maturité? Il est clair que tant la génétique que l'environnement influent sur l'âge et la maturité. Dans notre atelier, nous évaluons la contribution relative du génotype et de l'environnement ainsi que les interactions entre ces éléments. Il est démontré que l'arrivée à maturité du tacon et que les stades marins peuvent se faire plus tôt ou plus tard ou peuvent être empêchés par la manipulation de l'environnement, c'est-à-dire par détermination du moment de la première alimentation et par gestion thermique. La « décision » d'entreprendre le processus qui conduit à maturité semble dépendre des conditions physiologiques–biochimiques, lesquelles semblent à leur tour être déterminées génétiquement. L'influence génétique semble donc prendre la forme d'une capacité possédant une latitude plutôt large, dans l'attente des conditions environnementales et physiologiques–biochimiques appropriées plutôt qu'un réseau préétabli de réactions et de développements biochimiques destinés à se produire à un moment ou à un âge donnés.

Atlantic salmon (*Salmo salar*) shows great variability in several aspects of its life cycle: sexual maturation of male parr; age at smolting; seasonal patterns of adult return from the sea; sea-age and size at sexual maturity and short and long interval between maiden and subsequent spawning (Saunders 1981). Sea-age at maturity has been the subject of many scientific investigations dealing with *S. salar* (Gardner 1976) and has important implications in management for optimum value in commercial and angling fisheries and in the aquaculture industry. The length of sea life before first spawning varies commonly from 1 to 3 and rarely to 4 or 5 yr. Salmon maturing after one sea-winter (14–17 mo at sea) are called grilse. Multiple-sea-winter (MSW) fish are referred to as larger salmon. Grilse commonly weigh from 1.5 to 3.0 kg, while maiden 2- and 3-sea-winter salmon weigh from 3 to 7 and 7 to 12 kg, respectively.

Stocks of Atlantic salmon are characterized as having grilse, multiple-sea-winter (MSW), or a combination of the two spawning types. There may be year-to-year variation in the grilse—MSW salmon ratio and long- or short-term trends towards one type or the other. While MSW salmon may weigh 2–3 times more than grilse, the total biomass contribution of grilse often exceeds that of MSW salmon owing to stock differences in the grilse:MSW salmon ratio or to greater natural and fishing mortality of MSW salmon (Bailey and Saunders 1984). Irrespective of biomass considerations, MSW salmon are usually considered more valuable than grilse in both commercial and angling fisheries because of their larger size.

The period of greatest natural mortality of post-smolts is probably the first few weeks after they enter the sea (Larsson 1983). Grilse and MSW salmon share this period of heavy mortality plus a reduced and perhaps similar rate of natural mortality during the next year until grilse leave their feeding grounds and return to fresh water. MSW salmon continue to suffer natural and fishing mortality until they mature and return to fresh water; this must be taken into account when comparing yields of the two spawning types.

Management of the Atlantic salmon resource is focused largely on the grilse—MSW salmon phenomenon owing to possible genetic implications and consequences of size-selective fisheries. Important correlates are allocation of grilse and MSW salmon to commercial and angling fisheries and sea-age makeup of the spawning escapement. The Miramichi, the largest salmon producing river in Atlantic Canada, has numerous stocks with diverse spawning types (Møller 1970; Elson 1973; Saunders 1981), has had alarming reduction in numbers of returning salmon during the last decade or more and is in serious need of effective management to safeguard and rebuild these stocks. The Anadromous and Catadromous Subcommittee of the Canadian Atlantic Fisheries Scientific Advisory Committee (CAFSAC) has charged this workshop with the task of assessing the genetic and environmental factors which affect age and size at maturity with the aim of providing a more enlightened management approach to the salmon resource in the Miramichi and other rivers of Atlantic Canada.

The observation has frequently been made that deliberate selection of larger salmon by commercial fisheries has resulted in reduced age and size of those that survive to spawn; it has been suggested that this has resulted in gradual reductions in age and size of adults in subsequent generations. Gardner (1976) summarizes the results of many studies documenting changes in predominant sea-ages and seasonal pattern of adult return of *S. salar* over most of its range. Many, but not all, of the documented changes have been in the direction of increased proportions of grilse. However, environmental changes and reduced population density may have operated through changed growth rates to produce younger or older, smaller or larger smolts which affected patterns of sea age and size at maturity. Although Ricker (1981) concluded that genetic changes owing to size-selective fisheries on some Pacific salmon (*Oncorhynchus*) species are most likely responsible for declining age and size of returning adults during recent years, there is no conclusive evidence in the case of Atlantic salmon that the observed increases in runs of grilse and reduced numbers of MSW salmon are the result of genetic change in stocks owing to size-selective fisheries.

The excellent reviews of the literature dealing with genetic and environmental factors affecting age and size at maturity of Pacific (Ricker 1972) and Atlantic salmon (Gardner 1976) and recent studies of Atlantic salmon by Naevdal (1983) and Gjerde (1984) leave no doubt that there is a clear genetic influence on sea-age at maturity. However, both reviewers and subsequent researchers acknowledge an important environmental influence as well. A reasonable approach to the age-at-maturity problem is to evaluate the relative contributions of and interaction between genotype and environment. In this workshop, we assess recent and ongoing research on genetic and environmental influence and the interplay of these two factors on the timing of maturation in order to improve our understanding of the dynamics of age-size composition of maturing salmon, to improve stock assessment, to provide more precise estimates of spawning requirements and to indicate needs for further research.

Accepting that each river has its own stock of salmon and that large rivers may have a number of stocks, one or more in each tributary and various numbers along the main stem of the river (Ståhl 1980), rational management should be in recognition of the stock-specific characteristics such as seasonal pattern of adult return and the grilse—larger salmon status (Saunders 1981). Distant and local commercial fisheries tend to remove selectively the potential MSW component from runs of returning adults. Stocks contributing to the Greenland fishery would lose potential MSW spawners; mainland salmon contributing to the Newfoundland commercial fishery are mainly MSW with lesser numbers of grilse being taken. Local commercial fisheries, like those in the Miramichi Bay and estuary, are focused on MSW salmon and take place during early summer. Moreover, these early run components are mainly MSW salmon and are the most prized fish for angling. They are available to the angling fishery longer than grilse which typically arrive somewhat later. Tagging studies based on naturally produced smolts in the N.W. Miramichi in the early 1960's showed that 90% or more of the potential MSW salmon were removed from the fishery and that the spawning escapement was composed largely of grilse (Saunders 1969). The ratio of grilse to larger salmon among total recaptures during the early-to-mid 1960's was ca. 2:1; the ratio in the spawning escapement was ca. 28:1. There has not been a clear demonstration (among the early studies summarized by Gardner (1976) or subsequently) that grilse are permanently replacing MSW salmon in the Miramichi or other rivers. Relative proportions of grilse and MSW salmon produced by a single stock or collection of stocks in a river such as the Miramichi are difficult to evaluate because MSW fish undergo a longer period of natural and fishing mortality. In the example above for the Miramichi, the ratio of grilse to MSW salmon actually produced may have been closer to 1:1 than 2:1 had natural and fishing mortality not reduced numbers of MSW salmon during their second year at sea. Any changing trends in contribution of grilse and MSW salmon from a stock or collection of stocks in a river system can only be evaluated effectively by demonstrating to what extent production of both potential spawning types is changing from year to year and over longer periods. I know of no way of accomplishing this other than through annual tagging of naturally produced smolts. If the majority of MSW salmon are removed from the population before they can spawn and there is a high degree of heritability for age and size at maturation, what extent of annual removal of MSW spawners would be necessary, and for how many years and generations, before MSW salmon would disappear from the population? Long-term tagging studies need to be done to answer these questions. We need such information in order to respond with certainty to the questions asked by the CAFSAC Steering Committee: how does the proportion of total egg deposition contributed by MSW salmon influence the production of MSW salmon by the Miramichi stock; does age at maturity of male salmon (MSW vs grilse vs mature parr) influence the proportion of grilse and MSW salmon produced by Miramichi stocks and how should this be considered in establishing target numbers of spawners?

There is another significant question, perhaps to be answered in this workshop. When is the "decision" made concerning age at maturity, before smolts enter the sea or at some time thereafter? There is clear evidence that sexual maturation of *S. salar*, including male parr, is a heritable trait (Naevdal 1983; Thorpe et al. 1983), and a suggestion that maturation of parr may be under different genetic control from that of later stages in the sea (Gjerde 1984). It has also been demonstrated that environmental influences, both during juvenile life in fresh water and during marine life, can alter the expression of age at maturity. Saunders et al. (1982) give evidence that it is possible, through manipulation of the time of hatching and early growth rate, to produce 1-yr (1+) smolts with few or no male parr having matured the previous autumn. Early hatching and commencement of feeding by mid-May is likely to promote many males to mature by their first autumn. Later commencement of feeding (June) appears to preclude maturation during the first summer. Although maturation is thereby delayed, it is still possible to produce a high percentage of 1+ smolts if growing conditions are appropriate during summer and autumn. Bailey et al. (1980) and Saunders et al. (1982) suggest that the threshold size for precocious maturation is lower than that for smolting. Thorpe et al. (1982), Kristinsson et al. (1985) and Villarreal and Thorpe (1985) describe the relationship between growth rate and the processes of parr maturation and smoltification. They conclude that smoltification, not sexual maturation, is the primary cause of bimodality in length−frequency distribution.

Kristinsson et al. (1985) showed, in populations of individually marked salmon parr, that individuals which entered the upper mode and were the presumptive smolts in the population were faster growing for a period before bimodality was evident. Maturing male parr entered the upper growth mode rarely and, when they did, later than immature males and females. Ritter and Newbould (1977) report that 1+ smolts gave comparatively fewer grilse and more MSW salmon than 2+ smolts of the same strain. Saunders et al. (1983) show that Atlantic salmon of a given strain and with a common hatchery rearing background produce sharply different ratios of grilse to MSW salmon when sea ranched (released to migrate and feed naturally) than when reared in sea cages. In the example given, sea-ranched salmon produced grilse to MSW salmon in a ratio of about 1:1 in comparison with 1:100 for cage-reared fish. They suggest that low winter temperature (1-2°C) in sea cages results in a "decision" to postpone maturation. Free ranging salmon, presumably in locations with higher winter temperature (Templeman 1968; Lear 1976; Reddin 1985), had a high incidence of grilse. These observations show that the "decision" to commence sexual maturation may be made after smolts enter the sea, or that if a decision is made before

the fish leave fresh water, it may not be a firm decision to mature after a specified length of sea life but rather to mature when the environmental and the fish's physiological−biochemical conditions are appropriate. Although sexual maturity of *S. salar* is completed under periods of decreasing photoperiod, Scott and Sumpter (1983) suggest that initiation of maturation in this and other salmonid species takes place under the influence of increasing daylength. If overwintering conditions (such as low temperature in sea cages) are unfavorable for feeding and growth, salmon may not have the metabolic resources to commence maturation when the "decision" time is reached. Perhaps genetic determination of age at maturity goes only as far as prescribing that the animal may commence maturation at a time when specified physiological and biochemical conditions have been met but does not specify a season (year) for the event. It has been suggested that there are threshold sizes and/or developmental states for parr−smolt transformation (Elson 1973; Refstie et al. 1977; Bailey ct al. 1980; Kristinsson 1985) and sexual maturation of male parr (Bailey et al. 1980; Saunders et al. 1982; Thorpe et al. 1982; Kristinsson et al. 1985). These threshold conditions for maturation of *S. salar* can be met early in life and at small sizes. Male Atlantic salmon commonly mature at the parr stage while females only occasionally do so (Sutterlin and MacLean 1984; Baglinière and Maisse 1985).

Age at smolting has also been shown to be a heritable trait (Refstie et al. 1977; Thorpe et al. 1983). Naturally produced salmon in eastern Canadian rivers commonly smolt at 2−4 yr and sometimes at 5−7 yr. As with sexual maturation, it is possible under culture conditions to manipulate smolt age. Under ideal rearing conditions, it is possible to have >90% 1+ smolts (Goff and Forsyth 1979). Smoltification, like sexual maturation, is under genetic control; both of these traits appear to require threshold conditions (size or physiological−biochemical state) which may be quite inflexible. The flexibility is in when these conditions are met; it is difficult to conceive that genetic control can be tied to a time scale in respect to such once-a-year phenomena as smolting and maturation. Would it be appropriate, therefore, that we speak of the genetic basis for stage and size rather than age and size at sexual maturation? This acknowledges a certain genetic control of these physiological processes without tying them to a particular year.

In the foregoing, I have stressed plasticity in the life cycle of *S. salar*, particularly in respect to age and size at maturation. In a given year-class of Atlantic salmon, some members of which may live for 8−10 yr, there may be spawning individuals nearly every year (Saunders and Schom 1985). Although male parr may mature at age 0+ under culture conditions, mature 0+ males are rare in nature. The evidence suggests that sexual maturation in male parr and in subsequent life stages requires that there be an appropriate balance between somatic and gonadal development. We have seen that, in a group of salmon, maturation can occur at a given age and size under one set of environmental conditions but be precluded or postponed under a different set of conditions. I suggest that annual variations in the grilse:MSW salmon ratio in nature may reflect subtle environmental changes owing to fluctuations in oceanographic conditions or occurrence of the salmon at different places in the ocean from year to year, or at least during critical periods for food gathering and physiological decision making. It is likely that in spite of the demonstrated heritability for age at maturity of *S. salar*, the genetic influence is in the form of a capability with rather wide latitude and flexibility awaiting appropriate environmental and physiological—biochemical conditions rather than a preset array of biochemical reactions and developments ordained to take place during a given time. If the conditions are not appropriate, the animal appears to have the "choice" not to begin or perhaps even to arrest the process and wait until next year.

Acknowledgments

I thank John E. Thorpe, Robert G. Randall, Robert L. Stephenson, and Eugene B. Henderson for constructive criticism of the manuscript.

References

BAGLINIÈRE, J. L., AND G. MAISSE. 1985. Precocious maturation and smoltification in wild Atlantic salmon in the Armorican massif, France. Aquaculture 45: 249−263.

BAILEY, J. K., AND R. L. SAUNDERS. 1984. Returns of three year-classes of sea-ranched Atlantic salmon of various river strains and strain crosses. Aquaculture 41: 259−270.

BAILEY, J. K., R. L. SAUNDERS, AND M. I. BUZETA. 1980. Influence of parental smolt age and sea age on growth and smolting of hatchery-reared Atlantic salmon (*Salmo salar*). Can. J. Fish. Aquat. Sci. 37: 1379−1386.

ELSON, P. F. 1973. Genetic polymorphism in northwest Miramichi salmon, in relation to season of river ascent and age at maturation and its implications for management of the stocks. ICNAF Res. Doc. 73/76, Ann. Meet. 1973.

GARDNER, M. L. 1976. A review of factors which may influence the sea-age and maturation of Atlantic salmon, *Salmo salar* L. J. Fish Biol. 9: 289−327.

GJERDE, B. 1984. Response to individual selection for age at sexual maturity in Atlantic salmon. Aquaculture 38: 229−240.

GOFF, T. R., AND L. S. FORSYTH. 1979. Production of Atlantic salmon smolts in one year without artificial heating of water, Mersey Hatchery, Nova Scotia. Fish. Mar. Serv. Tech. Rep. 841: 20 p.

KRISTINSSON, J. B., R. L. SAUNDERS, AND A. J. WIGGS. 1985. Growth dynamics during the development of bimodal length—frequency distribution in juvenile Atlantic salmon (*Salmo salar* L.). Aquaculture 45: 1−20.

LARSSON, P.-O. 1983. Salmon ranching in Sweden, p. 127−137. *In* C. Eriksson, M. P. Ferranti, and P.-O. Larsson [ed.] Proc. Comm. European Communities COST 46/4 Workshop. Sea Ranching of Atlantic Salmon.

LEAR, W. H. 1976. Migrating Atlantic salmon (*Salmo salar*) caught by otter trawl on the Newfoundland Continental Shelf. J. Fish. Res. Board Can. 33: 1202−1205.

MØLLER, D. 1970. Transferrin polymorphism in Atlantic salmon (*Salmo salar*). J. Fish. Res. Board Can. 27: 1617−1625.

NAEVDAL, G. 1983. Genetic factors in connection with age at maturation. Aquaculture 33: 97−106.

REDDIN, D. G. 1985. Atlantic salmon (*Salmo salar* L.) to the east of the Grand Bank of Newfoundland. J. Northw. Atl. Fish. Sci. (in press)

REFSTIE, T., T. A. STEINE, AND T. GJEDREM. 1977. Selection experiments with salmon. II. Proportion of Atlantic salmon smoltifying at 1 year of age. Aquaculture 10: 231−242.

RICKER, W. E. 1972. Hereditary and environmental factors affecting certain salmonid populations, p. 19−160. *In* R. C. Simon and P. A. Larkin [ed.] H. R. MacMillan Lectures in Fisheries, The Stock Concept in Pacific Salmon, Univ. British Columbia, Vancouver, B.C.

    1981. Changes in the average size and average age of Pacific salmon. Can. J. Fish. Aquat. Sci. 38: 1636−1656.

RITTER, J. A., AND K. NEWBOULD. 1977. Relationships of parent-age and smolt age to age at first maturity of Atlantic salmon (*Salmo salar*). Int. Counc. Explor. Sea C.M.1977/M:32, 5 p.

SAUNDERS, R. L. 1969. Contributions of salmon from the northwest Miramichi River, New Brunswick, to various fisheries. J. Fish. Res. Board Can. 26: 269−278.

    1981. Atlantic salmon (*Salmo salar*) stocks and management implications in the Canadian Atlantic Provinces and New England. Can. J. Fish. Aquat. Sci. 38: 1612−1625.

SAUNDERS, R. L., AND C. B. SCHOM. 1985. Importance of the variation in life history parameters of Atlantic salmon (*Salmo salar*). Can. J. Fish. Aquat. Sci. 42: 615−618.

SAUNDERS, R. L., E. B. HENDERSON, AND B. D. GLEBE. 1982. Precocious sexual maturation and smoltification in male Atlantic salmon (*Salmo salar*). Aquaculture 28: 211−229.

SAUNDERS, R. L., E. B. HENDERSON, B. D. GLEBE, AND E. J. LOUDENSLAGER. 1983. Evidence of a major environmental component in determination of the grilse:larger salmon ratio in Atlantic salmon (*Salmo salar*). Aquaculture 33: 107−118.

SCOTT, A. P., AND J. P. SUMPTER. 1983. The control of trout reproduction: basic and applied research on hormones, p. 176−199. *In* J. C. Rankin, T. J. Pitcher and R. Duggan [ed.] Control Processes in Fish Physiology. Croom Helm, London and Canberra.

SUTTERLIN, A. M., AND D. MacLEAN. 1984. Age at first maturity and the early expression of oocyte recruitment processes in two forms of Atlantic salmon (*Salmo salar*) and their hybrids. Can. J. Fish. Aquat. Sci. 41: 1139−1149.

STÅHL, G. 1980. Genetic differentiation among natural populations of Atlantic salmon (*Salmo salar*) in northern Sweden, p. 95−105. *In* N. Ryman [ed.] Fish gene pools. Ecol. Bull. (Stockholm) 34.

TEMPLEMAN, W. 1968. Distribution and characteristics of Atlantic salmon over ocean depths and on the Grand Bank and shelf slope areas off Newfoundland, March—May, 1966. Int. Comm. Northwest Atl. Fish. Res. Bull. 5: 62−85.

THORPE, J. E., C. TALBOT, AND C. VILLARREAL. 1982. Bimodality of growth and smolting in Atlantic salmon (*Salmo salar* L.). Aquaculture 28: 123−132.

THORPE, J. E., R. I. G. MORGAN, C. TALBOT, AND M. S. MILES. 1983. Inheritance of developmental rates in Atlantic salmon, *Salmo salar* L. Aquaculture 33: 119−128.

VILLARREAL, C. A., AND J. E. THORPE. 1985. Gonadal growth and bimodality of length frequency distribution in juvenile Atlantic salmon (*Salmo salar*). Aquaculture 45: 265−288.

Age at First Maturity in Atlantic Salmon, *Salmo salar*: Freshwater Period Influences and Conflicts with Smolting

J. E. Thorpe

Freshwater Fisheries Laboratory, Pitlochry, PH16 5LB, Scotland

Abstract

THORPE, J. E. 1986. Age at first maturity in Atlantic salmon, *Salmo salar:* freshwater period influences and conflicts with smolting, p. 7–14. *In* D. J. Meerburg [ed.] Salmonid age at maturity. Can. Spec. Publ. Fish. Aquat. Sci. 89.

Salmon are opportunistic, phenotypically plastic generalists, which have highly variable life-history strategies within species, notably through variable developmental rates. Atlantic salmon, *Salmo salar*, frequently mature as parr (especially males) — a form of miniaturization comparable to that known for *Tilapia* spp., in which maturity is achieved at a small size and at a rapid rate. Growth rate and maturation rate are positively correlated, leading to physiological conflict, since smolting implies the abandonment of freshwater adaptations while maturation implies their retention. The two processes are mutually inhibitory in amago salmon, *Oncorhynchus rhodurus*, and in masu, *O. masou*, and there is circumstantial evidence of similar mutual inhibition in Atlantic salmon. Demographers have shown in several salmonids that fish mature at that age which maximizes their lifetime reproductive potential. However, individual fish make their developmental conversions in response to specific proximate cues. Photoperiod changes act as zeitgebers for such events, and it is suggested that the physiological decision is mediated internally using growth-rate, or rate of acquisition of surplus energy, rather than absolute size as the criterion. Some demographic consequences of increased freshwater growth rates leading to maturation before smolt emigration are illustrated by examples from the Atlantic salmon of the Matamek River and the sockeye salmon of Lakes Dalneye and Uyeginsk.

Résumé

THORPE, J. E. 1986. Age at first maturity in Atlantic salmon, *Salmo salar:* freshwater period influences and conflicts with smolting, p. 7–14. *In* D. J. Meerburg [ed.] Salmonid age at maturity. Can. Spec. Publ. Fish. Aquat. Sci. 89.

Les saumons sont des géneralistes opportunistes et phénotypiquement plastiques qui possèdent des stratégies d'antécédents biologiques fortement variables à l'intérieur de l'espèce, notamment en ce qui concerne les vitesses variables de développement. Le saumon de l'Atlantique (*Salmo salar*) mature fréquemment en tant que tacon (particulièrement pour les mâles) — une forme de miniaturisation comparable à celle que l'on connaît pour *Tilapia* spp., pour qui la maturité est atteinte à une taille petite et à une vitesse rapide. La vitesse de croissance et la vitesse de maturation sont positivement corrélées, ce qui donne lieu à un conflit physiologique, puisque la transformation en saumoneau implique l'abandon des adaptations en eau douce tandis que le cheminement vers la maturité implique leur rétention. Les deux processus sont mutuellement inhibiteurs chez *Oncorhynchus rhodurus* et chez le saumon japonais (*O. masou*), et il existe des preuves circonstancielles d'inhibition mutuelle analogue chez le saumon atlantique. Les démographes ont montré que chez plusieurs salmonidés, les poissons maturent à l'âge qui maximise leur potentiel de reproduction en fonction de la durée de leur existence. Toutefois, certains poissons opèrent leurs conversions évolutives en réaction à certains signaux proches. Les changements de photopériodes agissent comme synchroniseurs temporels pour de tels événements et les auteurs estiment que la décision physiologique intervient de façon interne en fonction de la vitesse de croissance, ou de la vitesse d'acquisition d'un surplus énérgétique, plutôt qu'en fonction de la taille absolue comme critère fondamental. Certaines conséquences démographiques des vitesses de croissance en eau douce accrues conduisant à la maturité avant l'émigration des saumoneaux sont illustrées par des exemples tirés du saumon atlantique de la rivière Matamek et du saumon rouge des lacs Dalneye et Uyeginsk.

Margalef (1959) distinguished two types of animal community: the initial and the mature. The former was made up of animals which were phenotypically plastic, opportunistic, and highly adaptable: the latter comprised animals which were specialized, efficient in a restricted niche, but relatively intolerant of environmental change. Among fishes Fryer and Iles (1969) quoted examples of these in Africa: *Tilapia* species exemplified the initial type, able to colonize and occupy a wide range of habitats, in contrast to the *Haplochromis* species, which were highly specialized forms restricted to very limited habitats of single lakes, and which represented mature communities. Balon (1983) has recently categorized these evolutionary patterns as altricial (generalists) and precocial (specialists).

Salmonids show the characteristics of initial community members, in that they are opportunistic, phenotypically plastic generalists, which have highly variable life-history strategies even within species. But the development of discrete spawning stocks (STOCS Symposium papers, 1981) has led to narrower specialization of populations adapted to specific sets of environmental conditions, which approaches the mature community condition of specialists. However, the ability of most salmonids to colonize new habitats (e.g. the worldwide plantings of *Salmo gairdneri* and *S. trutta*, and the establishment of *Oncorhynchus tschawytscha* populations in New Zealand) suggests that despite their ancient evolutionary lineage and divergent adaptation of distinct stocks, these fish retain sufficient heterozygosity to respond successfully to radically changed environmental conditions, possibly by virtue of their polyploid origins (Ohno et al. 1969; Roberts 1970; Allendorf and Thorgaard 1984). Conspicuous among these plastic traits are variable developmental rates, in particular for growth and sexual maturation.

TABLE 1. Maturity in *Tilapia* (Fryer and Iles 1969).

	Mature at	
	Length (cm)	Age
T. variabilis		
Lake Victoria	21	4 yr
Ponds	16	<7 mo
T. esculenta		
Lake Victoria	20–25	2–3 yr
Ponds	16	6 mo
Aquaria	10	5 mo

TABLE 2. Reports of positive correlation of growth rate and maturation rate in salmonids.

Species	Authority
Oncorhynchus kisutch	Bilton (1980)
O. masou	Utoh (1976, 1977)
O. nerka	Ricker (1938) Krokhin (1967) Nikulin (1970) Kato (1980)
O. rhodurus	Nagahama et al. (1982)
Salmo clarki	Jonsson et al. (1984)
S. gairdneri	Alm (1959) Kato (1975) Naevdal et al. (1979)
S. salar	Alm (1959) Leyzerovich (1973) Mitans (1973) Simpson and Thorpe (1976) Glebe et al. (1978) Naevdal et al. (1978) Lundqvist (1980) Murphy (1980) Thorpe and Morgan (1980) Saunders et al. (1982) Dalley et al. (1983) Thorpe et al. (1983)
S. trutta	Alm (1959) Jonsson (1977, 1981)
Salvelinus alpinus	Alm (1959) Jonsson and Hindar (1982)
S. fontinalis	Jonsson and Hindar (1982)
S. malma	Jonsson and Hindar (1982)
S. namaycush	Alm (1959)

Opportunism: Early Maturation

Generalists are opportunists. The *Tilapia* species are well-known for their ability to invade a wide range of habitats, and in many to reproduce when they are still very small. For example, Fryer and Iles (1969) noted that *T. variabilis* which normally matured at a length of 21 cm at 4 yr in Lake Victoria, did so at 16 cm and <7 mo in fish ponds (Table 1). Likewise, *T. esculenta*, of similar size and performance in the lake, reduced this to 10 cm and 5 mo in aquaria. These fish have been called "stunts" but the authors emphasized the inappropriateness of this name, which implied retardation, when in fact the fish showed specific growth rates to maturity higher than found in "normal" individuals. Fryer and Iles preferred the term miniaturization, that is, a marked speeding up of both growth rate and maturation rate, in a form of neoteny in which individuals which attained maturity at a very small size were not subsequently precluded from growing to a "normal" size, should conditions change. Balon (1968) discussed evidence for neotenic development among forms of *Salmo trutta*, and concluded that the landlocked ones (brown trout, European lake trout) had arisen by neoteny from the fully anadromous type (sea trout). He later extended this argument to salmonines in general, and attributed to neoteny the deveopment of iteroparity in *Salmo* species as compared to the semelparity of the evolutionarily older *Oncorhynchus* species (Balon 1980).

Basic Specializations

Salmonids are relatively primitive fishes (Greenwood et al. 1966; Cavender 1970) whose principal specializations are related to reproduction and early life in protected riverine environments (Thorpe 1982, 1984). Use of this freshwater environment requires adaptation of two general types: physiological, where the main problem is the maintenance of hydromineral balance in a hypotonic medium; and behavioural, the chief problems being maintenance of station in a rapidly moving unidirectional environment, and acquisition of adequate nourishment to meet the costs involved as well as to grow and develop. Since freshwater is relatively unproductive compared with the marine environment, prey density is relatively low. But the advantage of the trade-off of a productive habitat for a protected one is temporary, since at some point this advantage is outweighed by the disadvantage of food scarcity. At this stage full growth potential can only be achieved by emigration to a more fertile environment, which is only permitted if freshwater specializations are abandoned. Later in life these adaptations have to be reactivated if the adult fish is to re-enter freshwater to spawn.

Conflict: Maturation Versus Smolting

In hatchery production of salmonids it is commonplace that growth is more rapid than under local wild conditions. Among Atlantic salmon in hatcheries maturation of males as parr in freshwater occurs regularly, but its frequency varies among stocks, years and rearing conditions (Thorpe 1975; Glebe et al. 1978, 1979; Bailey et al. 1980; Saunders et al. 1982). In particularly favourable growth conditions, such as those in Bailey et al. (1980) experiments with heated water in winter, some of the fastest growing males matured at 0+ (Saunders et al. 1982). This has also occurred occasionally in U.K. hatcheries without supplementary heating (Turner, pers. comm.; Morgan, pers. comm.), again under relatively favourable growing conditions. Baglinière and Maisse (1985) found wild mature parr at 0+ in the River Scorff, France, but only in the relatively productive lower reaches where growth rate of salmon was higher than upstream. It is also commonplace that high growth rate in hatcheries leads to smolting 1 or more years sooner than under local wild conditions. But smolting represents a collection of changes which results in abandonment of freshwater adaptations, whereas maturation leads to the retention of such adapta-

TABLE 3. Age at maturation in sibling Atlantic salmon populations at Almondbank, Scotland (after Thorpe 1982).

| Spawning season | Age (yr) | Growth group | |
		Upper modal	Lower modal
	0	hatch	hatch
*	0.7		
	1.2	smolt	
*	1.7		mature male parr
	2.2		smolt
*	2.7	mature	
	3.2		
*	3.7	mature	mature

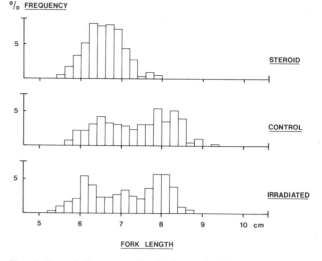

FIG. 1. Length-frequency distributions of sibling populations of Atlantic salmon, sterilized by irradiation, or fed methyltestosterone.

tions. So, conditions which promote rapid development in freshwater lead to physiological conflict.

Half a century ago Alm carried out a long series of experiments on the growth of *S. trutta* in ponds in Sweden (Alm 1959). He was the first to show that fish which grew fastest in a population matured earliest. This general finding has since been recorded in a wide range of salmonid species (Table 2), so that the positive correlation of growth rate and maturation rate in this group of fishes is well established. In particular in Atlantic salmon, it has been shown experimentally that the progeny of males which matured very young (as 1+ parr in freshwater) grew faster and matured earlier than did the progeny of males which matured at older ages (after 1 and 2 yr at sea) (Thorpe and Morgan 1980; Thorpe et al. 1983). Hence these positively correlated developmental rates were heritable, and the same experiments showed that increased incidence of early maturity could be selected for rapidly (6.8 to 30.1% in 2 generations).

Although both the processes of smolting and maturation in salmonids are incompletely understood (see papers on smolting in *Aquaculture* 1982, vol. 28 (1 and 2); *Aquaculture* 1985, vol. 45; and on maturation in *Aquaculture* 1984, vol. 43), evidence is accumulating that the two processes are mutually inhibitory. Thorpe and Morgan (1980) and Thorpe (1982), noted that Atlantic salmon which smolted at age 15 mo did not return as mature adults until aged 30 mo, whereas some of their smaller siblings which did not emigrate matured at age 21 mo (Table 3). Myers (1984) noted that the proportion of 1+ male parr that matured at 2+ was high in the Little Codroy River, Newfoundland, when the proportion of immature 1+ fish smolting at age 2 was low. In amago salmon, *O. rhodurus*, Nagahama (1985) found that plasma testosterone and 11-ketotestosterone which were at high levels in maturing males before spawning, were non-detectable or at very low levels in smolts, but increased in desmolting fish. Recently it has been shown experimentally in masu salmon, *O. masou*, that feeding methyltestosterone (MT) in February–April prevented silvering, seawater adaptation and change of caudal shape (condition factor reduction), whereas all these changes occurred in the smolting controls (Ikuta et al. 1985). Likewise in amago salmon (Miwa and Inui 1985) feeding MT or estradiol-17β (E2) to sterilised fish intensified parr characteristics, and prevented the silvering and seawater tolerance which was evident among the controls, which smolted. Both sex steroids reduced gill Na−K−ATPase activity, reduced the number and size of gill chloride cells, and thickened the skin and gill epithelium. These inhibitory effects on smolting were greater with MT than with E2. In the reverse

experiment, castrated masu salmon smolted, whereas sham operated controls did not (Aida et al. 1984). In Atlantic salmon at the Almondbank hatchery, Scotland, the development of bimodality in the length frequency distribution of sibling populations has been suppressed by feeding MT such that no treated fish began smolting at 0+, whereas 58% of control fish did, but sterilization by irradiation with cobalt-60 did not increase that rate of smolting within the population (Villarreal and Thorpe 1985) (Fig. 1).

It appears, then, that fish under favourable growing conditions are faced with a physiological choice — to smolt and emigrate to sea, or to mature and stay in freshwater. There is some evidence that in Atlantic salmon the latter choice does not totally preclude the former, but may interfere with the successful completion of smolting, or may reduce the probability of survival after the smolt stage (Forsythe 1967; Osterdahl 1969; Saunders 1976; Leyzerovich 1973; Mitans 1973; Leyzerovich and Melnikova 1969; Dalley et al. 1983). Baglinière and Maisse (1985) have reported on the widespread occurrence of spawning marks on the freshwater parts of scales of adult Atlantic salmon returning to rivers in Brittany, where growth conditions are so favourable that even a small proportion of the female population may achieve sexual maturity as parr.

Regulation of Physiological Choice

Smolting

Elson (1957) suggested that Atlantic salmon must reach a threshold length of 10 cm in autumn if they were to smolt in the following spring. The approximate constancy of length of migration of these smolts over broad geographical areas, and from year to year, lends credence to the idea of critical sizes. In a range of experiments (Thorpe 1977; Thorpe and Morgan 1978; Thorpe and Wankowski 1979; Thorpe et al. 1980, 1982) it has been shown that the physiological decision which regulates growth in the months immediately preceding smolt emigration is taken in the previous summer. In sibling populations, fish which maintain relatively high food intake after midsummer continue to grow throughout the winter. Those which reduce their food intake slow down in growth more rapidly, and cease grow-

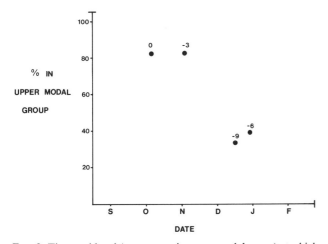

FIG. 2. Time and level (percentage in upper modal group) at which bimodal segregation of growth groups became apparent, in sibling populations of Atlantic salmon reared under controlled photoperiod regimes 0, 3, 6, and 9 mo out of phase with the natural light regime.

ing through the winter (Higgins 1985a; Higgins and Talbot 1985), effectively a developmental arrest (Smith-Gill 1983). The result is a bimodal segregation of the length frequency distribution of the population, the majority of the upper modal group smolting in spring, and the lower modal group remaining as parr. Analysis throughout the first summer of RNA:DNA ratios of skeletal muscle, of cross-sectional area of fibres and frequency of fibre size, has shown that this growth change occurs in early July, very soon after the solstice (Thorpe et al. 1982; Villarreal 1983; Villarreal and Thorpe 1986; Higgins 1985b, and in preparation). Hence, if a size threshold for this physiological decision exists, it is the length of the fish in July which will be critical.

Saunders and Henderson (1970) and Komourdjian et al. (1976) have shown that smolting itself was influenced directly by the photoperiod regime under which the fish were reared. Higgins and Talbot (1985) have shown that growth responses of these young fish were correlated more directly with photoperiod than with temperature, since fish on increasing photoperiods and low temperatures (ca. 1°C) in January and February grew more than on decreasing photoperiods but higher temperatures (2−7°C) in November and December. In preliminary experiments in which sibling salmon populations were reared at the same ambient water temperature but under photoperiod regimes which were 0, 3, 6, and 9 mo out of phase with the natural photoperiod cycle, the timing of the development of a stable bimodal segregation in length frequency distribution was delayed according to the phase relationship to natural daylength (Fig. 2). These findings provide strong evidence that photoperiod plays a major role in regulating the decision to maintain or to reduce growth rate in midsummer.

Maturation

Schaffer and Elson (1975) suggested that the decision taken by adult salmon at sea whether or not to mature and return to spawn at a particular age, depended on their effective fecundity at that age and their probability of survival for another year. In a similar way, Jonsson et al. (1984) concluded from data on experimental transfers of cutthroat trout (*Salmo clarki*) and Dolly Varden (*Salvelinus malma*), that the fish matured at that age which maximized their lifetime

reproductive potential. Such judgements can be made *post hoc* by demographers, in a population sense, but not immediately by individual fishes. The motivation for change must arise from proximate cues.

Maturation in salmonids has been shown to be photoperiod regulated (reviewed by Lam 1983; and Lundqvist 1983). Bailey et al. (1980) suggested that the decision whether or not to mature at the parr stage was size-threshold dependent. Thorpe et al. (1980), and Saunders et al. (1982) have argued that if this maturation threshold was at a larger size than the smolting one, then populations with high proportions of small 1-yr smolts would show little or no evidence of maturing parr in the first autumn, whereas populations with high proportions of large 1-yr smolts would also show high incidence of mature 0+ parr. One-year smolts at Almondbank, Scotland were small (10−12 cm) and maturation at 0+ did not occur: 1-yr smolts at St. Andrews, New Brunswick were large (15−25 cm) and parr maturation at 0+ did occur. The evidence, therefore, was consistent with the two-threshold hypothesis (see also fig. 2 in Baglinière and Maisse 1985).

Critical Sizes

It has been shown (Thorpe et al. 1980) that, under specific hatchery conditions, 2+ smolts (lower modal group) were longer than were their siblings which smolted at 1+, which paralleled wild conditions where size tended to increase with smolt age within stocks (e.g. Forsythe 1967, 1968). Likewise, salmon maturing young tended to do so at sizes smaller than those maturing later (e.g. Shearer 1972). Hence, even within populations evidence is lacking for a fixed size beyond which the fish inevitably become smolts or mature. Also, Jonsson et al. (1984) rejected the hypothesis of a specific size for maturation in their cutthroat and Dolly Varden, because the transferred populations matured at a different length than did the donor stocks.

In general, Policansky (1983), considering the question whether developmental transitions were triggered by attainment of a certain size or age, concluded that under stable conditions with abundant food supply, fish should grow rapidly and mature as soon as they are developmentally able to do so.

By contrast, the evidence given above for the implication of growth rate as a modifier of the age at which both smolting and maturation occur is analogous to that for the miniaturization process in *Tilapia* spp. Jonsson et al. (1984) rejected the hypothesis that age at maturity was adjusted by growth-rate alone, on the grounds that their trout matured at a younger age in one lake where they were of a smaller size than in another. From their data it was not possible to assess this conclusion adequately, since no within-season growth information was given. Hence specific growth rates at the time of triggering of gonadal development are not known, and could have been higher at the appropriate time in the fish which matured young and at small size than in the other population at that same time, as Fryer and Iles (1969) pointed out was the case for *Tilapia* spp.

The concept of a critical size at which a major developmental conversion (Smith-Gill 1983) may occur begs the question of how the organism recognises how large it is. It needs some reference standard. The size that a fish achieves at any particular age depends on the quantity of food it has consumed, the efficiency with which that has been assimi-

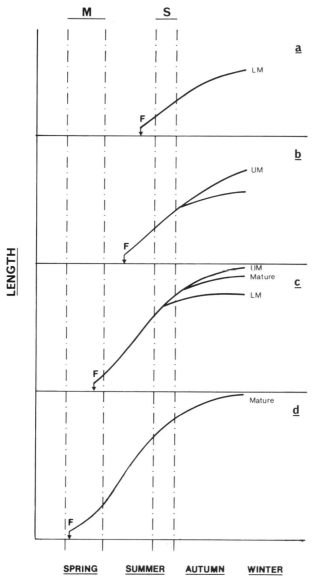

FIG. 3. Hypothetical growth curves for Atlantic salmon. M: sensitive period for maturation trigger; S: sensitive period for growth arrest trigger; F: first feeding; UM: upper modal growth group; LM: lower modal growth group. (a) Poor developmental conditions: F late; growth-rate low during S-period; whole population arrests growth. (b) moderate deveopmental conditions: F early summer; growth-rate higher during S-period; faster part of population maintains growth, remainder arrests. (c) good developmental conditions: F late spring; growth-rates in both S- and M-periods high; fastest part of male population maintains growth but then slows as the individuals mature; faster part of female population, and average part of male population, maintain growth; slower part of population (both sexes) arrest growth. (d) exceptionally good developmental conditions: F early spring; growth-rate of whole population high in both sensitive periods: all males mature, and females mature 1 yr later.

lated, and the way in which that acquired energy and material has been allocated. For example, Higgins' (1985b) data showed that within sibling Atlantic salmon populations those fish which formed the upper modal growth group in bimodal length frequency distributions not only consumed more food, but they fed for longer in the day, converted that food to body tissue more efficiently than did the lower modal group fish, and kept intake high enough to permit growth while the lower modal group fed at a maintenance level. Size by itself is a

measure of past performance: instantaneous growth-rate is a measure of current performance, and would provide a better basis on which to make the developmental decision, than would size alone. Smith-Gill and Berven (1979) noted that metamorphosis in amphibians was not predicted by size or age alone, but that "differentiation rate" was the best predictor.

Calow and Townsend (1981) viewed growth of an animal as its developmental means of achieving the reproductive state, and considered its biochemical production processes were adapted to optimize rather than maximize its developmental rates. Optimization implies that these rates were regulated below their physiological maxima. The pattern of regulation was fixed genetically, so that the animal showed programmed development, achieved via hormonal feedback mechanisms in relation to resource availability and functional demand (Bullough 1967).

The hypothesis is therefore proposed that salmon are physiologically aware of their growth-rate through their rate of acquisition of surplus energy (*sensu* Ware 1980), and hormone kinetics associated with its storage: that, provided this rate is above a genetically determined level in the early spring when the fish are sensitive to photoperiodic stimulation of their gonadotrophic hormone systems (cf. Scott and Sumpter 1983), gonadal maturation will be triggered and reallocation of energy resources to include maturation will be set in train.[1] (Such a mechanism would apply during the marine phase also [cf. Saunders 1986]). The decision to maintain or curtail growth, which leads to smolting or its postponement for a year, will be achieved in a similar manner, through hypothalamic activation in early July of hormones regulating output of growth hormone, thyroxine and corticosteroids. If the appropriate thresholds are exceeded in spring maturation will ensue, and smolting will be inhibited (Fig. 3). Values for these threshold levels, and precise times of sensitivity to activation, are not yet known, but should be expected to vary both within and between stocks.

Demographic Consequences

Maturation of Atlantic salmon in freshwater before smolting has been reported from throughout their geographical range, but its incidence varies among localities and years. It is possible that it occurs among males in most stocks, as it has been found in most populations in which it has been sought carefully. In extreme cases whole populations appear to have evolved this particular strategy, dispensing with the sea phase altogether (Power 1958; Sutterlin and MacLean 1984), whereas in others the females were found to migrate to sea while the males remained as freshwater parr (Nikolskii et al. 1947). Baglinière and Maisse (1985) have reported on the variable occurrence of mature female parr in rivers of N.W. France. Schiefer (1971) considered that participation of mature male parr at spawning in St. Lawrence North Shore rivers influenced the maturation age structure of progeny generations by increasing the grilse proportion among returning adults. Myers (1983) argued that increases in the proportion of parr maturing, which could result as a consequence of increased fishing pressure, could have a profound effect on the yield of a fishery, since early maturity increased parr mortality (Leyzerovich 1973; Dalley et al. 1983) and so reduced the number of adults available for exploitation.

[1]This is the same as Pauly's (1984) rate of oxygen consumption hypothesis, published after submission of this paper.

TABLE 4. Lake Dalneye sockeye salmon (Krogius 1979).

	1935–46	1947–56	1957–65	1966–76
Spawning migrants	62 000	10 000	5 700	1 600
% as grilse	0.2	0.6	4.3	37.5
Smolt output	197 000	59 000	31 200	27 200
Parr: % mature males	7.0	11.2	15.6	16.9
% of male spawners	26.0	49.4	74.2	88.8
Male spawners: parr:adult	0.35	0.98	2.88	7.93

TABLE 5. Lake Uyeginsk sockeye salmon (Nikulin 1970).

	1930	1968
Spawning migrants	100 000	300
% male	?50	39
Parr: % mature male	12.8	81.7
% mature female	0.0	5.0

Myers (1984) showed that in the Little Codroy River 60% of the adult male production was lost due to maturation as parr.

Gibson (1978) has shown a general reduction in male age at maturity in recent years in the Matamek River, Quebec. Using a matrix population model Caswell et al. (1984) suggested that the increase in male parr maturation (from 31 to 75%) in that river, was a consequence of natural selection in response to increased fishing pressure at sea. This can be supported with circumstantial evidence from a 42-yr study of the sockeye salmon (*O. nerka*) population of Lake Dalneye, Kamchatka (Krogius 1979), where there was a substantial decrease in the abundance of sea-run spawners (from 62 600 annually in 1935–46, to 1 600 annually in 1966–76) also attributed to heavy fishing pressure at sea (Table 4). The response in the lake ecosystem was dramatic: phosphate levels fell by 75%, primary production by 40%, smolt output by 86%, and the proportion of mature males among the juveniles rose from 7 to 16.9%. The numbers of males returning annually from the sea fell from 30 000 (60 as "grilse") to only 500 (190 as "grilse"), and the ratio of mature parr:sea-run males rose from 0.35:1 to 7.93:1. It is clear that a 97% reduction in the total population was accompanied by a reduction in mean age at maturity in the males, and a 20-fold increase in the proportion of mature parr in the spawning stock.

It is not clear from either Caswell et al. or Krogius' papers whether early maturity was achieved as a consequence of increased individual growth rate. However, in Lake Uyeginsk (Okhotsk Region, USSR), where Nikulin (1970) documented an even more drastic decline in the sockeye population from ca. 100 000 sea-run spawners in 1930 to 300 in 1968, he did record an increase in growth rate of juvenile fish in freshwater accompanying a dramatic increase in maturation at this stage (Table 5). In 1930, 12.8% of the juvenile population had matured (all males): in 1968, 86.7% matured, and 5.8% of these were females.

Taken together, laboratory data and field evidence would suggest that, given improved individual developmental conditions through reduced density (Matamek, Dalneye, Uyeginsk) or increased productivity (Scorff), the increased rate of acquisition of energy and materials leads to earlier maturation and changes in life-history strategy in salmonids, favouring rapid turnover of generations at small body size, (even dispensing with the sea phase altogether), through the inhibitory effects of maturation on smolting.

References

AIDA, K., T. KATO AND M. AWAJI. 1984. Effects of castration on the smoltification of precocious male masu salmon *Oncorhynchus masou*. Bull. Jap. Soc. Sci. Fish. 50: 565–571.

ALLENDORF, F. W., AND G. H. THORGAARD. 1984. Tetraploidy and the evolution of salmonid fishes, p. 1–53. *In* B. J. Turner [ed.] Evolutionary genetics of fishes. Plenum Press, New York, NY.

ALM, G. 1959. Connection between maturity, size and age in fishes. Rep. Inst. Freshwat. Res. Drottningholm 40: 5–145.

BAILEY, J. K., R. L. SAUNDERS, AND M. I. BUZETA. 1980. Influence of parental smolt age and sea age on growth and smolting of hatchery reared Atlantic salmon (*Salmo salar*). Can. J. Fish. Aquat. Sci. 37: 1379–1386.

BAGLINIÈRE, J. L., AND G. MAISSE. 1985. Observations on precocious maturation and smoltification relationships in wild Atlantic salmon populations in the Armorican Massif (France). Aquaculture 45: 249–263.

BALON, E. K. 1968. Notes on the origin and evolution of trouts and salmons with special reference to the Danubian trouts. Vest. Cs. Spol. Zool. 32: 1–21.

1980. Early ontogeny of the Lake charr, *Salvelinus (Cristivomer) namaycush*, p. 485–562. *In* E. K. Balon [ed.] Charrs. Dr. W. Junk, The Hague.

1983. Epigenetic mechanisms: reflections on evolutionary processes. Can. J. Fish. Aquat. Sci. 40: 2045–2058.

BILTON, H. T. 1980. Experimental releases of coho salmon in British Columbia. p. 305–324. *In* J. E. Thorpe [ed.] Salmon ranching. Academic Press, London.

BULLOUGH, W. S. 1967. The evolution of differentiation. Academic Press, London.

CALOW, P., AND C. R. TOWNSEND. 1981. Resource utilization in growth. p. 220–244. *In* C. R. Townsend and P. Calow [ed.] Physiological ecology. Blackwell, Oxford.

CASWELL, H., R. J. NAIMAN, AND R. MORIN. 1984. Evaluating the consequences of reproduction in complex salmonid life cycles. Aquaculture 43: 123–134.

CAVENDER, T. M. 1970. A comparison of coregonines and other salmonids with the earliest known teleostean fishes, p. 1–32. *In* C. C. Lindsey and C. S. Woods [ed.] Biology of coregonid fishes. Univ. of Manitoba Press, Winnipeg, Man.

DALLEY, E. L., C. W. ANDREWS, AND J. M. GREEN. 1983. Precocious male Atlantic salmon parr (*Salmo salar*) in insular Newfoundland. Can. J. Fish. Aquat. Sci. 40: 647–652.

ELSON, P. F. 1957. The importance of size in the change from parr to smolt in Atlantic salmon. Can. Fish Cult. 21: 1–6.

FORSYTHE, M. G. 1967. Analysis of the 1965 smolt run in the Northwest Miramichi River, New Brunswick. Fish. Res. Board Can. Tech. Rep. 4: 1–73.

1968. Analysis of the 1966 smolt run in the Northwest Miramichi River, New Brunswick. Fish. Res. Board Can. Tech. Rep. 91: 1–33.

FRYER, G., AND T. D. ILES. 1969. Alternative routes to evolutionary success as exhibited by African cichlid fishes of the genus *Tilapia* and the species flocks of the Great Lakes. Evolution 23: 359−369.

GIBSON, R. J. 1978. Recent changes in the population of juvenile salmon in the Matamek River, Quebec, Canada. J. Cons. Int. Expl. Mer 38: 201−207.

GLEBE, B. D., R. L. SAUNDERS, AND A. SREEDHARAN. 1978. Genetic and environmental influence in expression of precocious sexual maturity of hatchery-reared Atlantic salmon (*Salmo salar*) parr. Can. J. Genet. Cytol. 20: 444.

GLEBE, B. D., T. D. APPY, AND R. L. SAUNDERS. 1979. Variation in Atlantic salmon (*Salmo salar*) reproductive traits and their implications in breeding programs. Int. Coun. Expl. Sea CM1979/M23: 1−11.

GREENWOOD, P. H., D. E. ROSEN, S. H. WEITZMANN, AND G. S. MYERS. 1966. Phyletic studies of teleostean fishes with a provisional classification of living forms. Bull. Am. Mus. Nat. Hist. 131: 339−456.

HIGGINS, P. J. 1985a. Metabolic differences between Atlantic salmon parr and smolts (*Salmo salar*). Aquaculture 45: 33−53.

1985b. Growth, metabolism and feeding in juvenile Atlantic salmon. Ph.D. thesis, University of Aberdeen, Scotland.

HIGGINS, P. J., AND C. TALBOT. 1985. Feeding and growth in juvenile Atlantic salmon, p. 243−263. *In* C. B. Cowey, A. M. Mackie, and J. G. Bell [ed.] Nutrition and feeding in fish. Academic Press, London.

IKUTA, K., K. AIDA, N. OKUMOTO, AND I. HANYU. 1985. Effects of thyroxine and methyltestosterone on the smoltification of masu salmon *Oncorhynchus masou*. Aquaculture 45: 289−303.

JONSSON, B. 1977. Demographic strategy in a brown trout population in Western Norway. Zool. Scr. 6: 255−263.

1981. Life history strategies of trout (*Salmo trutta* L.). Ph.D. Thesis, Univ. of Oslo, Norway.

JONSSON, B., AND K. HINDAR. 1982. Reproductive strategy of dwarf and normal Arctic charr (*Salvelinus alpinus*) from Vangsvatnet Lake, Western Norway. Can. J. Fish. Aquat. Sci. 39: 1404−1413.

JONSSON, B., K. HINDAR, AND T. G. NORTHCOTE. 1984. Optimal age at sexual maturity of sympatric and experimentally allopatric cutthroat trout and Dolly Varden charr. Oecologia (Berlin). 61: 319−325.

KATO, T. 1975. The relation between growth and reproductive characters of rainbow trout. Bull. Freshwater Fish. Res. Lab. Tokyo. 25: 83−115.

1980. Relation between age at maturity and growth of Kokanee, *Oncorhynchus nerka*, in Lake Towada. Bull. Natl. Res. Inst. Aquaculture. 1: 7−19.

KOMOURDJIAN, M. P., R. L. SAUNDERS, AND J. C. FENWICK. 1976. Evidence for the role of growth hormone as a part of a 'light-pituitary axis" in growth and smoltification of Atlantic salmon (*Salmo salar*). Can. J. Zool. 54: 544−551.

KROGIUS, F. V. 1979. O vzaimosvyazi presnovodnogo i morskogo period zhizni krasnoi nerki ozera Dalnego. Biologiya morya. 3: 24−29. (In Russian)

KROKHIN, E. M. 1967. Materialy k poznaniyu karlikovoi krasnoi *Oncorhynchus nerka* Walb. v Dalnyem ozere (Kamchatka). Vopr. Ikhtiol. 7: 433−445. (In Russian)

LAM, T. J. 1983. Environmental influences on gonadal activity in fish. p. 65−116 *In* W. S. Hoar, D. J. Randall, and E. M. Donaldson [ed.] Fish physiology: reproduction. Vol. IXB. Academic Press, New York, NY.

LEYZEROVICH, K. A. 1973. Dwarf males in hatchery propagation of the Atlantic salmon. J. Ichthyol. 13: 382−292.

LEYZEROVICH, K. A., AND M. N. MELNIKOVA. 1979. The seaward migration of the Atlantic salmon, *Salmo salar*, and their return to the river. J. Ichthyol. 19: 164−167.

LUNDQVIST, H. 1980. Influence of photoperiod on growth in Baltic salmon (*Salmo salar* L.) with special reference to the effect of precocious sexual maturation. Can. J. Zool. 58: 940−944.

1983. Precocious sexual maturation and smolting in Baltic salmon (*Salmo salar*): Photoperiodic synchronization and adaptive significance of annual biological cycles. Ph.D. thesis, Umea University, Sweden.

MARGALEF, R. 1959. Mode of evolution of species in relation to their places in ecological succession. Proc. Int. Cong. Zool. 15: 787−789.

MITANS, A. R. 1973. Dwarf males and the sex structure of a Baltic salmon (*Salmo salar*) population. J. Ichthyol. 13: 192−197.

MIWA, S., AND Y. INUI. 1985. Inhibitory effects of 17α-methyltestosterone and estradiol-17β on smoltification of sterilised amago salmon (*Oncorhynchus rhodurus*). (Abstract only) Aquaculture 45: 383.

MURPHY, T. M. 1980. Studies on precocious maturity in artificially reared 1+ Atlantic salmon parr *Salmo salar* L. Ph.D. thesis, Univ. of Stirling, Scotland.

MYERS, R. A. 1983. Evolutionary change in the proportion of precocious parr and its effect on yield in Atlantic salmon. I.C.E.S. CM1983/M13: 16 p.

1984. Demographic consequences of precocious maturation of Atlantic salmon (*Salmo salar*). Can. J. Fish. Aquat. Sci. 41: 1349−1353.

NAEVDAL, G., M. HOLM, R. LEROY, AND D. MOLLER. 1978. Individual growth rate and age at first sexual maturity in Atlantic salmon. Fiskeridir. Skr. Ser. Havsunders. 16: 519−529.

1979. Individual growth rate and age at first sexual maturity in rainbow trout. Fiskeridir. Skr. Ser. Havsunders. 17: 1−10.

NAGAHAMA, Y. 1985. Involvement of endocrine systems in smoltification in the amago salmon, *Oncorhynchus rhodurus*. (Abstract only) Aquaculture 45: 383−384.

NAGAHAMA, Y., S. ADACHI, F. TASHIRO, AND E. G. GRAU. 1982. Some endocrine factors affecting the development of seawater tolerance during parr−smolt transformation of the amago salmon *Oncorhynchus rhodurus*. Aquaculture 28: 81−90.

NIKOLSKII, G. V., N. A. GROMCHEVSKAYA, G. I. MOROZOVA, AND V. A. PIKULEVA. 1947. Ryby basseina verkhnei Pechory. Mater. Poznaniyu Fauny Flory SSSR Otd. Bot. 6: 1−202. (In Russian)

NIKULIN, O. A. 1970. O svyazi mezhdu snizheniem absolyutnoi chislennosti krasnoi *Onchorhynchus nerka* (Walb.) i uvelicheniem otnositelnoi chislennosti karlikov sredi nagulivayuscheisya molodi v ozere Uyeginskom (Okhotskii raion). Izv. TINRO. 71: 205−217. (In Russian)

OHNO, S., J. MURAMOTO, J. KLEIN, AND N. B. ATKIN. 1969. Diploid-tetraploid relationship in clupeoid and salmonoid fish, p. 139−147. *In* C. D. Darlington and K. R. Lewis [ed.] Chromosomes today. Vol. 21. Oliver and Boyd, Edinburgh.

OSTERDAHL, L. 1969. The smolt run of a small Swedish river, p. 205−215. *In* T. G. Northcote [ed.] Salmon and trout in streams. H. R. MacMillan Lectures in Fisheries, Univ. of British Columbia, Vancouver, B.C.

PAULY, D. 1984. A mechanism for the juvenile-to-adult transition in fishes. J. Cons. Int. Explor. Mer 41: 280−284.

POLICANSKY, D. 1983. Size, age and demography of metamorphosis and sexual maturation in fishes. Am. Zool. 23: 57−63.

POWER, G. 1958. The evolution of the freshwater races of the Atlantic salmon (*Salmo salar* L.) in Eastern North America. Arctic 11: 86−92.

RICKER, W. E. 1938. "Residual" and kokanee salmon in Cultus Lake. J. Fish. Res. Board Can. 4: 192−218.

ROBERTS, F. L. 1970. Atlantic salmon (*Salmo salar*) chromosomes and speciation. Trans. Am. Fish. Soc. 99: 105−111.

ROFF, D. A. 1983. An allocation model of growth and reproduction in fish. Can. J. Fish. Aquat. Sci. 40: 1395−1404.

SAUNDERS, J. W. 1976. Fate of Atlantic salmon parr and smolts after descending from a small tributary to the Northwest Miramichi River. I.C.E.S. CM176/M:13. 7 p.

SAUNDERS, R. L. 1986. The scientific and management implications of age and size at sexual maturity in Atlantic salmon (*Salmo salar*), p. 3−6. *In* D. J. Meerburg [ed.] Salmonid age at maturity. Can. Spec. Publ. Fish. Aquat. Sci. 89.

SAUNDERS, R. L., AND E. B. HENDERSON. 1970. Influence of photoperiod on smolt development and growth in Atlantic salmon (*Salmo salar*). J. Fish. Res. Board Can. 27: 1295−1311.

SAUNDERS, R. L., E. B. HENDERSON, AND B. D. GLEBE. 1982. Precocious sexual maturation and smoltification in male Atlantic salmon (*Salmo salar*). Aquaculture 28: 211−229.

SCHAFFER, W. M., AND P. F. ELSON. 1975. The adaptive significance of variations in life history among local populations of Atlantic salmon in North America. Ecology 56: 577−590.

SCHIEFER, K. 1971. Ecology of Atlantic salmon, with special reference to occurrence and abundance of grilse in North Shore Gulf of St. Lawrence Rivers. Ph.D. thesis, Univ. of Waterloo, Ont. Canada. 129 p.

SCOTT, A. P., AND J. P. SUMPTER. 1983. The control of trout reproduction: basic and applied research on hormones, p. 200−220. *In* J. C. Rankin, T. J. Pitcher, and R. T. Duggan [ed.]. Control processes in fish physiology. Croom Helm, London.

SHEARER, W. M. 1972. A study of the Atlantic salmon population of the North Esk 1961−1970. M.Sc. thesis, Univ. of Edinburgh, Scotland.

SIMPSON, T. H., AND J. E. THORPE. 1976. Growth bimodality in the Atlantic salmon. Int. Coun. Expl. Sea CM 1976/M22: 7 p.

SMITH-GILL, S. J. 1983. Developmental plasticity: developmental conversion *versus* phenotypic modulation. Am. Zool. 23: 47−55.

SMITH-GILL, S. J., AND K. A. BERVEN. 1979. Predicting amphibian metamorphosis. Am. Nat. 113: 563−585.

STOCS SYMPOSIUM PAPERS. 1981. Stock Concept International Symposium, Alliston, Ontario. 1980. Can. J. Fish. Aquat. Sci. 38: 1457−1914.

SUTTERLIN, A. M., AND D. MACLEAN. 1984. Age at first maturity and the early expression of oocyte recruitment processes in two forms of Atlantic salmon (*Salmo salar*) and their hybrids. Can. J. Fish. Aquat. Sci. 41: 1139−1149.

THORPE, J. E. 1975. Early maturity in male Atlantic salmon. Scott. Fish Bull. 42: 15−17.

1977. Bimodal distribution of length of juvenile Atlantic salmon (*Salmo salar* L.) under artificial rearing conditions. J. Fish. Biol. 11: 175−184.

1982. Migration in salmonids, with special reference to juvenile movements in freshwater, p. 86−97. *In* E. L. Brannon and E. O. Salo [ed.] Proceedings of the salmon and trout migratory behavior symposium, Seattle, Washington.

1984. Downstream movements of juvenile salmonids: a forward speculative view, p. 387−396. *In* J. D. McCleave, G. P. Arnold, J. J. Dodson, and W. H. Neill [ed.] Mechanisms of migration in fishes. Plenum Press, New York, NY.

THORPE, J. E., AND R. I. G. MORGAN. 1978. Parental influence on growth rate, smolting rate and survival in hatchery reared juvenile Atlantic salmon, *Salmo salar* L. J. Fish. Biol. 13: 549−556.

1980. Growth-rate and smolting-rate of progeny of male Atlantic salmon parr, *Salmo salar* L. J. Fish. Biol. 17: 451−460.

THORPE, J. E., R. I. G. MORGAN, E. M. OTTAWAY, AND M. S. MILES. 1980. Time of divergence of growth groups between potential 1+ and 2+ smolts among sibling Atlantic salmon. J. Fish. Biol. 17: 13−21.

THORPE, J. E., R. I. G. MORGAN, C. TALBOT, AND M. S. MILES. 1983. Inheritance of developmental rates in Atlantic salmon, *Salmo salar* L. Aquaculture 33: 119−128.

THORPE, J. E., C. TALBOT, AND C. VILLARREAL. 1982. Bimodality of growth and smolting in Atlantic salmon, *Salmo salar* L. Aquaculture 28: 123−132.

THORPE, J. E., AND J. W. J. WANKOWSKI. 1979. Feed presentation and food particle size for juvenile Atlantic salmon, *Salmo salar* L. p. 501−513. *In* J. E. Halver and K. Tiews [ed.] Finfish nutrition and fishfeed technology. Volume 2. Heinemann, Berlin.

UTOH, H. 1976. Study of the mechanism of differentiation between the stream resident form and the seaward migratory form in masu salmon, *Oncorhynchus masou* Brevoort. I. Growth and sexual maturity of precocious salmon parr. Bull. Fac. Fish., Hokkaido Univ. 26: 321−326.

1977. Study of the mechanism of differentiation between the stream resident form and the seaward migratory form of masu salmon, *Oncorhynchus masou* Brevoort. II. Growth and sexual maturity of precocious salmon parr (2). Bull. Fac. Fish., Hokkaido Univ. 28: 66−73.

VILLARREAL, C. A. 1983. The role of light and endocrine factors in the development of bimodality in the juvenile Atlantic salmon (*Salmo salar* L.). Ph.D. thesis, University of Stirling, Scotland.

VILLARREAL, C. A., AND J. E. THORPE. 1985. Gonadal growth and bimodality of length frequency distribution in juvenile Atlantic salmon, *Salmo salar*. Aquaculture 45: 265−288.

1986. Content of nucleic acids as indices of growth in juvenile Atlantic salmon. (in preparation)

WARE, D. M. 1980. Bioenergetics of stock and recruitment. Can. J. Fish. Aquat. Sci. 37: 1012−1024.

Ovarian Development of Atlantic Salmon (*Salmo salar*) Smolts and Age at First Maturity

E. Michael P. Chadwick, Robert G. Randall, and Claude Léger

Fisheries Research Branch, Department of Fisheries and Oceans, P.O. Box 5030, Moncton, N.B. E1C 9B6

Abstract

CHADWICK, E. M. P., R. G. RANDALL, AND C. LÉGER. 1986. Ovarian development of Atlantic salmon (*Salmo salar*) smolts and age at first maturity, p. 15–23. *In* D. J. Meerburg [ed.] Salmonid age at maturity. Can. Spec. Publ. Fish. Aquat. Sci. 89.

The hypothesis that sea age of adult Atlantic salmon (*Salmo salar*) can be determined from the ovarian development of smolts before they enter the sea was tested. Smolts were selected from six stocks, with parents ranging in sea age from entirely 1-sea-winter (1SW) salmon to entirely 3SW salmon. The modal ovarian development stage of smolts from the 1SW stock was greater ($P < 0.01$) than the other stocks. Over 30% of the oocytes of the 1SW stock were at development stages five and six (with yolk vesicles); for smolts from the other stocks, there were few oocytes at these stages. It appeared that mean ovarian development of smolts was inversely correlated to sea age of parents. These results were corroborated by samples of smolts collected from 34 rivers in insular Newfoundland in 1973, where fork length and ovarian weight of smolts were inversely correlated ($P < 0.01$) to sea age of parents. Finally, significant correlations for three stocks between the number of 1SW salmon and the number of 2SW salmon in the following year suggest that the proportion of smolts destined to be both 1SW and 2SW salmon remained constant from one year to the next and that sea age of Atlantic salmon is influenced by factors in freshwater.

Résumé

CHADWICK, E. M. P., R. G. RANDALL, AND C. LÉGER. 1986. Ovarian development of Atlantic salmon (*Salmo salar*) smolts and age at first maturity, p. 15–23. *In* D. J. Meerburg [ed.] Salmonid age at maturity. Can. Spec. Publ. Fish. Aquat. Sci. 89.

L'hypothèse selon laquelle on peut déterminer le nombre d'années en mer du saumon adulte de l'Atlantique (*Salmo salar*) par le degré de développement des ovaires de saumoneaux en avalaison fut testée. Six populations de saumoneaux furent échantillonnées. La gamme du nombre d'années en mer des géniteurs s'étendait d'une population entièrement unibermarine à une population entièrement triribermarine. Les ovaires des saumoneaux dont les parents étaient tous des castillons étaient plus avancés, quant au stade modal de développement des ovocytes, que ceux des autres populations ($P < 0,01$). Plus de 30 % des ovocytes de cette même population avaient atteint les stades cinq ou six (début de la vitellogénèse); très peu des ovocytes des saumoneaux provenant des autres populations étaient si développés. Il sembla y avoir une relation inverse entre le développement ovarien moyen des populations de saumoneaux et le nombre d'années en mer des géniteurs. Une étude effectuée sur 34 rivières de Terre-Neuve en 1973, où il fut trouvé que la longueur à la fourche ainsi que le poids des ovaires des saumoneaux étaient inversement liés au nombre d'années en mer des parents ($P < 0,01$), vient appuyer nos résultats. Finalement, pour trois populations du saumon de l'Atlantique, une corrélation significative entre le nombre de castillons et celui de saumons diribermarins l'année suivante suggère que les proportions de saumoneaux qui deviendront castillons et diribermarins demeurent constantes d'une année à l'autre, et il s'en suit que des facteurs proximaux qui influencent le nombre d'années en mer du saumon de l'Atlantique.

Introduction

Is sea age of Atlantic salmon (*Salmo salar*) determined in freshwater? This question is difficult to examine directly in wild populations, as opposed to hatchery populations (Naevdal et al. 1978), partly becauser wild populations are rarely sampled well enough to determine exact parentage of eggs spawned, not to forget the importance of precocious male parr (Jones 1959). Secondly, progeny which would return to their natal rivers as adults are never fully accounted for because of complex interceptory fisheries (Pippy 1982) and the greater exploitation of larger and older salmon (Anon. 1978; Saunders 1969).

The second problem can be avoided by ignoring adults and focusing attention on smolts. If factors in freshwater, as opposed to factors at sea, determine the sea age of a wild population, then smolts destined to be adults of different sea ages could be morphologically distinct. Observations of wild smolts in rivers of England (Calderwood 1925), Wales (Hutton 1937), Iceland (Gudjonsson 1978), and Canada

(Ritter 1975) indicated that the age of smolts was negatively correlated to the sea age of returning adults. It has been demonstrated in well-sampled populations that smolt size increases with freshwater age (Murray 1968; Chadwick 1981), thus both age and size of smolts might be inversely correlated to sea age. Similar observations have been made for other species: Hager and Noble (1976) and Bilton (1980) described that large smolts of *Oncorhynchus kisutch* produced significantly greater returns of jacks (one winter at sea) than younger smolts, and Khalturin (1972) found a similar situation for *O. nerka* in the Soviet Union.

The objective of this paper is to examine wild smolts from several populations which vary in sea age. To avoid the complicating phenomenon of parr maturation which occurs frequently among male salmon (Dalley et al. 1983), we restricted our attention to female smolts. We test the hypothesis that sea age of a population can be determined from the ovarian development of sea-going smolts. Patterns of ovarian development were determined from histological sections. This technique has been used to predict time of

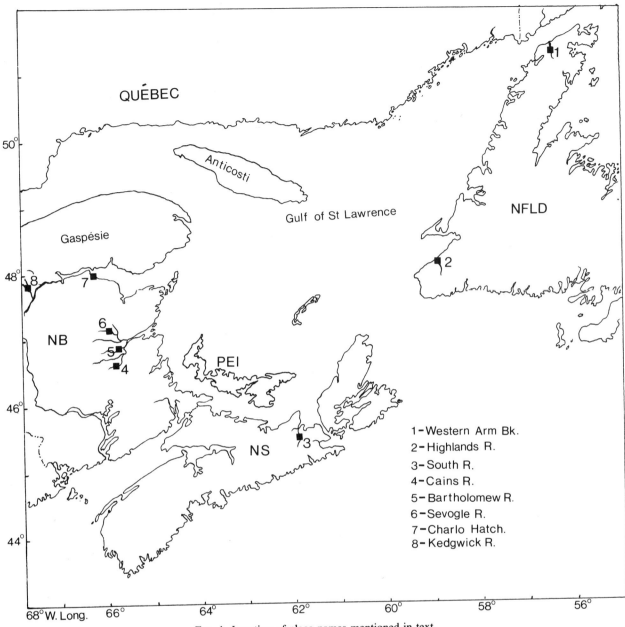

FIG. 1. Location of place names mentioned in text.

1 - Western Arm Bk.
2 - Highlands R.
3 - South R.
4 - Cains R.
5 - Bartholomew R.
6 - Sevogle R.
7 - Charlo Hatch.
8 - Kedgwick R.

spawning of capelin (Forberg 1982) and to discriminate among stocks of Atlantic salmon (Sutterlin and McLean 1984).

Methods

Smolts were sampled from seven populations. The populations were selected to provide a range in sea age of female parents: two rivers with primarily 1-sea-winter (1SW) spawners, Sevogle River and Western Arm Brook; two rivers with primarily 2-sea-winter (2SW) spawners, Cains and Bartholomew rivers; two rivers with primarily 3-sea-winter (3SW) spawners, South and Highlands rivers; and one hatchery-reared (Charlo) population of 3SW parentage (both males and females), Kedgwick River (Fig. 1). Unfortunately, the samples from Sevogle River were spoiled and could not be used.

The sea age, sex, and fork length of female spawners was estimated for each population. Samples were taken from

bright or spawning fish, in all rivers except Highlands where samples were taken from kelts. Sea age was determined from scales. Sex was determined from external characteristics on South, Highlands and Bartholomew Rivers. On the other three rivers, sex was determined surgically. On four rivers, fecundity was calculated for the mean fork length at each sea age using the following equation:

$$\ln F = 1.7276 + 1.6587 \ln FL,$$

where F is fecundity and FL is fork length (cm) (from 106 Miramichi salmon examined in 1983, Randall unpublished data). On Western Arm Brook, fecundity was determined from 107 samples in 1983 (Chadwick unpublished data). On Kedgwick River, fecundity was determined from egg counts in the hatchery.

The proportion of eggs contributed by each sea age was calculated for a given spawning year. The mean sea age of parents was weighted by the year in which the smolts in our samples were spawned. On South River, we were unable to

16

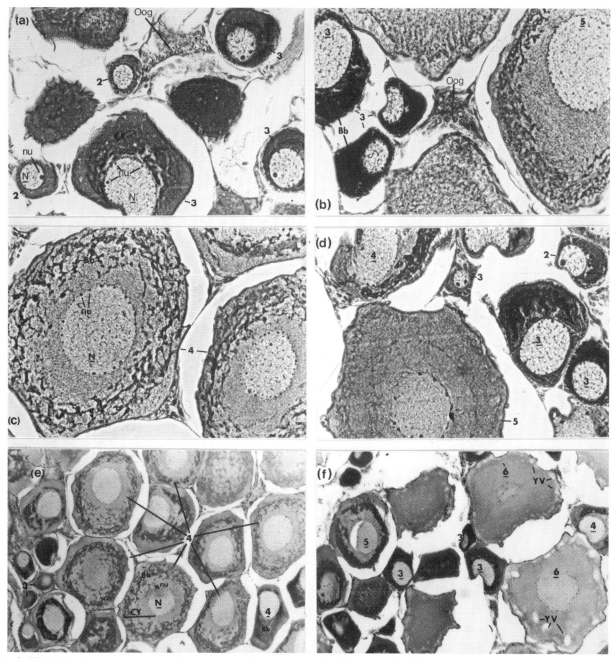

FIG. 2. Histological appearance of smolt (*Salmo salar*) oocytes (a)−(d) 250×; (e)−(f) 100×; 2, 3, 4, 5, 6 oocyte development stages (Bb — Balbiani bodies; Cy — cytoplasm; N — nucleus; nu — nucleoli. Oog — oogonia; YV — yolk vesicles).

obtain samples of the parents of the smolts in our sample and we assumed that the adults sampled one year later (1982) would be representative.

In late May and early June 1984, a sample of approximately 30 female smolts was collected in each of the five rivers. Fish were captured by angling on the Highlands, with a trap net on the Cains and at fish counting fences on the other three rivers. Smolts from Charlo Hatchery were collected in April.

In most cases, the left gonad was removed immediately after the fish were killed, but when this was impractical, the fish were kept on ice until the gonad could be removed.

The gonads were weighed (0.01 g) fixed in Bouin's solution and stored in 70% ethanol. At the time of sampling, the fish were measured (FL), weighed (0.1 g) and a scale sample taken for ageing.

Histological Procedure

Following dehydration and clearing (ethanol and xylene), the gonads were embedded in paraplast (TM) (56°C melting point) and sectioned at 8 μm. Four series of transverse sections were obtained from the anterior portion of each gonad at 0.4 mm intervals. The sections were mounted and stained with Erlich hematoxylin and eosin (Humason 1979).

Stained sections were studied using a compound microscope (250×) and all nucleated oocytes in a transect through one section in each series were counted and identified as to their development stages. Thus, four sections were studied for each specimen. Oogonia "nests" were counted and the numbers of cells within each was estimated.

The separation of oocyte development stages (Fig. 2) was based on cellular structure, staining characteristics and rela-

TABLE 1. Mean sea age of parents.

River	Percent			Mean sea age	Code
	1SW	2SW	3SW		
Western Arm Brook	100	0	0	1.00	1
Cains River	53	43	4	1.51	2
Highlands River	21	71	8	1.87	3
Bartholomew River	13	87	0	1.87	4
South River	0	77	23	2.23	5
Kedgwick River	0	0	100	3.00	6

TABLE 2. Percent-at-age and mean age of female smolts collected from the six rivers.

River	n	Age (%)				Mean age
		2	3	4	5	
1. Western Arm	31	0	7	77	16	4.1
2. Cains	28	93	7	0	0	2.1
3. Highlands	25	8	88	4	0	3.0
4. Bartholomew	27	67	33	0	0	2.3
5. South	16	63	31	6	0	2.4
6. Kedgwick	11	100	0	0	0	2.0

tive size of the oocytes, adapted from previous studies (Funk et al. 1972; Beams and Kessel 1973; Foucher and Beamish 1980; van den Hurk and Peute 1979; Wallace and Selman 1981; Forberg 1982; Groman 1982; Robb 1982; Howell 1982; Sutterlin and MacLean 1984).

Stage 1: Oogonia — 5–6 μm in size, round to oval in shape with a small centrally located nucleus; usually in groups or "nests" of 5–40 cells.

Stage 2: Primary oocyte — nucleus occupies most of the cell and contains one large nucleolus. Cell size 10–20 μm.

Stage 3: Early perinucleolus — nucleoli small, numerous and located around the periphery of the nucleus. Intensely staining "Balbiani bodies" concentrated around or adjacent to nucleus. Cell size 20–100 μm.

Stage 4: Mid perinucleolus — "Balbiani bodies" fragmented, no longer concentrated near the nucleus but are migrating toward the periphery of the cell. Intensity of cytoplasm staining fades. Cell size 100–200 μm.

Stage 5: Late perinucleolus — "Balbiani bodies" concentrated in a ring at the periphery of the oocyte, are usually faded and tend to disappear. Periphery of nucleus becomes irregular in later part of stage. Cell size 250–400 μm. End of previtellogenic phase of development.

Stage 6: Yolk vesicle stage — Clear "yolk vesicles" appear in cytoplasm, usually towards periphery.

Analysis

The first step in our analysis was to compare the biological characteristics of smolts in each river. Fork length (FL), weight (w), condition (FL^3/w) and gonadosomatic index

TABLE 3. Biological characteristics of female smolts collected from the six rivers. GSI means were calculated after arcsine transformations.

River	n	Mean length (mm)	Mean weight (g)	K	GSI
1. Western Arm	31	163.5	38.3	0.86	0.0764
2. Cains	28	123.7	18.4	0.96	0.0745
3. Highlands	25	145.0	27.7	0.90	0.0746
4. Bartholomew	27	126.7	18.5	0.90	0.0776
5. South	16	144.5	28.7	0.93	0.0685
6. Kedgwick	11	158.7	42.1	1.04	0.0802

(GSI, 2 × weight of left gonad/w) were compared among populations using unbalanced analysis-of-variance (SAS 1979). Significantly different means among rivers were identified using the Student–Newman–Keuls multiple range test. The gonadosomatic index was transformed (arcsine, Sokal and Rohlf 1981) before analysis.

The second step was to test the null hypothesis that gonadal development was equal in all populations. For each smolt within rivers, a modal oocyte stage was identified. Frequencies of smolts in each mode were arranged by river in a contingency table and analysed using a log-likelihood ratio G-test (Sokal and Rholf 1981). In addition, for all rivers combined, frequencies of smolts in each modal oocyte stage were analysed (i) by smolt age and (ii) by 10 mm intervals of fork length.

Results

Generally, the mean sea age of parents fell into four categories (Table 1): on Western Arm Brook, all parents were 1SW salmon; on Cains River, over half of parents were 1SW salmon; on Highlands, Bartholomew, and South rivers, over 70% of parents were 2SW salmon; and on Kedgwick River, all parents were 3SW salmon. The relative fecundities for all stocks were lower in 1979 than in 1980 (Appendix 1).

Although sample sizes were small, the biological characteristics of smolts were different among rivers. Smolt ages were significantly different ($P < 0.01$) and usually tended to be inversely correlated to sea age of the parents (Table 2): Western Arm Brook (1SW parents) had predominantly 4-yr-old smolts; Highlands River had predominantly 3-yr-old smolts; and the other rivers had predominantly 2-yr-old smolts. Smolts were also significantly different ($P < 0.01$) in fork length, weight., and condition (Table 3), but there was no obvious correlation with sea age of parents. The longest and heaviest smolts were from Western Arm Brook and Kedgwick River, stocks with the youngest and oldest parents (Table 4), and also stocks with the greatest total age, 5 years (Tables 1 and 2). At an intermediate size, the length and weight of smolts from Highlands and South rivers were not different. The smallest smolts were from Cains and Bartholomew rivers, both tributaries of the Miramichi River. The condition factor of hatchery-reared smolts was significantly greater than the others (Tables 3 and 4). Finally, there was little difference in gonadosomatic index among five rivers, but it was significantly less ($P < 0.01$) for South River (Tables 3 and 4).

The ovarian development of smolts appeared to be inversely related to sea age of parents. The modal devel-

TABLE 4. Means for biological characteristics of female smolts sampled in six rivers: 1 — Western Arm Brook, 2 — Cains, 3 — Highlands, 4 — Bartholomew, 5 — South, and 6 — Kedgwick rivers. Results of Student−Newman−Keuls tests are also given.

Means (decreasing left to right)						
Fork length						
River	1	6	3	5	4	2
Significance*						
Weight						
River	6	1	5	3	4	2
Significance						
Condition						
River	6	2	5	4	3	1
Significance						
Gonadosomatic index						
River	6	4	1	3	2	5
Significance						
Oocyte stage						
River	1	2	3	5	4	6
Significance*						

*Underlined means are not significantly different.

TABLE 5. Modal oocyte development by age and intervals of fork length for female smolts sampled on all six rivers combined.

Variable	Mode			G-test
	3	4	5	
a) Age				
2	12	55	0	
3	16	20	4	P < 0.01
4	15	5	11	
b) Fork length (mm)				
120	3	14	0	
121−130	6	26	0	
131−140	7	15	0	P < 0.01
141−150	6	11	0	
151−160	10	12	3	
160	10	5	11	

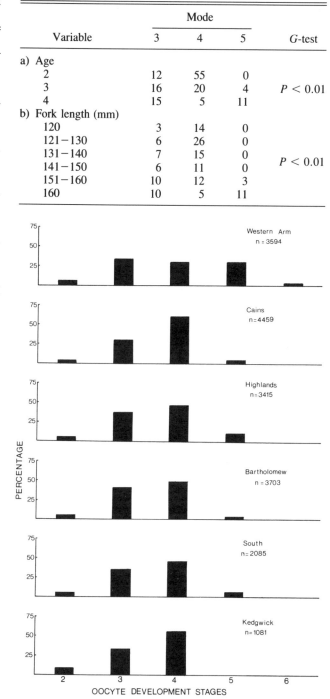

FIG. 4. Percentage of oocytes at each oocyte development stage for the six rivers.

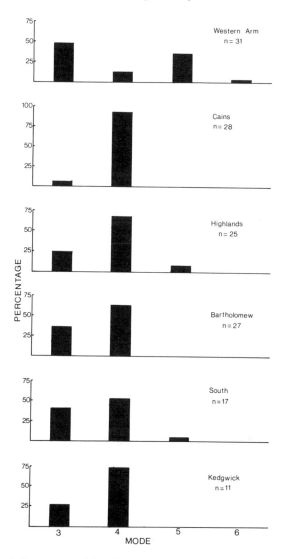
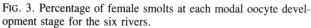

FIG. 3. Percentage of female smolts at each modal oocyte development stage for the six rivers.

opment stage on Western Arm Brook (1SW parents) was significantly greater (P < 0.01) than the other stocks (Fig. 3). Over 30% of the oocytes from Western Arm Brook smolts were at development stages five and six (Fig. 4); for smolts from the other rivers, there were few oocytes at these stages; and for smolts from Kedgwick River (3SW parents), there were none. There were also significant differences (P < 0.01) between ages and 10 mm intervals of fork length for all smolts combined (Table 5) which may partly account for the greater maturity of Western Arm Brook smolts.

TABLE 6. Biological characteristics of smolts sampled in 34 rivers around insular Newfoundland in 1973 (Chadwick 1982). An index of large salmon abundance for the year which produced the predominant age-group of smolts is also given for each river.

River	Map no.	Sample size	Fork length (cm)	Condition	Mean age	Percent male	Weight (g) ovaries	Weight (g) body	Index of large salmon abundance
Beaver Brook	1	75	13.8	1.17	4.0	25	0.30	31	1.0
Sops Arm River	2	24	13.0	1.14	4.1	29	0.25	25	3.0
Burlington River	3	28	15.1	0.95	3.6	21	0.31	34	1.5
Riverhead Brook	4	75	16.0	0.97	3.4	28	0.46	44	0.5
Pt. Leamington R.	5	7	15.6	1.12	3.4	43	0.37	46	1.5
Cambellton River	6	100	16.1	1.09	3.2	29	0.44	46	1.0
Gander River	7	24	14.4	1.05	3.8	8	0.32	32	5.0
Ragged Harbour R.	8	63	17.4	0.96	3.2	24	0.59	60	0.5
Indian Bay Brook	9	76	16.7	1.06	3.0	37	0.38	51	1.0
Gambo River	10	49	16.7	1.16	3.0	24	0.55	55	3.0
Terra Nova River	11	41	14.9	1.10	3.5	37	0.33	37	2.0
Northwest River	12	47	17.2	1.00	4.0	34	0.56	55	6.0
Champney's River	13	34	15.5	1.06	3.4	15	0.33	40	0
Trouty Brook	14	53	16.7	1.11	3.2	11	0.69	53	0
Renews River	15	22	17.8	1.06	2.7	41	1.06	65	0
Salmonier River	16	54	16.0	1.03	3.1	24	0.49	45	0.2
Branch River	17	97	15.8	1.03	3.1	7	0.40	41	0
Northeast River	18	32	13.9	1.35	3.2	69	0.52	37	3.0
Pipers Hole R.	19	37	16.4	1.16	3.4	32	0.46	52	1.0
Red Harbour R.	20	99	14.7	1.18	3.2	4	0.41	38	1.0
Taylor Bay Brook	21	80	17.5	1.83	3.3	15	0.75	92	0.0
Terrenceville R.	22	112	13.9	1.12	3.3	9	0.27	31	0.0
Grandy's River	23	9	17.7	0.96	3.8	—	—	53	0.0
Farmers River	24	103	16.6	0.89	3.1	—	—	41	0.0
Garia River	25	19	15.7	1.13	2.9	26	0.37	45	10.0
Highlands River	26	56	13.7	0.94	2.7	64	0.15	25	11.0
Robinsons River	27	44	13.5	1.06	3.0	34	0.21	26	20.0
Fischells River	28	35	14.0	1.04	2.6	26	0.22	29	10.0
Southwest Brook	29	40	13.4	1.07	3.0	50	0.25	26	10.0
Harry's River	30	10	12.7	1.21	3.4	20	0.20	24	10.0
River of Ponds	31	86	16.2	1.09	3.2	29	0.42	47	3.0
Little Bk. Ponds	32	29	17.4	1.16	3.1	48	0.57	61	0.0
East River	33	104	13.6	1.01	4.0	34	—	25	8.0
St. Genevieve R.	34	99	17.0	0.84	4.2	34	—	41	6.0

There appeared, however, to be a continuum between mean ovarian development of smolts and sea age of parents (Fig. 5), which was not as apparent for age or size of smolts.

Discussion

The age at first maturity of Atlantic salmon appeared to be associated with the ovarian development of smolts. The results are not entirely robust, however, and the experiment should be repeated with more replicates of smolts from 1SW, 2SW, and 3SW parents of discrete stocks and an analysis of a continuous variable such as oocyte size. In this experiment, some shrinkage and cytoplasmic retraction occurred during fixation in some of our samples and we decided to only count cells and not to measure them. Nevertheless, these results support the hypothesis that the sea age of adults can be determined from the ovarian development of smolts, before they enter the sea.

Although there was some indication that sea age was related to oocyte development and perhaps fork length of wild smolts (Table 4), it was not apparent for gonadosomatic index or smolt age. The association between smolt size and sea age of parents was also suggested in a series of

samples collected from 34 rivers in insular Newfoundland in 1973. The methods used to collect and sample the smolts are given in Chadwick (1982). Sea age of parents was determined for the spawning year which produced the predominant age-group of smolts; it was calculated for each river as the percent large salmon (> 2.7 kg), by smolt-class, taken in the sport fishery (Moores et al. 1978). A smolt-class is the year a salmon migrates to sea as a smolt; a smolt-class of adults would include 1SW salmon captured in one year and 2SW salmon captured in the following year. The major results of this survey were: first, fork length and ovarian weight of smolts were correlated ($P < 0.01$) to sea age of parents (Table 6 and Fig. 6); and second, fork length explained 65% of the variation in ovarian weight. These results are supported by Lee and Power (1976) and Sutterlin et al. (1978), who found some evidence of exceptionally large smolts maturing in the first summer at sea. Other biological attributes of smolts, such as age, condition and sex ratio, were not correlated to sea age of parents. It is also interesting to note that in 29 out of 32 rivers, females predominated males (Table 6); this is similar to the findings of our samples in 1984.

One explanation for predominantly female smolt

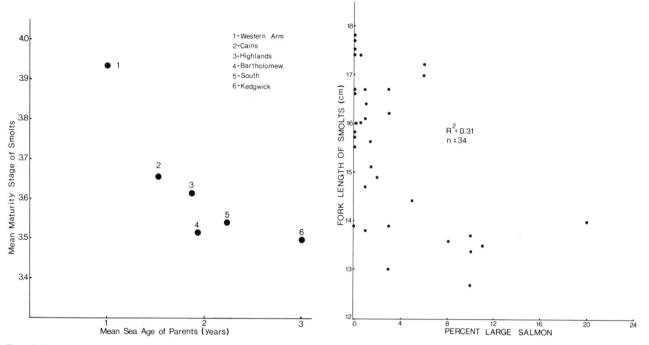

FIG. 5. Relationship between mean maturity stage of female smolts and mean sea age of parents on the six rivers.

FIG. 6. Relationship between mean fork length of smolts and mean sea age of parents on 34 rivers sampled in insular Newfoundland, 1973.

TABLE 7. Relationships between 1SW salmon captured in the sport fisheries of Cascapédia and Bonaventure rivers and in Millbank Trap (Miramichi River) and 2SW salmon captured in the following year.

| Year i | Cascapédia[a] | | Bonaventure[a] | | Millbank[b] | |
	1SW salmon year i	2SW salmon year $i+1$	1SW salmon year i	2SW salmon year $i+1$	1SW salmon year i	2SW salmon year $i+1$
1970	17	27	147	197	2 484	399
1971	8	72	120	370	1 962	1 151
1972	31	110	93	436	2 543	1 132
1973	51	132	159	355	2 450	1 791
1974	20	71	118	252	4 038	1 208
1975	33	139	234	305	3 548	943
1976	48	147	289	509	4 939	1 934
1977	37	136	65	229	1 505	693
1978	3	30	35	76	1 268	318
1979	53	247	210	556	2 500	1 093
1980	36	71	172	423	2 139	199
1981	70	188	349	442	2 174	408
1982					2 665	245
R^2	0.70		0.42		0.36	
df	10		10		11	
p	<0.01		<0.05		<0.05	

[a]1SW salmon <2.3 kg; 2SW salmon >2.3 <5.4 kg.
[b]Sea age determined from scales.

migrations is that many males remain in the river as precocious parr (Chadwick 1982; Dalley et al. 1983). Our assumption in the introduction, that precocious males are ubiquitous among rivers of Atlantic Canada, is probably valid, but nevertheless it leaves the problem of male parentage unresolved. Our results would have been more definitive if exact parentage could be determined; in fact, it is perhaps surprising that we were able to find any differences in oocyte development among our six rivers without knowl-

edge of the male parent.

There is one further line of evidence that supports the hypothesis that sea age is determined before smolts enter the sea. Dempson and Furey (1983) and Marshall et al. (1982) reported that the number of large salmon (2SW salmon and older) in fisheries of Labrador and Miramichi River, respectively, could be predicted from the number of 1SW salmon in the preceding year. We would not find these relationships unless the proportion of smolts destined to be both 1SW and 2SW salmon remained constant from one year to the next. It is unlikely that these relationships would exist if sea age was determined by factors in the marine environment (Saunders et al. 1983). We have included recent angling harvest data on Bonaventure and Cascapédia Rivers and scientific samples at Millbank Trap (Miramichi River). In each case, sea age was determined from scales or weight frequency distributions and in each case, the number of 2SW salmon could be predicted from the number of 1SW salmon in the preceding year (Table 7). These correlations were significant inspite of many interceptory fisheries which confounded our attempts to account for the production of large salmon by individual stocks.

In summary, we found that smolts had different patterns of ovarian development; and it appeared that sea age of a stock was related to the degree of ovarian development. Our results suggest that sea age of Atlantic salmon is largely determined by factors in freshwater. Our results are preliminary, however, and we provided little insight into the relative importance of either genetic (Naedval et al. 1978) or environmental influences in freshwater. Ideally, experimentally controlled comparisons should be made within stocks of known parentage among different freshwater and sea conditions. We would encourage any research in this direction.

Acknowledgements

We wish to thank the following people: M. Hambrook, E. Schofield, W. McGuiness, P. Caines, and C. MacInnes for assistance in collecting samples of smolts; J. Rice and R. Myers for providing statistical advice; D. MacLean provided advice on oocyte stage identification; S. Gauthier and P. Collette for the typing. D. E. Waldron kindly provided information on the smolts collected in 1973. Y. Côté kindly provided angling harvest data on Cascapédia and Bonaventure rivers.

References

ANON. 1978. Atlantic salmon review task force. Biological Conservation Subcommittee Report. Fish. Mar. Serv. Newfoundland and Maritimes Region. 203 p. (Mimeo).

BEAMS, H. W., AND R. G. KESSEL. 1973. Oocyte structure and early vitellogenesis in the trout, Salmo gairdneri. Am. J. Anat. 136: 105−122.

BILTON, H. T. 1980. Returns of adult coho salmon in relation to mean size and time at release of juveniles to the catch and the escapement. Can. Tech. Rep. Fish. Aquat. Sci. 941: 41 p.

CALDERWOOD, W. L. 1925. The relation of sea growth and spawning frequency in Salmo salar. Proc. R. Soc. Edinb. 45: 142−148.

CHADWICK, E. M. P. 1981. Biological characteristics of Atlantic salmon smolt in Western Arm Brook, Newfoundland. Can. Tech. Rep. Fish. Aquatic Sci. 1024: 45 p.

1982. Dynamics of an Atlantic salmon stock (Salmo salar) in a small Newfoundland river. Ph.D. thesis, Memorial University of Newfoundland, Nfld. 267 p.

DALLEY, E. L., C. W. ANDREWS, AND J. M. GREEN. 1983. Precocious male Atlantic salmon parr (Salmo salar) in insular Newfoundland. Can. J. Fish. Aquat. Sci. 40: 647−652.

DEMPSON, J. B., AND G. FUREY. 1983. Summary of catch and effort statistics in the recreational and commercial Labrador Atlantic salmon, Salmo salar, fishery 1982. CAFSAC Res. Doc. 83/9: 14 p.

FORBERG, K. G. 1982. A histological study of development of oocytes in capelin Mallotus villosus villosus (Muller). J. Fish Biol. (1982) 20: 143−154.

FOUCHER, R. P., AND R. J. BEAMISH. 1980. Production of nonviable oocytes by Pacific hake (Merluccius productus). Can. J. Fish. Aquat. Sci. 37: 41−48.

FUNK, J. D., E. M. DONALDSON, AND H. M. DYE. 1973. Induction of precocious sexual development in female pink salmon (Oncorhynchus gorbuscha). Can. J. Zool. 51: 493−500.

GROMAN, D. B. 1982. Histology of striped bass. Am. Fish. Soc. Mono. No. 3: 53−56.

GUDJONSSON, T. 1978. The Atlantic salmon in Iceland. J. Agr. Res. Icel. 10(2): 11−39.

HAGER, R. C., AND R. E. NOBLE. 1976. Relation of size at release of hatchery-reared coho salmon to age, size and sex composition of returning adults. Prog. Fish. Cult. 38: 144−147.

HOWELL, W. H. 1982. Seasonal changes in the ovaries of adult yellowtail flounder, Limanda ferruginea. Fish. Bull. 81(2): 341−355.

HUMASON, G. L. 1979. Animal tissue techniques. Fourth ed., W. H. Freeman & Co., San Francisco, CA. 661 p.

HUTTON, J. A. 1937. Wye parr and smolts: the inverse ratio theory of river and sea life. Salmon Trout Mag. 84: 119−123.

JONES, J. W. 1959. The salmon. Collins. London, 192 p.

KHALTURIN, D. K. 1972. Growth patterns of Pacific and Atlantic salmon in relation to early ontogenesis. Ekologiya. No. 2, 21−35. (Translated from Russian by Plenum Publ. Corp., New York, NY.)

LEE, R. L. G., AND G. POWER. 1976. Atlantic salmon (Salmo salar) of the Leaf River, Ungava Bay. J. Fish. Res. Board Can. 33: 2616−2621.

MARSHALL, T. L., J. L. PEPPAR, AND E. J. SCHOFIELD. 1982. Prediction of 2SW and older Atlantic salmon returning to the Millbank Trap, Miramichi River, NB. CAFSAC Res. Doc. 83/21.

MOORES, R., B., R. W. PENNEY, AND R. J. TUCKER. 1978. Atlantic salmon angled catched and effort data Newfoundland and Labrador, 1953−77. Fish. Mar. Serv. Data Rep. 84: 274 p.

MURRAY, A. R. 1968. Smolt survival and adult utilization of Little Codroy River, Newfoundland, Atlantic salmon. J. Fish. Res. Board Can. 25: 2165−2218.

NAEVDAL, N., M. HOLM, O. INGEBRIGTSEN, AND D. MØLLER. 1978. Variation in age at first spawning in Atlantic salmon (Salmo salar). J. Fish. Res. Board Can. 35: 145−147.

PIPPY, J. H. C. 1982. Report on the Working Group on the interception of mainland salmon in Newfoundland. Can. MS. Rep. Fish. Aquat. Sci. 1654: 196 p.

RITTER, J. A. 1975. Relationships of smolt size and age with age at first maturity in Atlantic salmon. Environ. Can. Res. Dev. Br. Tech. Rep. Mar/T-75-5.

ROBB, A. P. 1982. Histological observations on the reproductive biology of the haddock, Melanogrammus aeglefinus (L.). J. Fish Biol. 20: 397−408.

SAS. 1979. SAS user's guide 1979 edition. SAS Institute Inc. North Carolina 27511, 494 p.

SAUNDERS, R. L. 1969. Contributions of salmon from the Northwest Miramichi River, New Brunswick, to various fisheries. J. Fish. Res. Board Can. 26: 269−278.

SAUNDERS, R. L., E. B. HENDERSON, B. D. GLEBE, AND E. J. LOUDENSLAGER. 1983. Evidence of a major environmental component in determination of the grilse: larger salmon ratio in Atlantic salmon (salmo salar). Aquaculture 33: 107−118.

SOKAL, R. R., AND F. J. ROHLF. 1981. Biometry: the principles and practice of statistics in biological research. Second Ed. W. H. Freeman and Co., San Francisco, CA. 859 p.

SUTTERLIN, A. M., AND D. MACLEAN. 1984. Age at first maturity and the early expression of oocyte recruitment processes in two forms of Atlantic salmon (Salmo salar) and their hybrids. Can. J. Fish. Aquat. Sci. 41: 1139−1149.

SUTTERLIN, A. M., P. HARMON, AND B. YOUNG. 1978. Precocious sexual maturation in Atlantic salmon (Salmo salar) postsmolts reared in a seawater impoundment. J. Fish. Res. Board Can. 35: 1269−1271.

VAN DEN HURK, R., AND J. PEUTE. 1979. Cyclic changes in the ovary of the rainbow trout, *Salmo gairdneri*, with special reference to sites of steroidogenesis. Cell Tissue Res. 199: 289–306.

WALLACE, R. A., AND K. SELMAN. 1981. Cellular and dynamic aspects of oocyte growth in teleosts. Am. Zool. 24: 325–343.

Appendix 1

Biological attributes of adult salmon in the various rivers.

Year of spawning	Sea age	No.	%	Fork length (cm)	Fecundity	% F	Eggs/fish
Western Arm Brook							
1979	1SW	206	100	51.3	3 388	61	2 067 (100%)
	2SW	0	0				
	3SW	0					
		206					
1980	1SW	58	100	53.6	3 388	88	2 981 (100%)
	2SW	0					
	3SW	0					
		58					
Cains River							
1979	1SW	144	72	51.8	3 925	27	763 (30%)
	2SW	42	21	72.5	6 855	91	1 310 (51%)
	3SW	15	7	81.2	8 273	83	481 (19%)
		201					2 554
1980	1SW	237	40	52.0	3 950	19	300 (7%)
	2SW	333	56	73.3	6 981	95	3 714 (90%)
	3SW	21	4	83.0	8 580	38	130 (3%)
		591					4 144
1981	1SW	170	84	51.4	3 875	25	814 (56%)
	2SW	24	12	71.4	6 684	73	586 (40%)
	3SW	9	4	75.4	7 316	20	59 (4%)
		203					1 459
Highlands River							
1979	1SW	34	59	53.7	4 166	41	1 088 (29%)
	2SW	20	34	87.9	9 436	56	1 797 (51%)
	3SW	4	7	97.1	11 130	88	686 (20%)
		58					3 491
1980	1SW	23	40	53.8	4 180	70	1 170 (21%)
	2SW	32	56	82.1	8 426	83	3 916 (71%)
	3SW	2	4	100.5	11 784	88	415 (8%)
		57					5 501
Bartholomew River							
1979	1SW	298	87	51.8	3 925	3	102 (12%)
	2SW	45	13	72.5	6 855	84	749 (88%)
	3SW	0	0				
		343					851
1980	1SW	403	75	52.0	3 950	0	—
	2SW	135	25	73.3	6 981	77	1 344 (100%)
	3SW	0	0				
		538					1 344
1981	1SW	620	86	51.4	3 875	5	167 (20%)
	2SW	101	14	71.4	6 684	70	655 (80%)
	3SW	0	0				
		721					822
South River							
1982	1SW	50	43	53.4	—	0	0
	2SW	54	47	74.3	7 140	75	2 517 (77%)
	3SW	12	10	89.2	9 668	80	773 (23%)
							3 290
Kedgwick River							
1981	1SW	0	0	—	—	—	0
	2SW	0	0	—	—	—	0
	3SW	8	100	—	10 010	63	10 010 (100%)
							10 010

Genetic Factors in Sexual Maturity of Cultured Atlantic Salmon (*Salmo salar*) Parr and Adults Reared in Sea Cages

Brian D. Glebe

The Huntsman Marine Laboratory and the Salmon Genetics Research Program, St. Andrews, N.B. E0G 2X0

and Richard L. Saunders

Department of Fisheries and Oceans, Fisheries and Environmental Services, Fisheries Research Branch, Biological Station, St. Andrews, N.B. E0G 2X0

Abstract

GLEBE, B. D., AND R. L. SAUNDERS. 1986. Genetic factors in sexual maturity of cultured Atlantic salmon (*Salmo salar*) parr and adults reared in sea cages, p. 24–29. *In* D. J. Meerburg [ed.] Salmonid age at maturity. Can. Spec. Publ. Fish. Aquat. Sci. 89.

Variation in incidence of mature parr was examined among hatchery-reared strains and family groups. The mean incidence of mature parr within diallel strain sets ranged from 2.0 to 40.8% of all males. Heterosis for incidence of maturity and growth was evident in most strain crosses. Mean parental sea age at sexual maturity was a factor in maturation among parr, late maturing parents yielding fewer mature parr progeny. Similarly, strains with low incidences of mature parr produced fewer grilse returns after sea ranching. At the family level, more mature parr were found among the progeny of grilse and mature parr sires than among those of 2-sea-winter salmon sires (48% compared with 27%). Although strains having high incidences of mature parr were associated with proportionately greater grilse returns when sea ranched, there was no comparable relationship at the family level between incidence of mature parr and grilse in sea cages. The suggestion is that maturity in fresh water and seawater are independent genetic events.

Résumé

GLEBE, B. D., AND R. L. SAUNDERS. 1986. Genetic factors in sexual maturity of cultured Atlantic salmon (*Salmo salar*) parr and adults reared in sea cages, p. 24–29. *In* D. J. Meerburg [ed.] Salmonid age at maturity. Can. Spec. Publ. Fish. Aquat. Sci. 89.

La variation dans l'incidence du tacon mature a été examinée parmi certaines lignées piscicoles et certains groupes de familles. L'incidence moyenne de tacon mature à l'intérieur d'ensembles de lignées diallèles a oscillé entre 2,0 et 40,8 % de tous les mâles. L'hétérosis pour l'incidence de la maturité et de la croissance était évident dans la plupart des croisements de lignées. L'âge-mer parental moyen à maturité sexuelle était un facteur dans le cheminement vers la maturité parmi les parents de tacons qui maturent tardivement et donnent une progéniture de tacons matures moins nombreuse. De la même façon, les lignées possédent de faibles incidences de tacons matures ont produit un moins grand nombrre de retours de madeleineaux après un pâturage en mer. Sur le plan familial, des tacons plus matures ont été trouvés parmi la progéniture des géniteurs de madeleineaux et de tacons matures que parmi ceux des géniteurs de saumons dibermarins (48 % comparativement à 27 %). Bien que les lignées possédant de fortes incidences de tacons matures aient été associées à des retours de madeleineaux proportionnellement supérieurs dans les cas de pâturages marins, il n'existait aucune corrélation comparable sur le plan familial entre l'incidence de tacons matures et de madeleineaux en cages marines. L'explication tiendrait au fait que la maturité en eau douce et celle en eau de mer sont des événements génétiques indépendants.

Introduction

Age at maturity of cultured Atlantic salmon (*Salmo salar*) is considered an important economic trait. Poor growth and carcass quality associated with early maturity among cage-reared fish has been, and continues to be, a constraint to development of this industry (Naevdal 1983; Gjerde 1984). Similarly, reduced growth and delayed smoltification of hatchery-reared, sexually mature male parr (Saunders et al. 1982) and higher mortality among wild mature parr (Leyzerovitch 1973; Mitans 1973) indicates that freshwater maturity also influences population structure.

Stock specificity of age at first maturation (Berg 1964; Saunders and Sreedharan 1978; Naevdal et al. 1978) and breeding studies (Elson 1973; Piggins 1974; Thorpe and Morgan 1980; Gjerde 1984) provide conclusive evidence for a genetic component in this trait both among parr and among larger salmon grown in seawater. Estimated heritabilities

(Gjedrem 1983; Gjerde 1984) indicate that a rapid response to selection within cultured stocks should occur in both environments. Recent reports have further indicated that different genes may be determining freshwater and seawater maturation and that selection should proceed independently for these traits (Glebe et al. 1980; Gjerde 1984). However, Naevdal (1983) suggested from his breeding studies that the degree of parr maturity and sea age at maturity may not be completely independent and that a genetic correlation may exist between these traits.

In this study, evidence is presented for a genetic and environmental (through growth rate) involvement in freshwater maturation among parr and sea age at maturity. Variation in these traits among hatchery-reared strains and family groups is examined. The influence of different sire types (mature parr, grilse (mature after 1-sea-winter [1SW]) and 2-sea-winter [2SW] salmon) on progeny age at maturity of progeny is also investigated.

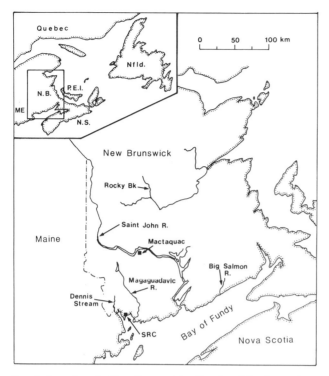

FIG. 1. Locations in New Brunswick, Canada of the donor rivers from which wild broodstock were collected (SRC, Salmon Research Center).

Material and Methods

Strain Variation in Incidence of Parr Maturity

Wild Atlantic salmon broodstock were collected in 1974, 1975, and 1976 from five New Brunswick rivers: the Magaguadavic (M), Saint John (S), Big Salmon (B), Rocky Brook (R), and Dennis Stream (D) (Fig. 1). The sea age of each broodfish was determined by scale reading and validated according to McPhail (1973). Gametes from these fish were combined in a number of 4 × 4 (1975, 1976) or 3 × 3 (1974) diallel mating sets, producing a total of 16, or nine different strains with 10–12 families per strain. Details of the mating design and initial rearing procedures are described by Friars et al. (1979) with the exception that no heated water was used to rear the 1974 year-class (year-class refers to spawning year). All spawning was done in late autumn and each cross (full sib family) was reared in an individual tank until June. The 1975 and 1976 year-class families (average individual weight 4 g) were then microtagged (Jefferts et al. 1963) and combined by strain in outdoor rearing tanks (8-m diam.) where they remained until release as 1+ smolts the following spring. Ambient rearing temperatures resulted in slower growth of the 1974 year-class and a delay in microtagging and relocation to outdoor rearing tanks until October. Individual weights at this time ranged from 4 to 5 g. Release as 2+ smolts was accomplished in May 1977. Recapture procedures for sea-ranched smolts returning as adults are described by Bailey and Saunders (1984).

The size and incidence of mature male parr were determined for strains at various times during freshwater rearing. The lengths (±0.1 cm) of 100 individuals randomly selected from the 1975 and 1976 year-class strains were measured in July. Random samples of 50 yearling 1974 year-class parr and 100 underyearling 1975 and 1976 year-class parr were collected during November. The length (±0.1 cm), weight (±0.1 g), sex, and state of maturity were determined for each individual. The lack of external identifying marks precluded assignment of individuals to specific families at this time.

Comparison of the mean length (immature parr) and the percentage of mature individuals (expressed as % of total males) of the reciprocal crosses with the mean values for the parental or pure strains was used as a measure of heterosis ("hybrid" vigor). The relationship among incidence of mature parr, immature parr length and parental age at maturity (all mean values by strain) was determined by multiple regression analysis. Strain was not used as a dummy variable in the analysis due to concordance with parental age at maturity. Parental age at maturity was strain-specific (i.e. parents tended to be grilse in some strains and 2SW salmon in others) and, therefore, more appropriate for inclusion than a dummy variable.

Family Variation in Incidence of Mature Parr

A nested (males within females) mating design was used to evaluate the effect of sire age at maturity on incidence of mature male progeny. During November 1980, artificial spawning of individual Saint John River strain (Mactaquac Federal Fish Culture Station origin) 2SW salmon females with each of a mature parr, a grilse and a maiden spawning 2SW male from the same strain was completed. During the same period, individual wild female grilse from the Big Salmon River were spawned with three males of different ages at maturity. Three and six mating sets of this type were produced for the Saint John and Big Salmon strains, respectively. Ova from each female were divided into 1000–1500 egg lots. Each lot was then fertilized by a different sire type. An excess of eggs from the Saint John Strain families permitted a single replication. Incubation and early rearing techniques were similar to those described by Friars et al. (1979) with the exception that there was no supplemental heating of water. Late in October, 50 fish (0+ parr) per family (Big Salmon strain) or per replicate family (Saint John strain) were killed and the length (±0.1 cm), weight (±0.1 g), sex and state of maturity determined. At this time, up to 500 individuals per family were microtagged, branded, and combined in an 8-m diam. outdoor rearing tank. In December 1982, the 1+ parr were sorted by brand until the length, weight, and maturity (indicated by the issue of milt with abdominal pressure) of 50 individuals per family were recorded. Parr age (0+, 1+) refers to years from hatching.

The mean incidence of mature males (as a percentage of total males only) was calculated by strain and sire type for the two age categories of parr.

Relationship Between Incidence of Mature Male Parr and Grilse in Sea Cages

In 1977, a 2 × 2 diallel cross involving the Big Salmon River and Saint John River broodstock was completed (Glebe et al. 1980). Only mature parr sires (six from each strain) were used to fertilize replicated egg lots of approximately 1000 from each of three 2SW females from each strain. The result was an array of six family groups within each of two pure strains and two reciprocal hybrid strains.

TABLE 1. Mean percentage of mature male parr (% mp) and mean length (Len) of immature parr by pure strain (diagonal) and strain cross (*1974 year-class; **1975 year-class; ***1976 year-class; SE — standard error). B = Big Salmon R., D = Dennis Stream, S = Saint John R., R = Rocky Brook, M = Magaguadavic R.

Strains	B		D		S		Female
Male	% mp	Len(SE)	% mp	Len(SE)	% mp	Len(SE)	
B	*22.3	16.2(0.8)	40.8	18.2(0.2)	26.0	17.6(0.3)	
D	*34.0	17.5(0.4)	25.2	15.1(0.3)	20.7	17.6(0.3)	
S	*34.6	19.4(0.7)	30.0	20.0(0.5)	8.7	14.9(0.4)	

	B		R		S		M	
	% mp	Len(SE)	% mp	Len(SE)	% mp	Len(SE)	% mp	Len(SE)
B	**18.8	12.8(0.7)	25.6	17.0(0.7)	37.9	17.2(0.4)	22.3	17.7(0.5)
	***12.0	13.8(0.3)	22.0	16.1(0.2)	14.0	15.4(0.4)	4.0	16.6(0.4)
R	**21.7	16.6(0.2)	8.0	17.8(0.2)	14.2	17.9(0..3)	17.8	18.7(0.3)
	***7.0	14.3(0.3)	2.0	15.4(0.3)	16.0	17.4(0.4)	2.0	15.4(0.4)
S	**22.6	16.7(0.3)	14.4	17.5(0.2)	20.9	17.7(0.4)	19.8	16.9(0.4)
	***6.0	12.3(0.3)	3.0	15.2(0.4)	3.0	14.3(0.4)	2.4	16.1(0.5)
M	**13.9	16.7(0.4)	9.0	18.3(0.3)	19.8	18.9(0.2)	4.7	18.2(0.3)
	***2.0	14.4(0.3)	19.0	16.3(0.4)	3.0	14.3(0.4)	2.2	16.0(0.4)

TABLE 2. Contrasts between pure strain means (length (cm) and percentages of mature male parr (% mp)) and the equivalent reciprocal cross means (e.g. B × R, reciprocal cross involving parental strains B and R, difference calculated as

$$\frac{(B \times B) + (R \times R)}{2} - \frac{(B \times R) + (R \times B)}{2}$$

where ( ) is the strain mean; positive values indicate heterosis). B = Big Salmon R., D = Dennis Stream, S = Saint John R., R = Rocky Brook, M = Magaguadavic R.

	Year-class					
	1974		1975		1976	
Strain cross	% mp	Len	% mp	Len	% mp	Len
B × D	13.7	2.2				
B × R			10.2	1.5	7.5	0.6
B × S	14.8	3.0	10.4	1.7	2.5	-0.2
B × M			6.4	1.7	-4.1	0.6
R × S			-0.1	0.0	7.0	1.5
R × M			7.1	0.5	8.4	0.1
S × M			7.0	0.0	0.1	0.1
S × D	8.4	3.8				

Heated water was used (as described earlier) to accelerate growth and enhance the proportion of 1+ smolts. Approximately 100 individuals were selected at random (including mature parr) from each of the surviving 21 families (80% overall mean incidence of 1+ smolts; average smolt length for all families: 17.2 cm, SD = 0.8). The smolts were placed without acclimation in a sea cage at Deer Island, New Brunswick. The 2100 smolts were reared under an agreement with Marine Products Ltd., a private aquaculture company. During November and December 1980, the 1500 remaining 1SW fish were killed for market. At this time, the family origin, sex, and state of sexual maturity of each fish were determined. If brands could not be read, then microtags were used to identify families. Correlation analysis was used to examine the relationship between family incidence of mature male parr and the proportion of male grilse.

Results

Heterosis for Parr Maturity and Size

The mean incidence of mature parr within diallel strains was highly variable, ranging from 2.0 to 40.8% of all males (Table 1). Of the pure strains, the Magaguadavic River stock produced the fewest mature parr, while the Big Salmon River stock produced the greatest number. Heterosis for incidence of mature male parr was evident in all but two strain crosses (Table 2). Similarly, the mean lengths indicated heterosis for growth of 12 of 15 reciprocal strain crosses. A positive and significant correlation ($r=0.64$, $P<0.01$, 13 df.) was was found between calculated values for heterosis for mature male parr and the mean length for reciprocal strain crosses.

Comparison of the mean length (8.5 cm, SD = 0.36) of 1975 year-class strains with the mean length of (6.9 cm, SD + 0.15) of 1976 year-class strains in July indicated growth was more rapid in 1975. Comparable mean incidences of mature parr for these year-classes were 18.2% (SD = 7.8) and 7.5 (SD = 6.8), respectively.

Multiple regression analysis identified mean strain length of progeny and the cross product of parental mean age at maturity as contributing significantly to the variation in incidence of mature parr. The variables, mean female parent age and mean male parent age at sexual maturity, were not significant. The equation was:

$$y = -75.3 + 7.6x - 11.0z$$
$$(F = 12.5,\ df = 38,\ \text{multiple } R^2 = 39.7)$$

where y = % mature parr
x = length of immature parr (November)
z = cross product of parental sea age at maturity.

Figure 2 (A,B) illustrates the relationships between % mature parr and strain length (November) and % mature parr and the cross-product of parental sea age at maturity. These data were used to generate the regression equation described above.

TABLE 3. Incidence of mature male parr (% mp) (expressed as % of all males) by strain, dam and sire type within the 0+ and 1+ parr groups.

Strain	Dam	Sire	% mp (0+)	% mp (1+)	Total
Saint John	salmon × parr		0.28	0.20	0.48
	salmon × grilse		0.12	0.13	0.25
	salmon × salmon		0.12	0.13	0.25
Big Salmon	grilse × parr		0.55	0.46	1.01
	grilse × grilse		0.70	0.56	1.26
	grilse × salmon		0.38	0.64	1.02

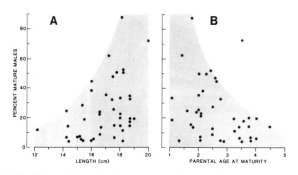

FIG. 2. The relationship between incidence of mature parr and mean length of parr (A) and the cross product of mean male and female parental sea age at maturity in years (B).

The correlation between incidence of mature parr and the proportion of grilse from each strain when sea-ranched was positive and significant ($r=0.37$, $n=33$, $P<0.05$). The overall mean incidence of grilse was 76%. The remaining 24% matured as 2SW or 3SW spawners. The overall mean incidence of mature parr was 15.5%.

Incidence of Mature Parr Among Families

Mature parr were found in families produced by all sire types (mature parr, grilse, and 2SW salmon). The Saint John strain produced the fewest mature parr (Table 3), with one female parent producing no 1+ mature parr regardless of sire type. The total number maturing as 0+ and 1+ parr (assuming once mature, a parr did not mature the following year) yielded ratios of mature to immature of approximately 0.25 and 0.50 for the Saint John strain and 1.0 for the Big Salmon strain. Orthogonal contrasts indicated that among 0+ parr, the grilse and mature parr sires produced significantly ($P<0.05$) different incidences of mature parr progeny relative to those of 2SW salmon sires (mean values: parr = 0.47, grilse = 0.49, salmon = 0.27). No significant differences in the ratios for 1+ parr of various sire types were detected (overall mean = 0.34). Similarly, dam type (grilse or 2SW salmon) was found to contribute to significant variation in incidence of mature parr ($P<0.05$) among both 0+ and 1+ parr groups. However, dam type is confounded with strain effect. Hence, strain differences and not dam type may have resulted in the detected significant variation.

No stock-specific differences in parr size were apparent. However, orthogonal contrasts indicated that among 1+ parr the grilse sires produced significantly larger progeny than did 2SW salmon and mature parr sires (mean lengths of 1+ progeny sired by grilse, 2SW salmon and mature parr are 17.7, 16.9, and 16.7 cm, respectively). Similarly, immature parr were significantly larger than mature parr at age 0+ and 1+ (mean lengths: 0+ mature = 7.7 cm, 0+ imma-

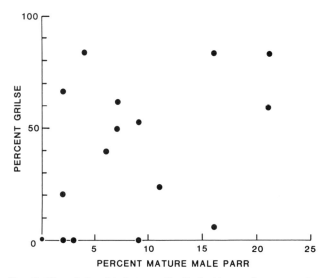

FIG. 3. The relationship between family incidence of mature male parr and the proportion of male grilse among males reared in marine cages.

ture = 7.9 cm, 1+ mature = 16.5 cm, 1+ immature = 17.5 cm).

Family Incidence of Mature Parr and Grilse

Correlation analysis indicated there was no significant relationship between family incidence of mature parr and male grilse within the same family when reared in a sea cage ($r = 0.2$, df = 14, $P > 0.05$). Figure 3 illustrates the data used in this analysis. Of the 21 family groups originally placed in the sea cage, only 16 families had 25 or more representatives among the market sample 20 mo later. Only these 16 families were included in the correlation analysis.

Discussion

Maturation of Parr

Saunders and Sreedharan (1978) first described the wide variation in incidence of maturing parr among Salmon Research Center strains. This variation was implied to be strain specific. However, the significant positive correlation between calculated values for heterosis for length (November) and parr maturity suggests that parr size and strain genetic integrity may both contribute to this observed variability. The calculation for heterosis removes the individual effect of strains when the parental strain mean is compared with the mean of the reciprocal hybrid crosses. Further evidence of the modifying effect of growth on parr maturation is the increased incidence of maturity among parr strains having larger individuals in July when, according to Villarreal and Thorpe (1985), male gonadal development is instituted. Incidence of maturity was three times greater in the 1975 year-class than in the 1976 year-class. The mean size differential between year-classes in July was 1.6 cm. This suggests that the propensity to mature is greater when a certain threshold size is exceeded early during the maturation cycle. Saunders et al. (1982) have also proposed a size threshold hypothesis regulating age at maturity as parr. Murphy (1980) provided evidence that larger individuals within sib groups have a tendency to mature, based on sampling of parr in April–June. A parallel, size-related influence on maturity among sea-ranched, hatchery-reared smolts has been reported by Ritter et al. (1986). Larger hatchery smolts produced proportionately more grilse than did smaller smolts.

Parental sea age at maturity and growth of progeny influence the incidence of mature parr. With increasing sea age of both parents (Fig. 2), the scope for parr maturity within strains is reduced. This agrees well with reports that sea age at maturity is similarly constrained; Elson (1973), Piggins (1974), and Ritter et al. (1986) reported that grilse parents produced earlier maturing (grilse) progeny than did 2SW parents. Thorpe et al. (1983) provided evidence that male parr parents yielded higher incidences of mature parr progeny.

When individual families are considered, mature parr and grilse parents produced more mature parr progeny as underyearlings than 2SW salmon parents. Gjerde (1984) reported that more maturing parr were found among offspring of mature male parr. Naevdal (1983) indicated that tagged mature parr tended to mature as grilse although many delayed maturation until after two or three sea winters. Therefore, when using grilse as sires, there is an increased likelihood that they had matured previously as parr. In this instance, these sire types would be expected to produce similar numbers of mature parr among offspring.

The interaction of sire and dam age to constrain incidence of mature parr among strains suggests both a male and female parent role in influencing maturation among parr. Gjerde (1984) also reported a significant interaction (indicative of non-additive genetic variation in age at sexual maturity) between age of sire and age of dam which constrained the incidence of mature parr at the family level.

Glebe (unpubl. data) found that only 6% of parr mature as underyearlings matured again as yearlings. This suggests that the incidences of mature parr over 2 yr can be summed to provide an estimate of the total numbers of parr maturing prior to smoltification (2+ smolts in this study). The calculated totals when expressed as ratios of total male parr, including both immature and mature (approximately 0.25, 0.50, and 1.00; Table 3) suggest simple genetic regulation of this trait. Blake (1981) reviewed various simple genetic models, sex linked and autosomal, which predict similar ratios of mature progeny based on sire and dam types. Maturation among parr may be determined by a single gene analogous to that controlling maturation in platyfish (Kallman and Bao 1982).

Interpretation of variation in parr size by family is difficult due to growth depression associated with parr maturation. Saunders et al. (1982), Lundqvist (1980), and Gjerde (1984) and this study have shown reduced growth among maturing parr. Thorpe and Morgan (1980) and Thorpe et al. (1983) have shown that mature parr were initially among the fastest growing individuals in a population. However, subsequent retarded growth associated with gonadal development depresses the growth of mature parr. The net effect, if the incidence of mature parr is sufficiently high, would be to reduce the mean size of parr in that population. Until family mean lengths and weights can be adjusted to compensate for parr maturity (Saunders et al. 1982), conclusions concerning the relationship between maturation and growth must be prudent.

Sea Age at Maturity

Conflicting reports over the effect of smolt age on incidence of grilse (Naevdal et al. 1978) suggest that smolt size and subsequent growth rate rather than age may be determining sea age at maturity. Naevdal et al. (1978) and Naevdal (1983) found a positive correlation between smolt size and incidence of grilse among sibs and that postsmolt growth also influenced maturity. In this study, the significant correlation between strain incidence of mature parr and grilse may be a consequence of generally larger smolt size among those strains having high proportions of mature parr. The positive correlation between heterosis for growth and parr maturity suggests this is the case.

At the family level, no relationship between incidence of mature parr and the proportion of grilse was found. This suggests that maturation in fresh water and seawater may be independent genetic events. As such, they would require consideration as separate traits in breeding programs. Glebe et al. (1980) and Gjerde (1984) provide evidence to support independence of these traits. Similarly, Naevdal (1983) concedes that maturation as parr is of minor importance as a grilse-producing factor. The positive relationship between incidence of mature parr and grilse among strains reported here and by Schiefer (1971) suggests that, although these traits may be unrelated genetically, natural selection may generally favour the same trend in age at maturity in both the freshwater and marine environments.

Acknowledgements

The assistance of all the technical and fish culture staff at the Salmon Research Center in data collection is greatly appreciated. Dr. G. Friars provided advice on evaluation of heterosis and suggestions for improving the manuscript. Joan Reed assisted in data analysis. We thank Dr. B. Riddell (Pacific Biological Station) and G. Naevdal (University of Bergen) for their constructive criticisms of an earlier draft of this manuscript. Special thanks are extended to Brenda Fawkes for typing services. Funding was provided by the Department of Fisheries and Oceans through the Salmon Genetics Research Program.

References

BAILEY, J. K., AND R. L. SAUNDERS. 1984. Returns of three year-classes of sea-ranched Atlantic salmon of various river strains and strain crosses. Aquaculture 41: 259–270.

BERG, M. 1964. Nord-norske lakseelver (north Norwegian salmon rivers). Johan Grundt Tanum forlay, Oslo, 300 p. (English summary).

BLAKE, R. L. 1981. Growth, respiration and sexual maturation of juvenile Atlantic salmon (*Salmo salar* L.). M.S. thesis, Univ. of Maine, Orono, Maine.

ELSON, P. F. 1973. Genetic polymorphism in Northwest Miramichi salmon in relation to season of river ascent and age at maturation and its implications for management of the stocks.

ICNAF Res. Doc. 73/76, Ann. Meet. 1973.

FRIARS, G. W., J. K. BAILEY, AND R. L. SAUNDERS. 1979. Considerations of a method of analyzing diallel crosses of Atlantic salmon. Can. J. Genet. Cytol. 21: 121−128.

GJEDREM, T. 1983. Genetic variation in quantitative traits and selective breeding in fish and shellfish. Aquaculture 33: 51−72.

GJERDE, B. 1984. Response to individual selection for age at sexual maturity in Atlantic salmon. Aquaculture 38: 229−240.

GLEBE, B. D., W. EDDY, AND R. L. SAUNDERS. 1980. The influence of parental age at maturity and rearing practice on precocious maturation of hatchery-reared Atlantic salmon parr. Int. Counc. Explor. Sea C.M. 1980/F:8, 8 p.

JEFFERTS, K. B., P. K. BERGMAN, AND H. F. FISCUS. 1963. A coded wire identification system for macroorganisms. Nature (London) 198: 460−462.

KALLMAN, K. D., AND I. Y. BAO. 1982. Genetic control of the hypothalamo-pituitary axis and the effect of hybridization on sexual maturity (Xiphophorus, Pisces, Poeciliidae). J. Exp. Zool. 220: 297−309.

LEYZEROVICH, K. A. 1973. Dwarf males in hatchery propagation of the Atlantic salmon (Salmo salar L.). J. Ichthyol. 13: 382−391.

LUNDQVIST, H. 1980. Influence of photoperiod on growth in Baltic salmon parr (Salmo salar L.) with special reference to the effect of precocious sexual maturation. Can. J. Zool. 58: 940−944.

MCPHAIL, D. 1973. Age comparisons of four Atlantic salmon stocks. Res. Dev. Branch, Environ. Can. MS Rep. 73−2.

MITANS, A. R. 1973. Dwarf males and the sex structure of a Baltic salmon (Salmo salar L.) population. J. Ichthyol. 2: 192−197.

MURPHY, T. M. 1980. Studies on precocious maturity in artificially reared 1+ Atlantic salmon parr, Salmo salar L. Ph.D. thesis, Univ. of Stirling, 232 p.

NAEVDAL, G. 1983. Genetic factors in connection with age at maturation. Aquaculture 33: 97−106.

NAEVDAL, G., M. HOLM, O. INGEBRIGTSEN, AND D. MØLLER. 1978. Variation in age at first spawning in Atlantic salmon (Salmo salar). J. Fish. Res. Board Can. 35: 145−147.

PIGGINS, D. J. 1974. Survival rates from the 1970 brood year ova to smolts and grilse. Ann. Rep. Salm. Res. Trust Ireland 19: 23−25.

RITTER, J. A., G. J. FARMER, R. K. MISRA, T. R. GOFF, J. K. BAILEY, AND E. BAUM. 1986. Parental influences and smolt size and sex ratio effects on sea age at first maturity of Atlantic salmon (Salmo salar), p. 30−38. In D. J. Meerburg [ed.] Salmonid age at maturity. Can. Spec. Publ. Fish. Aquat. Sci. 89.

SAUNDERS, R. L., AND A. SREEDHARAN. 1978. The incidence and genetic implications of sexual maturity in male Atlantic salmon parr. Int. Counc. Explor. Sea C.M. 1978/M:23, 8 p.

SAUNDERS, R. L., E. B. HENDERSON, AND B. D. GLEBE. 1982. Precocious sexual maturation and smoltification in male Atlantic salmon (Salmo salar). Aquaculture 28: 211−229.

SCHIEFER, K. 1971. Ecology of Atlantic salmon, with special reference to occurrence and abundance of grilse in north shore Gulf of St. Lawrence rivers. Ph.D. thesis, Univ. of Waterloo, Waterloo, Ont. 129 p.

THORPE, J. E., AND R. I. G. MORGAN. 1980. Growth rate and smolting rate of progeny of male Atlantic salmon parr, Salmo salar L. J. Fish Biol. 17: 451−460.

THORPE, J. E., R. I. G. MORGAN, C. TALBOT, AND M. S. MILES. 1983. Inheritance of developmental rates in Atlantic salmon, Salmo salar L. Aquaculture 33: 119−128.

VILLARREAL, C. A., AND J. E. THORPE. 1985. Gonadal growth and bimodality of length frequency distribution in juvenile Atlantic salmon (Salmo salar). Aquaculture 45: 265−288.

Parental Influences and Smolt Size and Sex Ratio Effects on Sea Age at First Maturity of Atlantic Salmon (*Salmo salar*)

J. A. Ritter, G. J. Farmer, R. K. Misra, T. R. Goff, J. K. Bailey[1], and E. T. Baum[2]

Department of Fisheries and Oceans, Fisheries Research Branch,
P.O. Box 550, Station M, Halifax, N.S. B3J 2S7

Abstract

RITTER, J. A., G. J. FARMER, R. K. MISRA, T. R. GOFF, J. K. BAILEY, AND E. T. BAUM. 1986. Parental influences and smolt size and sex ratio effects on sea age at first maturity of Atlantic salmon (*Salmo salar*), p. 30–38. *In* D. J. Meerburg [ed.] Salmonid age at maturity. Can. Spec. Publ. Fish. Aquat. Sci. 89.

Releases of hatchery smolts were used to assess parental influences and smolt size and sex ratio effects on sea age at first maturity of Atlantic salmon (*Salmo salar*). Progeny of 1-sea-winter (1SW) salmon produced proportionately more salmon that matured after one winter at sea (grilse) than offspring from 2-sea-winter (2SW) and older salmon. This relationship between parent and offspring was observed for releases of early-run and late-run population components of the Northwest Miramichi River, New Brunswick and for one year (1+) and two year (2+) smolts released in a river in Nova Scotia. Larger hatchery smolts produced proportionately more grilse than did smaller smolts. The effect of variation in smolt size on the grilse proportion was greater for release groups which originated from pooled matings of grilse and multi-sea-winter (MSW) salmon than for progeny of either 1SW salmon or almost pure MSW salmon. Differences in the proportion of grilse produced by comparable groups of 1+ and 2+ hatchery smolts were related to differences in sex ratio and/or smolt size. Relationships reported in this paper show opportunity to regulate sea age at first maturity in cultured Atlantic salmon through broodstock selection and the manipulation of other hatchery practices.

Résumé

RITTER, J. A., G. J. FARMER, R. K. MISRA, T. R. GOFF, J. K. BAILEY, AND E. T. BAUM. 1986. Parental influences and smolt size and sex ratio effects on sea age at first maturity of Atlantic salmon (*Salmo salar*), p. 30–38. *In* D. J. Meerburg [ed.] Salmonid age at maturity. Can. Spec. Publ. Fish. Aquat. Sci. 89.

Des lâchages de smolts piscicoles ont été employés pour évaluer les influences parentales ainsi que les effets de la taille des smolts et du sexe-ratio sur l'âge-mer à la première maturité du saumon de l'Atlantique (*Salmo salar*). La progéniture du saumon unibermarin (UBM) a produit proportionnellement plus de saumons ayant atteint leur maturité après un hiver en mer (madeleineau) que les rejetons des saumons dibermarins (DBM) et des saumons plus âgés. Cette relation entre les parents et les rejetons a été observée pour des lâchages de composantes de population à course précoce et de population à course tardive de la rivière Miramichi du nord-ouest (Nouveau-Brunswick) et pour des smolts d'une année (1+) et de deux années (2+) lâchés dans une rivière de la Nouvelle-Écosse. Les smolts piscicoles plus gros ont produit proportionnellement plus de madeleineaux que les smolts plus petits. L'effet de la variation de taille chez les smolts sur la proportion de madeleineaux a été supérieur pour les groupes de lâchages provenant d'accouplements groupés de madeleineaux et de saumons polybermarins (PBM) que pour la progéniture provenant soit du saumons UBM ou du saumon PBM presque pur. Les différences dans la proportion de madeleineaux produites dans des groupes comparables de smolts piscicoles 1+ et 2+ ont été rapprochées des différences dans le sexe-ratio ou la taille des smolts. Les relations dont il est fait état dans la présente étude montrent l'utilité d'intervenir sur l'âge-mer à la première maturité chez le saumon atlantique par une sélection de nichée et la manipulation des autres pratiques piscicoles.

Introduction

Interest in sea age at first maturity in Atlantic salmon (*Salmo salar*) has increased in recent years as salmon management programs have become more purposeful and as the requirements of the new and rapidly expanding salmon aquaculture industry have increased. Fisheries workers are becoming increasingly aware of annual fluctuations and changing trends in the sea age composition of wild salmon populations (Kerswill 1971; Elson 1973; Ruggles and Turner 1973). A decline in sea age represents a decrease in the value of the public resource to both commercial and recreational industries. Aquaculturists have learned that profit margins are influenced by their ability or fortune to maintain low incidence of early maturation in their cultured

lots.

Parental influence on sea age at sexual maturity in Atlantic salmon has been reasonably demonstrated in aquaculture situations (Gunnes 1978; Naevdal et al. 1978; Naevdal 1983; Gjerde 1984; Gjerde and Gjedrem 1984; Gjerde and Refstie 1984) but evidence is sparse for salmon ranging free in the sea (Elson 1973; Piggins 1974; Ritter and Newbould 1977). Saunders et al. (1983) reported a difference in the sea age at first maturity of Atlantic salmon reared in sea cages and those of the same strain released into a river from which they were free to migrate and range in the sea. The results reported by Saunders et al. (1983) point to the presence of genotype-environment interaction in the determination of age at maturity in Atlantic salmon. Hence, one would not expect parental influences demonstrated under cage culture conditions to be similarly expressed among free ranging salmon.

Age of maturity in coho salmon (*Oncorhynchus kisutch*) is reported by Bilton et al. (1982) to be inversely related to

---

[1]Present address: North American Salmon Research Institute, St. Andrews, N.B. E0G 2X0.

[2]Present address: Atlantic Sea Run Salmon Commission, P.O. Box 1298, Bangor, Maine 04401, USA.

TABLE 1. Percentages of grilse produced by groups of smolts originating from pure matings of 1SW and 2SW salmon of early-run and late-run population components of the Northwest Miramichi River, N.B. Smolts were released into the Northwest Miramichi between 1965 and 1972. Age of smolts was 2+ except for four groups of 1+ smolts[a].

Parental run-timing	Smolt year	Parental age[b]	Total returns	Percent grilse
Early	1965	1SW	173	53.2[a]
		2SW	172	60.5
	1967	1SW	64	75.0
	1970	1SW	119	82.4
		2SW	121	66.1
	1971	2SW	67	59.7
	1972	1SW	69	79.7
		2SW	85	42.4
	Combined	1SW	425	68.9
		2SW	445	58.4
Late	1965	2SW	113	37.2
	1966	2SW	264	6.8[a]
	1967	1SW	84	38.1
		2SW	56	10.7
	1968	1SW	76	46.1[a]
		2SW	59	20.3[a]
	1970	1SW	80	58.8
		2SW	85	12.9
	1971	2SW	25	52.0
	Combined	1SW	240	47.5
		2SW	602	16.9

[a]Group of 1+ smolts.
[b]Parental age designated as either 1-sea-winter (1SW) or 2SW salmon.

juvenile size at release. Although smolt size of Atlantic salmon has been thought to influence sea age at first maturity, evidence is sparse and contradictory of the relationship reported for coho salmon (Ritter 1972). Common among some groups of hatchery smolts is a sex related size difference that has generally been attributed to maturation of the male parr (Bailey et al. 1980; Saunders et al. 1982).

In this paper we present information pertaining to parental influences and smolt size and sex ratio effects on sea age at first maturity of Atlantic salmon. Both smolt size and sex ratio effects are discussed in relation to smolt age and the perceived effect that it has on sea age at maturity of salmon. The effects of the different factors on age at maturity were assessed through releases of marked hatchery smolts.

Parental Influences

The relationship between parent and offspring sea age at first maturity in Atlantic salmon was examined through tag recapture data for releases of hatchery smolts in the Miramichi River, New Brunswick and the LaHave River, Nova Scotia.

Miramichi Releases

Data were derived from groups of smolts originating from selected parents captured at the Curventon counting fence situated on the Northwest Miramichi River 11.3 km above the head of tide (Elson 1973). A mating scheme was fol-

lowed which produced progeny representative of the four main components of the Northwest Miramichi salmon: early-run, 1-sea-winter (1SW); early-run, 2-sea-winter (2SW); late-run, 1SW; and late-run, 2SW salmon (Saunders 1967; Elson 1973). Early-run parents were fish that reached the Curventon fence prior to July 15. Occasionally the date was extended to July 31 to meet collection targets. Late-run parents were fish reaching the fence after August 31 and being of "bright" condition or having sea-lice (*Argulus* sp.). Separation of the parent fish into 1SW and 2SW age categories was based on scale characteristics (Elson 1973).

Seventeen groups of smolts were produced and released into the Northwest Miramichi River during the 1965 to 1972 period. The smolts were produced at three different federal hatcheries (i.e., South Esk on the Northwest Miramichi River, Saint John on Little River, N.B. and Kejimkujik on the upper Mersey River, N.S.). Thirteen of the release groups were two year (2+) smolts and four were one year (1+) smolts. Because it was not often possible to obtain sufficient parents for each of the four population components in a given year, progeny of all four components were liberated only in one year (1970). Numbers of smolts released as progeny of the parents representing the four components are:

Early-run	1SW	15 838	2SW	17 118
Late-run	1SW	13 342	2SW	44 801

All smolts were marked with Carlin tags (Saunders 1968). Comparisons of sea age at first maturity were based on the recovery of tagged salmon in commercial and sport fisheries and in river monitoring traps including the counting fence at Curventon. Sea age at first maturity is expressed as "Percent grilse", representing the number of 1SW salmon recovered in Maritime and Quebec waters as a percentage of the total adult salmon recoveries. Recaptures of 1SW salmon in both Greenland and Newfoundland fisheries were included in the total recoveries but excluded from the grilse category since those in the Greenland fishery were known to be non-maturing (Paloheimo and Elson 1974) while those in New-foundland were of uncertain maturity status (Pippy 1982).

Incidence of grilse for the seventeen release groups are detailed in Table 1 according to the run timing and parental sea age. These data were analysed to determine parental effects on the sea age at first maturity of the release groups partitioned according to the four population components. The analysis of variance procedure of mean proportions was not employed because in binomial populations variances of proportions are not independent of their means thereby violating the assumption of equality of variance inherent to the procedure (Armitage 1971). Differences between the mean proportions of the four populations components were tested therefore, by a weighted procedure which produced a chi-square statistic (Li 1964; Armitage 1971). By this procedure the weighting factor for the mean proportions is equal to the reciprocal of the estimated variance of a mean proportion. Two formulae for estimating the variance of a mean proportion are outlined in Snedecor and Cochran (1967). The choice between these formulae depended upon the homogeneity of individual proportion values within each population component which was examined by the variance test procedure described in Snedecor and Cochran (1967). These authors noted that this procedure is valid even when sample sizes are small, provided that not more than 20% of the expectations are as low as one. For this analysis, none of the expectations were lower than four. Chi-square values for homogeneity of individual proportions within population components were all significant ($P<0.05$).

The weighted procedure was used to test the following six comparisons of mean proportions of the four population components.

1. 1SW vs (i.e., versus) 2SW of early-run;
2. 1SW vs 2SW of late-run;
3. 1SW vs 2SW of early-run and late-run combined;
4. Early-run vs late-run of 1SW;
5. Early-run vs late-run of 2SW; and
6. Early-run vs late-run of 1SW and 2SW combined.

Chi-squares for all six comparisons were highly significant ($P<0.01$). Progeny of 1SW salmon produced proportionately more grilse than did progeny of 2SW salmon (61.2% vs 34.6%). This tendency was recorded for both early-run (68.9% vs 58.4% grilse) and late-run (47.5% vs 16.9%) components and, except for the 1965 releases, was consistent for comparable groups released in the same year. The exception where progeny of 1SW salmon produced proportionately fewer grilse than offspring of 2SW parents (53.2% vs 60.5%) was presumed to be the result of the difference in smolt ages (or a related function of smolt age such as size or sex ratio difference) since the progeny from the 1SW salmon were 1+ smolts while the progeny of the 2SW salmon were released as 2+ smolts. The tendency for 1+ hatchery smolts to produce proportionately fewer grilse than 2+ smolts is reported by others (Peterson 1971; Ritter 1975; Ísaksson 1982a, b; Bailey and Saunders 1984) and is shown and discussed in detail later in this paper. Removal of the four groups of 1+ smolts from the analysis of weighted mean proportions, because of the possible confounding effects of smolt age, did not markedly alter the levels of significance for the chi-squares of five of the six comparisons ($P<0.01$). The exception pertained to the chi-square for comparison 2, for which significance was reduced to $P = 0.059$. Analyses with and without data for groups of 1+ smolts demonstrated similar results and either may be viewed as evidence of genetic influence over sea age at first maturity in Atlantic salmon.

Progeny from early-run salmon produced proportionately more grilse than offspring of late-run parents (63.6% vs 25.7%). This tendency is most apparent within parental sea age classes (68.9% vs 47.5% for 1SW parents; 58.4% vs 16.9% for 2SW parents). These results are evidence of genetic difference between early-run and late-run components of the salmon population of the Northwest Miramichi River.

LaHave Releases

Broodfish for this study were collected from the Medway River, situated adjacent to the LaHave River in southwestern Nova Scotia. The release groups were distinguishable as progeny either of 1SW salmon parents or of large (LG) salmon parents. Separation of parents into these categories was based on size rather than age determination. Although ages of the parental broodstocks are available for three of the four release groups originating from LG salmon (MacPhail 1973), aging was done after spawning and individual ages of fish could not be linked to the matings which produced the release groups. These aging data revealed that the system of parental selection used permitted inclusion of some grilse as repeat spawners in the LG salmon matings

TABLE 2. Percentages of grilse produced by groups of 1+ and 2+ smolts originating from 1SW and LG salmon parents. Smolts were released into the LaHave River in 1973 and 1974.

Smolt year	Smolt age	Smolt fork length (cm)	Parental age[a]	Total returns	Percent grilse
1973	1+	16.4	LG	13	30.8
	2+	20.8	1SW	135	80.7
	2+	19.7	LG	128	66.4
1974	1+	15.8	1SW	43	69.8
	1+	16.2	LG	12	25.0
	2+	17.2	1SW	65	80.0
	2+	18.2	LG	48	47.9

[a]Parental age is designated as either 1-sea-winter (1SW) or large (LG) salmon. LG salmon include 2SW salmon, 3SW salmon, and some grilse as repeat spawners.

which otherwise were carried out with 2SW salmon and an occasional 3SW salmon. Based on readable scales, the incidences of repeat spawning grilse among the LG salmon broodfish were 20 and 29% respectively for the two years for which data are available (MacPhail 1973). Since the collection site and system of parental selection were the same in all years, it may be assumed that repeat spawning grilse were similarly abundant among the broodfish of the third year for which aging data are not available.

The releases were comprised of three groups of 1+ smolts and four groups of 2+ smolts. All groups were produced at Kejimkujik Hatchery which was situated on the Mersey River, N.S. within 30 km of the release sites on the LaHave River. The production of 1+ and 2+ smolts at this hatchery was accomplished by the grading and release of the faster growing fish in a given production lot as 1+ smolts and the slower as 2+ smolts.

All smolts were marked with modified Carlin tags (Saunders 1968) and released into the upper LaHave River, N.S. in 1973 and 1974. Percent grilse estimates, determined by the method described in the previous section, provided the basis for comparing the age at first maturity of progeny of 1SW and LG salmon matings (Table 2). The statistical procedure employed to analyse these data is similar to that described in the previous section. The analysis is based on partitioning of the release groups according to smolt age and parental sea age into four components, i.e., 1+ smolts 1SW, 1+ smolts LG, 2+ smolts 1SW and 2+ smolts LG. Only one observation on the proportion of grilse was available for the 1+ smolt 1SW component while two observations were available for each of the other three components. Individual proportion values within components were homogenous for 1+ smolts LG and 2+ smolts 1SW components but not for 2+ smolts LG.

The following seven comparisons of mean proportions of grilse were tested by the weighted procedure method:

1. 1SW vs LG of 1+ smolts;
2. 1SW vs LG of 2+ smolts;
3. 1SW vs LG of 1+ and 2+ smolts combined;
4. 1+ smolts vs 2+ smolts of 1SW;
5. 1+ smolts vs 2+ smolts of LG;
6. 1+ smolts vs 2+ smolts of 1SW and LG combined; and
7. Interaction of 1SW vs LG of 1+ smolts with 1SW vs LG of 2+ smolts.

Chi-square values were significant ($P<0.05$) for all but comparison 4. Releases of smolts in the LaHave River gave results relative to parental effect on sea age at first maturity which were consistent with the tendencies previously reported for smolts released in the Miramichi River (Tables 1 and 2). Progeny of 1SW salmon produced proportionately more grilse than did progeny of LG salmon, a tendency recorded for 1+ smolts (69.8% vs 28.0%) and 2+ smolts (80.5% vs 61.4%) separately and for 1+ and 2+ smolts combined (54.4% vs 71.5%). One year smolts produced proportionately fewer grilse than 2+ smolts, a tendency which appeared to be consistent for comparable release groups originating from both parental sea age types (69.8% vs 80.5% for 1SW parents; 28.0% vs 61.4% for LG salmon parents), but proved to be statistically significant ($P<0.05$) for only the smolt groups originating from LG salmon parents. Coincident with the tendency for 1+ smolts to produce proportionately fewer grilse than 2+ smolts was the difference in smolt size. One year smolts were consistently smaller than 2+ smolts from like parental age types (Table 2). The difference in the proportions of grilse produced by progeny of 1SW salmon and LG salmon was greater ($P<0.05$) for the 1+ smolts than for the 2+ smolts. Among the parental types and smolt age-groups, 2+ smolts of 1SW salmon produced the highest proportion of grilse (80.5%) while 1+ smolts of LG salmon produced by far the fewest grilse (28.0%).

Smolt Size Effects

Tag recapture data for 16 groups of hatchery smolts released into the LaHave River from 1978 to 1981 was examined for a relationship between the mean fork length of the smolts comprising the release group and the percentage of grilse in the total recoveries. All salmon releases were 1+ smolts (Goff and Forsyth 1979) originating from LG salmon parents taken from a trap in the Morgan Falls fishway situated at New Germany on the upper main LaHave River (Cutting and Gray 1984).

All release groups originated from pooled matings of LG salmon selected on the basis of size only. Although no estimate is available as to the contribution made by repeat spawning grilse to the matings producing the various release groups, a change in the incidence of repeat spawners is apparent in sample aging data for fish trapped at Morgan Falls between 1974 and 1983 (Cutting and Gray 1984). These data show the incidence of repeat spawning grilse and 2SW salmon in the population of salmon returning to Morgan Falls to have increased with build-up of the total adult returns to the fishway. The 1978 release groups originated from the 1976 spawning population of LG salmon returning to Morgan Falls. The incidence of repeat spawners among the LG salmon in 1976, as shown by sample aging data, was 3% compared to 23, 21, and 27% recorded for the donor populations from which the parents of the 1979, 1980, and 1981 releases were selected (Cutting and Gray 1984). Aging data for a recent (1983) collection of LG salmon made at the same trap, showed similarity in the incidence of repeat spawners among the fish collected for the hatchery program (41%) (D. K. MacPhail, personal communication)[3] and in the sampled returns of LG salmon to Morgan Falls (44%)

[3]Internal Report by D. K. MacPhail, Department of Fisheries and Oceans, P.O. Box 550, Station M, Halifax, N.S. B3J 2S7.

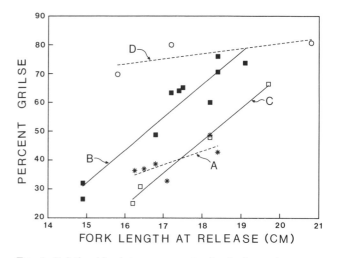

FIG. 1. Relationships between percent grilse in the total recovery and mean fork of the smolts at release for release groups categorized according to both the incidence of grilse amongst their parents and the river of origin. Designations for the four data sets are: low grilse incidence, LaHave(*, line A); intermediate grilse incidence, LaHave (■, line B); intermediate grilse incidence, Medway (□, line C); and 100% grilse, Medway (○, line D). Solid and broken lines fitted by unweighted regression correspond to presence of significant and nonsignificant regression coefficients, respectively.

(Cutting and Gray 1984). Although data was not available to differentiate the repeat spawners in the donor populations of the release groups into their maiden sea age categories, aging data for the 1983 collection showed grilse to dominate both the repeat spawning category (i.e., 30 of 32 repeat spawners) and the male spawners (i.e., 17 of 22 males). The inference of these data is that the contribution of grilse as repeat spawners to matings producing the 1978 release groups was low compared to grilse contributions to matings producing the release groups of 1979, 1980, and 1981.

The relationship between the incidence of grilse in the total recoveries and smolt size was examined through weighted regression of the grilse proportion on the mean fork length of the smolts comprising a release group (Li 1964; Snedecor and Cochran 1967; Armitage 1971). A plot of the data for the 16 release groups suggested independent linear relationships for groups of smolts originating from donor populations with low (3%) and higher (21−27%) incidences of repeat spawners, respectively (Fig. 1, lines A and B). Accordingly, data for the six groups originating from the low grilse incidence population (designated low grilse incidence, LaHave) were analyzed separate from the 10 groups which were progeny of higher grilse incidence populations (designated intermediate grilse incidence, LaHave). Estimates of the weighted coefficients of regression of the grilse proportions on smolt size and their standard errors are:

	Coeff.	SE
low grilse	0.0451	0.03335
intermediate grilse	0.1197	0.01981

Each regression coefficient was tested for significance by chi-square. The regression coefficient pertaining to the six releases from the low grilse incidence population was not significant ($P = 0.173$) while the coefficient for the ten releases originating from intermediate grilse incidence populations was highly significant ($P<0.001$).

The proportion of grilse among the adult returns increased with smolt size, a relationship demonstrated by the progeny of the higher grilse incidence populations, and also suggested, although not statistically supported ($P>0.05$), by progeny of the low grilse incidence population (Fig. 1, lines A and B). Consistent with evidence reported earlier in this paper, smolts originating from pooled matings to which grilse made low contribution yielded proportionately fewer grilse then smolts from matings to which grilse made an intermediate contribution. Similarly, the rate of change in the grilse proportion with an average increase of unity in the smolt size appeared to be lower among the release groups originating from the low grilse incidence population (i.e., the 1978 releases).

To further investigate the relationship between parental sea age at maturity and the responsiveness of the grilse proportion to variation in smolt size, data for the parentage trials carried out through smolt releases into the LaHave River (see Table 2) were examined in the same manner as data for the sixteen release groups. In this comparison the confounding effect of smolt age difference was ignored on the assumption that age is of little consequence relative to smolt size difference. Similarly, the difference in the rivers of origin of the parents (i.e., Medway and LaHave) was ignored since the Medway River salmon population was the primary source of gametes used to initially seed the upper LaHave River. One of the two data sets from the parentage trials represents smolts originating from 100% grilse parents (designated 100% grilse, Medway) while the other set represents progeny of LG salmon parents among which the incidence of repeat spawning grilse was probably between 20 and 30% (designated intermediate grilse incidence, Medway). The weighted regression coefficient for the four release groups originating from intermediate grilse incidence, Medway parents is significant ($P<0.01$) but the coefficient for the three release groups from 100% grilse, Medway parents is not significant ($P>0.05$) (Fig. 1, lines C and D). Trends in the four data sets displayed in Fig. 1 indicate that the responsiveness of the grilse proportion to variation in smolt size varies in relation to parental sea age. Sea age at maturity appears to have varied more in relation to variation in smolt size when parentage was a mix of grilse and multi-sea-winter (MSW) salmon than when parentage was comprised solely of grilse or almost pure MSW salmon. It is likely that the grilse contribution to matings producing the release groups originating from spawning populations of intermediate grilse incidence was higher than indicated by the percentages of repeat spawners reported for the donor populations because virgin MSW salmon males are generally scarce in LaHave and Medway populations and correspondingly repeat spawning grilse are relatively abundant among male spawners (i.e., among the 1983 broodfish, 17 of 22 males were repeat spawning grilse).

A perceived relationship between smolt age and sea age at first maturity is apparent in recapture data for tagged releases of 1+ and 2+ smolts (Table 3). These data, pertaining to three populations of salmon, were not subjected to statistical analysis because the number of observations was small given the numerous sources of variation. However, the general tendency observed in these data was for 1+ smolts to produce proportionately fewer grilse than comparable groups of 2+ smolts. The 1+ smolts were consistently smaller than 2+ smolts and for the single comparison where mean smolt sizes were almost equal (1+ − 17.6 vs

2+ − 18.3 cm for the 1976 releases of Medway smolts) the proportions of grilse produced by each were almost equal (1+ − 59.4% vs 2+ − 62.7%). The confounding effect of smolt size on comparisons between age at maturity and smolt age is further demonstrated by the groups of smolts released into the LaHave River under the parentage trials (see Parental Influences section). For these releases the weighted mean proportions of grilse produced by 1+ and 2+ smolts of LG salmon parents were significantly different ($P<0.05$). However, in the subsequent analysis of data for these same release groups, the weighted regression coefficient for the relationship between the grilse proportions and smolt size proved to be highly significant ($P<0.01$) (see Fig. 1, line C). These results, supported by the absence of a significant difference ($P>0.05$) between weighted mean proportions of grilse produced by 1+ and 2+ smolts of LaHave 1SW parents (refer to Parental Influences section), suggest that smolt age is not an important factor in the determination of sea age at first maturity of Atlantic salmon. According to these and other results reported earlier in the paper, the observed differences in the proportions of grilse produced by comparable groups of 1+ and 2+ smolts are at least partly the result of smolt size differences.

Another feature which was apparent in the data presented in Table 3 is the difference in grilse proportions recorded for the different source populations. Most striking are the releases of Penobscot River salmon which, in spite of the large size of the 2+ smolts released during the 1969−75 period (average 20.5 cm), produced very few grilse (1.4%). Although somewhat higher proportions of grilse were produced by both 1+ and 2+ smolts of Penobscot origin released during the 1976−81 period, grilse incidences among the adult recaptures were still low (7.0 and 10.9% respectively) relative to those recorded for the other two source populations. These data suggest that the potential of the Penobscot salmon population to produce grilse is low compared to that of either Saint John or Medway populations, a feature which is probably attributed to genetic difference.

Smolt Sex Ratio Effects

Examination of sex ratio data for yearling Saint John River salmon produced at the Mactaquac Hatchery provided evidence of a second factor contributing to the difference in proportions of grilse produced by 1+ and 2+ smolts. Size distributions for female, immature male and mature male yearling parr (Fig. 2 and 3) illustrate the effects of hatchery grading practices on the sex ratio of juveniles released as 1+ and 2+ smolts. The size distributions relative to sex and maturity status prior to grading are shown in Fig. 2 while the same information is presented for the small, medium and large grades after grading in Fig. 3. The general trends in these data are for the female fish to be proportionately more abundant in the large size classes and the males to be more abundant in the small size classes.

Precociously mature males accounted for roughly 0.4% of the ungraded population and were found in the middle size classes. The low incidence of mature parr indicates that the sex related growth rate difference recorded for these parr was not attributed to growth rate depression normally associated with precocious maturation (Saunders et al. 1982).

One of the purposes of late fall or early spring grading is to separate out the large fish for release as 1+ smolts. The

TABLE 3. Percentages of grilse produced by comparable groups of 1+ and 2+ hatchery smolts released in Canadian and American rivers during 1969−81.

Year of release	Parental Age[a]	Parental Type[b]	Smolt fork length (cm)	Total returns	Percent grilse by smolt age 1+	2+
Saint John smolt releases into Saint John River						
1971	—	wild	15.0	18	5.6	
			17.6	32	6.3	
			17.6	62	9.7	
			21.4	37		45.9
1976	LG	hatchery	15.2	42	35.7	
			21.6	232		67.7
1978	LG	hatchery	16.4	60	10.0	
			22.2	108		58.3
			21.5	108		57.4
	LG	wild	16.4	18	22.2	
			16.4	10	20.0	
			21.0	96		64.6
			21.0	42		54.8
1979	LG	—	16.8	18	22.2	
			16.8	13	23.1	
	LG	hatchery	21.2	172		69.8
			21.2	235		76.2
	LG	wild	20.7	266		84.6
			20.7	230		82.7
Medway smolt releases into LaHave River						
1973	LG	wild	16.4	13	30.8	
			19.7	128		66.4
1974	1SW	wild	15.8	43	69.8	
			17.2	65		80.0
	LG	wild	16.2	12	25.0	
			18.2	48		47.9
1976	1SW and LG	—	17.6	197	59.4	
			18.3	83		62.7
Penobscot smolt releases into Machias, Narraguagus, and Penobscot rivers						
1969−1975	LG	—	17.7	450	0.2	
			20.5	2 583		1.4
1976−1981	LG	—	—	371	7.0	
			—	1 375		10.9

[a]Parental Age is designated as either 1-sea-winter (1SW) or large (LG) salmon.

[b]Parental Type differentiates between release groups originating from wild or hatchery returning salmon.

small and medium parr are retained for an additional year and released as 2+ smolts. In this population, the grade structure was 11% large grade, 31% medium, and 58% small. Males comprised only 41% of the large grade, or as otherwise designated, potential 1+ smolts. This result is similar to both that observed in a sample (105) of 1+ smolts taken at Mactaquac Hatchery in 1976 and that reported by Bailey et al. (1980) for upper mode yearlings of Saint John River population origin reared at the Atlantic Salmon Research Institute, St. Andrews, N.B. Sexing of 2+ smolts produced at the Mactaquac Hatchery in 1980 (150 fish sampled) and 1981 (148 fish) showed male percentages of 54 and 52%, respectively.

Although sex ratio data does not exist for any of the smolt groups identified in Table 3, it is likely that the 1+ and 2+ smolts released into the Saint John River differed with re-spect to sex ratio since smolts of the two age-groups were the product of grading. A difference in the sex ratios of 1+ and 2+ smolts of the magnitude shown in recent sampling data would have markedly contributed to the observed differences in grilse proportions produced by 1+ and 2+ smolts of Saint John River origin since grilse from this population are more than 90% male and 2SW salmon are more than 70% female. The sea age at first maturity of salmon of Penobscot or Medway River origin would be less sensitive to variation in the sex ratio of smolts since the Penobscot smolts produce few grilse (i.e., generally <10%) while the Medway smolts produce proportionately many grilse which have a comparatively high female component (25%) (Cutting and Gray 1984).

The sex related growth rate difference recorded for parr of Saint John River origin may not apply to all salmon popu-

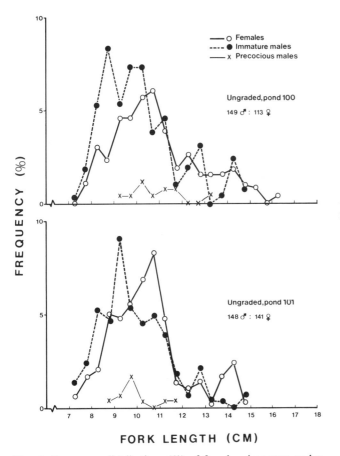

FIG. 2. Frequency distributions (%) of females, immature males and precocious males in yearling hatchery Atlantic salmon parr prior to grading, Mactaquac Hatchery, New Brunswick, April 24, 1980.

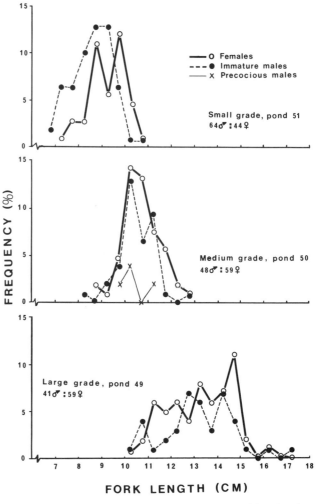

FIG. 3. Comparison of frequency distributions (%) of females, immature males and precocious males in small, medium and large grades of hatchery yearling Atlantic salmon parr, Mactaquac Hatchery, New Brunswick, April 24, 1980. Production at Mactaquac Hatchery following grading was divided into 170 000 parr of the small grade (58% of total population), 91 000 medium grade (31%), and 32 000 large grade (11%).

lations. The results do, however, show that hatchery grading practices can alter the sex ratio of smolt groups. For populations in which growth rate tendencies are similar to those observed for the Saint John River population, removal of the slower growing fish through grading, a common hatchery practice, would tend to enhance the female component among smolts and accordingly reduce the proportion of grilse in the adult return (i.e., for populations that produce both grilse and MSW salmon).

Discussion and Conclusions

Studies involving hatchery smolts have shown that sea age at first maturity in Atlantic salmon can be altered through parental selection. Grilse spawners tend to produce relatively higher proportions of grilse, while 2SW salmon parents produce proportionately more 2SW progeny (see also Piggins 1974). These observations along with those of Gjerde (1984), who also found offspring age at sexual maturity to vary in relation to parental age of Atlantic salmon, are evidence of genetic influence over sea age at first maturity. Parental selection of MSW salmon may be used to reduce the incidence of grilse in aquaculture lots and in the returns from hatchery plantings. Although fisheries effects on the population genetics of wild salmon stocks remain to be shown, the selectivity of the fisheries for MSW salmon (Paloheimo and Elson 1974) must be affecting the age at first maturity of stocks of the North Atlantic.

Investigation of the relationship between sea age at first

maturity and smolt size at release indicated a direct relationship between the grilse proportion and smolt size, i.e., large smolts produce proportionately more grilse than small smolts. Bilton et al. (1982) reported a similar relationship for coho salmon. These authors related recapture rates for both jacks (males that matured in their first sea year) and adults (males and females that matured in their second sea year) to juvenile size at release and release date. Through a response surface analysis they showed that jack production would be greatest for large juveniles released early. The effect of release time demonstrated by the coho salmon study is interpreted as a reflection of a size effect on sea age at first maturity. Coho and Atlantic salmon entering saltwater early may be expected to maintain a size advantage over salmon of comparable size entering the sea later. This size advantage would exist at the onset of maturation as jacks (coho salmon) or grilse (Atlantic salmon). The results of both the coho salmon study (Bilton et al. 1982) and this one suggest that age at maturation is influenced by the size of the individual at the time when maturation is triggered.

The relationship between sea age at first maturity and size at release has important implications for Atlantic salmon hatchery programs. It is generally accepted that large smolts are required to produce high survival rates. In the interest of efficiency many hatcheries are producing large smolts, a practice which may be expected to contribute to a reduction in the mean sea age of adult returns from hatchery releases. According to results presented in this paper, smolt size effect on sea age at first maturity will be largest in cultured lots originating from a hybridization of grilse and MSW salmon and lowest among progeny of parents that are of the same sea age.

The relationship between sea age at first maturity and smolt size reported in this paper contradicts Ritter's (1972) study which showed that the proportion of grilse among returning adults decreased with increasing smolt size within a given release group. It has been shown here that growth rates of males and females may differ during the parr stage thereby producing variations in sex ratio among different size classes of parr or smolts. Although the difference in growth rate reported here for male and female parr was independent of maturation of the male parr (i.e., incidence of mature parr was <1%), precocious maturation observed among hatchery parr (Saunders et al. 1982) may also have contributed to a size difference between male and female smolts in the release groups reported on by Ritter (1972). These growth rate differences would have resulted in male smolts being smaller than females thereby enhancing the proportion of grilse produced by the smaller size classes. Although sexing data is not available for the release groups reported on by Ritter (1972), results reported here and by others (Bailey et al. 1980; Saunders et al. 1982) suggest that the anomalous relationship between maturity and smolt size reported earlier is likely attributed to variations in sex ratio among the smolt size classes.

Differences in sea age at first maturity between 1+ and 2+ smolts have in part been attributed to differences in smolt sex ratio and/or to differences in smolt size. Although data does not exist to eliminate smolt age as a controlling factor, sex ratio and size differences can be expected to account for much and perhaps all of the differences in sea age at first maturity displayed by 1+ and 2+ smolts. We suggest that differences in sea age at first maturity reported by other authors for 1+ and 2+ hatchery smolts (Peterson 1971; Ísaksson 1982a, b; Bailey and Saunders 1984) may also be largely attributed to sex ratio and/or smolt size differences.

The results of this examination of data from various hatchery studies indicate that it is feasible to regulate sea age at first maturity in Atlantic salmon through broodstock selection and the manipulation of other hatchery practices. The opportunities to implement such practices are numerous and their application would benefit both public fisheries and private aquaculture.

Acknowledgements

Data for parentage trials conducted on the Northwest Miramichi River were obtained from Departmental computer files. Both the experimental design and the conduct of these trials are credited to Dr. P. F. Elson. Dr. R. L. Saunders contributed to the planning of the Miramichi trials, assisted with their conduct during the earlier years and also provided constructive review comments on an earlier draft of the manuscript. We thank H. T. Bilton, R. B. Morley, T. L. Marshall, R. A. Myers, and R. G. Randall for their constructive criticisms of earlier drafts of this manuscript. Special thanks goes to E. J. McLean for assisting with the collation and analysis of data, and D. K. MacPhail for preparing the figures.

References

ARMITAGE, P. 1971. Statistical methods in medical research. Blackwell Scientific Publications, 504 p.

BAILEY, J. K., AND R. L. SAUNDERS. 1984. Returns of three year-classes of sea-ranched Atlantic salmon of various river strains and strain crosses. Aquaculture 41: 259−270.

BAILEY, J. K., R. L. SAUNDERS, AND M. I. BUZETA. 1980. Influence of parental smolt age and sea age on growth and smolting of hatchery-reared Atlantic salmon (*Salmo salar*). Can. J. Fish. Aquat. Sci. 37: 1379−1386.

BILTON, H. T., D. F. ALDERDICE, AND J. T. SCHNUTE. 1982. Influence of time and size at release of juvenile coho salmon (*Oncorhynchus kisutch*) on returns at maturity. Can. J. Fish. Aquat. Sci. 39: 426−447.

CUTTING, R. E., AND R. W. GRAY. 1984. Assessment of the status of the Atlantic salmon stocks of the LaHave River, Nova Scotia. CAFSAC Res. Doc. 84/40: 44 p.

ELSON, P. F. 1973. Genetic polymorphism in Northwest Miramichi salmon, in relation to season of river ascent and age at maturation and its implications for management of the stocks. ICNAF Res. Doc. 73/76, Annual Meeting, June 1973: 6 p.

GJERDE, B. 1984. Response to individual selection for age at sexual maturity in Atlantic salmon. Aquaculture 38: 229−240.

GJERDE, B., AND T. GJEDREM. 1984. Estimate of phenotypic and genetic parameters for carcass traits in Atlantic salmon and rainbow trout. Aquaculture 36: 97−110.

GJERDE, B., AND T. REFSTIE. 1984. Complete dialled cross between five strains of Atlantic salmon. Livest. Prod. Sci. 11: 207−226.

GOFF, T. R., AND L. S. FORSYTH. 1979. Production of Atlantic salmon smolts in one year without artificial heating of water, Mersey Hatchery, Nova Scotia. Fish. Mar. Tech. Rep. 841: 13 p.

GUNNES, K. 1978. Genetic variation in production traits of Atlantic salmon. Eur. Assoc. Anim. Prod., Commission on Animal Genetics, Stockholm Meeting, 7 p.

ÍSAKSSON, Á. 1982a. Returns of microtagged Atlantic salmon (*Salmo salar*) to the Kollafjördhur Experimental Fish Farm in 1976−79 tagging experiments. Int. Coun. Explor. Sea, C.M. 1982/M: 34, 9 p.

1982b Returns of microtagged Atlantic salmon (*Salmo salar*) of Kollafjördhur stock to three different salmon ranching facilities. Int. Coun. Explor. Sea, C. M. 1982/M: 35, 9 p.

KERSWILL, C. J. 1971. Relative rates of utilization by commercial and sport fisheries of Atlantic salmon (*Salmo salar*) from the Miramichi River, New Brunswick. J. Fish. Res. Board Can. 28: 351−363.

LI, J. C. R. 1964. Statistical inference. Vol. I, Edward Brothers, Inc., 658 p.

MACPHAIL, D. 1973. Age comparisons of four Atlantic salmon stocks. Res. Dev. Br., Environ. Can., MS Rep. 73-2: 10 p.

NAEVDAL, G. 1983. Genetic factors in connection with age at maturation. Aquaculture 33: 97−106.

NAEVDAL, G., M. HOLM, O. INGERBRIGTSEN, AND D. MØLLER. 1978. Variation in age at first spawning in Atlantic salmon (*Salmo salar*). J. Fish. Res. Board Can. 35: 145−147.

PALOHEIMO, J. E., AND P. F. ELSON. 1974. Reduction of Atlantic salmon catches in Canada attributed to the Greenland fishery. J. Fish. Res. Board Can. 31: 1467−1480.

PETERSON, H. H. 1971. Smolt rearing methods, equipment and techniques used successfully in Sweden. International Atlantic Salmon Foundation. Spec. Publ. Ser. 2(1): 32−62.

PIGGINS, D. 1974. The results of selective breeding from known grilse and salmon parents. Annu. Rep. Salmon Res. Trust Ireland XVIII: 35−39.

PIPPY, J. 1982. Report of the Working Group on the Interception of Mainland Salmon in Newfoundland. Can. MS. Rep. Fish.

Aquat. Sci. Rep. 1654: 196 p.

RITTER, J. A. 1972. Preliminary observations on the influence of smolt size on tag return rate and age at first maturity of Atlantic salmon (*Salmo salar*). Int. Coun. Explor. Sea, C.M. 1972/M: 14, 10 p.

1975. Relationships of smolt size and age with age at first maturity in Atlantic salmon. Res. Dev. Br., Environ. Can., Tech. Rep. Ser. No. MAR/F-75-5: 7 p.

RITTER, J. A., AND K. NEWBOULD. 1977. Relationships of parentage and smolt age to age at first maturity of Atlantic salmon (*Salmo salar*). Int. Coun. Explor. Sea, C.M. 1977/M: 32: 5 p.

RUGGLES, C. P., AND G. E. TURNER. 1973. Recent changes in stock composition of Atlantic salmon (*Salmo salar*) in the Miramichi River, New Brunswick. J. Fish. Res. Board Can. 30: 779−786.

SAUNDERS, R. L. 1967. Seasonal pattern of return of Atlantic salmon in the Northwest Miramichi River, New Brunswick. J. Fish. Res. Board Can. 24: 21−32.

1968. An evaluation of two methods of attaching tags to Atlantic salmon smolts. Prog. Fish. Cult. 30: 104−109.

SAUNDERS, R. L., E. B. HENDERSON, AND B. D. GLEBE. 1982. Precocious sexual maturation and smoltification in male Atlantic salmon (*Salmo salar*). Aquaculture 28: 211−229.

SAUNDERS, R. L., E. B. HENDERSON, B. D. GLEBE, AND E. J. LOUDENSLAGER. 1983. Evidence of a major environmental component in determination of the grilse: larger salmon ratio in Atlantic salmon (*Salmo salar*). Aquaculture 33: 107−118.

SNEDECOR, G. W., AND W. G. COCHRAN. 1967. Statistical methods. Sixth edition, The IOWA State University Press, Iowa. 593 p.

Optimum Size and Age at Maturity in Pacific Salmon and Effects of Size-Selective Fisheries

M. C. Healey

Department of Fisheries and Oceans, Fisheries Research Branch
Pacific Biological Station, Nanaimo, B.C. V9R 5K6

Abstract

HEALEY, M. C. 1986. Optimum size and age at maturity in Pacific salmon and effects of size-selective fisheries, p. 39–52. *In* D. J. Meerburg [ed.] Salmonid age at maturity. Can. Spec. Publ. Fish. Aquat. Sci. 89.

The five species of Pacific salmon (*Oncorhynchus* spp.) endemic to North America are all anadromous and semelparous. Within this general life-history strategy the five species show considerable interspecific and intraspecific variation in life-history parameters, such as age and size at maturity. Sockeye, for example, display 22 mature age categories when the various combinations of freshwater and marine residence are taken into account. Average size of sockeye varies up to 40 cm among mature age classes. At the other extreme, pink salmon display only one mature age category and vary only about 9.5 cm in size among populations. Two life-history models based on demographic parameters give good qualitative prediction and, in some instances, good quantitative prediction of age and size at maturity. In general, however, these models underestimate age at maturity, presumably because they fail to account for multiple mature age classes in some populations. Historic information on size and age of Pacific salmon demonstrates that, for many populations, size declined between 1951 and 1975, but then increased somewhat between 1975 and 1981. The fisheries for salmon are selective for larger fish, and changes in size could be a consequence of genetic selection for slower growth. Recent increases in size in some populations and the failure of other populations to demonstrate expected changes in size are contrary to this hypothesis. The changes in size could also be a consequence of long-term variation in the ocean environment, and the observed changes in size are coincident with changes in some oceanic parameters.

Résumé

HEALEY, M. C. 1986. Optimum size and age at maturity in Pacific salmon and effects of size-selective fisheries, p. 39–52. *In* D. J. Meerburg [ed.] Salmonid age at maturity. Can. Spec. Publ. Fish. Aquat. Sci. 89.

Les cinq espèces de saumons du Pacifique (*Oncorhynchus* spp.) endémiques à l'Amérique du Nord sont tous des poissons anadromes et sémelpares. À l'intérieur de cette stratégie générale d'antécédents biologiques, les cinq espèces présentent des variations interspécifiques et intraspécifiques considérables en ce qui concerne les paramètres d'antécédents biologiques, comme l'âge et la taille à maturité. Ainsi, le saumon rouge comprend 22 catégories d'âges matures lorsque les diverses combinaisons de résidence en eau douce et en milieu marin sont prises en compte. La taille moyenne du saumon rouge atteint 40 cm parmi les classes d'âge mature. Á l'autre extrémité, le saumon rose ne possède qu'une catégorie d'âge mature et sa taille ne varie que d'environ 9,5 cm parmi les populations. Deux modèles d'antécédents biologiques basés sur certains paramètres démographiques donnent une bonne prédiction qualitative et, dans certains cas, une bonne prédiction quantitative de l'âge et de la taille à maturité. Toutefois, de manière générale ces modèles sous-estiment l'âge à maturité, probablement en raison de leur incapacité de tenir compte des multiples classes d'âges matures dans certaines populations. Des informations historiques concernant la taille et l'âge du saumon du Pacifique démontrent que, pour de nombreuses populations, la taille a diminué entre 1951 et 1975, mais qu'elle a ensuite augmenté quelque peu entre 1975 et 1981. La pêche au saumon est sélective dans le cas des poissons plus gros et certaines modifications dans la taille pourraient résulter d'une sélection génétique pour la croissance plus lente. De récentes augmentations de taille dans certaines populations et le fait que certaines autres populations se soient révélées incapables de confirmer les changements de taille prévus sont contraires à cette hypothèse. Les changements de taille pourraient aussi découler d'une variation à long terme dans le milieu marin tandis que les changements observés dans la taille coïncident avec des changements dans certains paramètres marins.

Introduction

There are seven species of Pacific salmon (genus: *Oncorhynchus*) endemic to the North Pacific. Five of the species (sockeye, *O. nerka*; pink, *O. gorbuscha*; chum, *O. keta*; coho, *O. kisutch*; chinook, *O. tshawytscha*) sustain breeding populations in North American rivers (Hart 1973). Neave (1958) argued that the genus and all the species had evolved during the past 500 000 – 1 000 000 years from a *Salmo*-like ancestor. Although the genus may be considerably older than this, the species are of relatively recent differentiation and share numerous life-history characteristics. All, for example, are anadromous and semelparous. The five North American species fall into two subgroupings, which again share similar morphological and ecological characteristics (Neave 1958; Tsuyuki et al. 1965; Tsuyuki

and Roberts 1966). Sockeye, chum, and pink form one subgrouping, of which sockeye is the most primitive and pink the most advanced member. These species are principally planktivorous and, during their marine life, live pelagically in the open ocean. Coho and chinook form the second subgroup, coho being the most primitive. These species are principally piscivorous and remain abundant in coastal and continental shelf waters throughout their marine life, except that one race of chinook salmon (the stream-type race) is a fish of the open ocean (Healey 1983). The evolution of seven species within a relatively short time implies an abundance of successful life-history options for the precursor species, and rather strong selection gradients favouring reproductive isolation, at least during the period of speciation.

The individual species are characterized by differences in

age and size at maturity. Sockeye mature mainly in their third to fifth years of life at 1−3 kg, chum in their third and fourth years of life at 4−6 kg, and pink in their second year of life at 2 kg. Coho mature in their third year of life at 3 kg and chinook in their third to fifth years of life at 3−10 kg. While these are the typical parameters for each species, there is, as I shall show later, tremendous variation in size and age at maturity, both within and between populations of Pacific salmon. The significance of this variation is a subject of concern and debate among fishery scientists. The prevalent belief is that the variation is adaptive and has been nurtured by environmental variation between reproductively isolated populations. There is no consensus, however, about how management agencies should react to this belief, or the extent to which gene pools should be preserved at the expense of other options (Calaprice 1969; Larkin 1981; Ihssen et al. 1981; MacLean and Evans 1981).

The five North American species of Pacific salmon are all commercially valuable and subject to intensive fisheries. These fisheries are selective for certain sizes and ages of salmon, although the direction of selection and its intensity have varied between fisheries and over time within fisheries (Ricker 1981). Evidence for declining size and age of fish in recent years has heightened concern about the genetic consequences of selecting for slower growth. The degree to which one should be concerned about the potential consequences of size and age-selective fisheries, however, depends on the selection differential imposed by the fisheries, the heritability of the traits in question, and the countervalent forces in the fishes' environment which resist selection away from the prevalent life-history patterns. These countervalent forces have not yet received much attention in the debate about the consequences of size-selective fisheries.

In this paper I consider how, in the context of life-history theory, the variation in reproductive parameters within and between Pacific salmon species may be accounted for, and what the effects of size-selective fisheries on age and size at maturity are likely to be. My analysis suggests that forces acting against change in the size and age of mature Pacific salmon may be significant.

Natural Variation Among Pacific Salmon

Variation in Age at Maturity

Descriptions of the life-history of anadromous salmon have focused on their allocation of time between freshwater and marine habitats, and considerable variation within as well as between species has been revealed. Sockeye, for example, mature in their third to eighth years of life, or at 6 different total ages. If age is split between freshwater and marine habitats, however, 22 different age categories are revealed, from 0.2 to 4.3 (Table 1). (Age designations in this paper, with one exception to be noted later, follow the European system in which freshwater annuli come before a decimal point and marine annuli after. For example, a fish aged 4.3 has 4 freshwater annuli and 3 marine annuli on its scales. This fish migrated to sea in the spring during its fifth year of life and returned to spawn in the fall during its eighth year of life.) Only 5 of the recorded age categories for sockeye (1.2, 1.3, 1.4, 2.2, 2.3) have, individually, comprised more than 50% in any spawning population, however, and 10 have occured only as rare variants (Table 1).

Individual spawning populations tend to be dominated by 2 or 3 age categories; nevertheless, 21 of the 22 known age categories have been observed in the Karluk River, Alaska (Rounsefell 1958).

Chum salmon also mature at 6 different total ages, from their second to seventh years (Table 1). Chum, however, show no significant variation in freshwater age, so that only 6 age categories are known to occur, and only 3 of these (ages 0.2−0.4) have individually comprised more than 50% of any spawning population.

Pink salmon, at the extreme, show essentially no variation in age of maturity or in freshwater age. All migrate to sea immediately after emerging from the spawning gravel in the spring, and mature at 2 years of age (Table 1), with the exception of the occasional, extremely rare, 3-year-old fish (Anas 1959; Turner and Bilton 1968). Three-year-old pink salmon have, however, been observed much more frequently in populations introduced to the Laurentian Great Lakes (Kwain and Chappel 1978; Wagner and Stauffer 1980; Nicolette 1984). The appearance of 3-year-old pink salmon in the Great Lakes demonstrates that the *Oncorhynchus* species still have the capacity to exploit new situations.

Coho and chinook, like sockeye, display variable freshwater age (Table 1). Coho mature at 5 different total ages (2−6) but, with 5 different freshwater ages, display 12 mature age categories. Three ages contribute most to spawning populations (1.0, 1.1, 2.1), while a fourth (3.1) is relatively common in some northern rivers. Chinook mature at 7 different total ages (2−8) and, with 3 different freshwater ages, display 16 mature age categories (Table 1). Seven age categories of chinook make a relatively strong contribution to spawning runs, and five (0.1, 0.3, 1.2, 1.3, 1.4) have contributed 50% or more to individual runs (Table 1).

Variation in Size at Maturity

Pacific salmon also vary considerably in size at maturity. Of the possible sources of this variation in size I shall consider only variation between age categories within populations and variation between populations.

Males show greater variation in size at maturity within populations than do females, probably because males often display more mature age-groups within a population. For sockeye, males vary 30−40 cm in average length among mature age classes and females, 15−20 cm. Chum show less variation, about 8−10 cm for both males and females. Pinks, having only one mature age, show no interage variation (Table 1). For coho, mature males vary 25−30 cm in length and females slightly more. Most coho females mature after 2 ocean-growing seasons so that it is difficult to generalize from the rare females which mature after 1 or 3 ocean-growing seasons. For chinook, most published size data do not differentiate between sexes, however, it may be assumed that the youngest mature ages classes are virtually all males since virtually no mature females aged 0.1, or 2.1 have been observed. On this basis, the variation in size of mature males is 60−70 cm for the ocean-type race (ages 0.) and 60−90 cm for the stream-type race (ages 1., 2.) (a few stream-type males mature precocially without ever going to sea). For females, the variation is about 40 cm for both races.

The age specific size distributions of mature fish overlap to a considerable degree. This is true both within and be-

TABLE 1. Interpopulation variation in age at maturity, average fork length of mature males and females and average fecundity of females for five species of Pacific salmon. For each age category the maximum percent contribution to any population is shown. For 5 yr old chum and all ages of chinook the size data are not differentiated by sex in the literature sources.

Species	Age	Maturity Max percent occurrence	Range in length at age (mm) Males	Range in length at age (mm) Females	Range in fecundity
Sockeye	0.2	+	508−592	544−571	
	0.3	0.1	627−635	584−617	
	0.4	+			
	1.1	2.2	399−470	472	
	1.2	89.2	537−602	546−582	2633−3118
	1.3	50.7	578−655	610−636	2755−3816
	1.4	66.5	665−724	643−691	3178
	1.5	7.2			
	2.0	+	300		
	2.1	1.4	394−511	466−525	1674
	2.2	58.3	547−640	534−617	2548−3708
	2.3	63.2	576−686	583−654	2926−3630
	2.4	8.9	633−737	609	4320
	3.0	+	320		
	3.1	1.7	544−610	520	1717
	3.2	15.4	550−655	535−638	2796−3668
	3.3	4.6	609−668	584−724	2802−3650
	3.4	+			
	4.0	+	340		
	4.1	+	534		
	4.2	0.3			
	4.3	+			
Chum	0.1	6.9			
	0.2	90.6	610−758	584−700	1988−3277
	0.3	94.9	577−806	555−776	2576−3707
	0.4	75.5	516−889	653−762	2804−3443
	0.5	19.8	617−724		
	0.6	0.5			
Pink	0.1	100.0	485−572	460−561	1316−2074
Coho	0.1	2.6			
	0.2	0.7			
	0.3	0.1			
	1.0	63.0	285−448	278	
	1.1	100.0	562−672	592−656	1983−4177
	1.2	3.0			
	2.0	19.0	210−372	521	
	2.1	93.0	558−670	510−670	2565−5286
	2.2	3.0			
	3.0	0.3	380		
	3.1	42.0	590−727	630−697	
	4.1	1.5	540	700	
Chinook	0.1	50.0	280−570		
	0.2	35.0	480−730		2648−4462
	0.3	53.0	630−880		3419−5355
	0.4	12.0	810−1030		4297−5724
	0.5	1.0	955−1150		4270
	1.0	1.0	102−401		
	1.1	19.0	358−635		
	1.2	56.0	572−909		4018
	1.3	77.0	727−1031		5388−9063
	1.4	60.0	828−1010		8716−10094
	1.5	12.0	967−1025		8196−12040
	2.1	+			
	2.2	+	602		
	2.3	+	749		

TABLE 1: (*Concluded*).

Species	Maturity		Range in length at age (mm)		Range in fecundity
	Age	Max percent occurrence	Males	Females	
	2.4	2.0	830−881		
	2.5	+	919−1055		

Sources of tabular data: Bakkala (1970); Beacham (1982); Bird (1982); Drucker (1972); Foerster (1968); Foerster and Pritchard (1941); Galbreath and Ridenhour (1964); Godfrey (1959a,b, 1965); Hamilton et al. (1970); Hanamura (1966); Healey and Heard (1984); Hunter (1959); Ishida (1966); Killick and Clemens (1963); Knudsen et al. (1983); Loeffel and Wendler (1969); Mesiar (1984); McBride et al. (1983); Pritchard (1937, 1943); Rich (1925); Rounsefell (1957); Sano (1966); Thorsteinson et al. (1963); Yancey and Thorsteinson (1963).

TABLE 2. Estimated natural and fishing mortality rates for five species of Pacific salmon during various life stages[e]. Mortality rates are instantaneous rates for the duration of the life stage (percent mortality in brackets), except as noted.

Life stage:	Freshwater[a]	Coastal marine[b]	Oceanic	
Mortality type:	Natural	Natural	Natural[c]	Fishing[d]
Species				
Pink	2.56−4.83 (87−99)	1.46−2.91 (77−95)	0.230 (21)	0.15−3.07 (14−95)
Chum	1.84−4.20 (84−98.5)	1.67−2.91 (81−95)	0.13−0.23 (12−21)	0.10−1.14 (10−68)
Sockeye	3.17−5.81 (96−99.7)	0.34−2.10 (29−88)	0.14−0.47 (13−37)	0.69−1.47 (50−77)
Coho	2.81 (94)	?	0.16−2.22 (15−89)	0.73−3.00 (52−95)
Chinook	2.38 (91)	?	0.42 (34)	0.205−1.304 (19−73)

[a]Stage length: Pink and chum 8 mo, sockeye and coho 20−32 mo, chinook 8−32 mo. Range of values reflects measured interannual variation as well as variation between populations.

[b]Stage length: Pink and chum 1−2 mo, sockeye 1 mo, coho and chinook 1−6 mo. Range of values represent mainly differences in estimation techniques.

[c]Mortality on an annual basis. Values from Ricker (1976), many of which are biased high especially in coho.

[d]Instantaneous rates of exploitation reported in the literature for different stocks. For chinook the range of values reflects between age and between stock differences.

[e]Data sources: Bakkala (1970); Cleaver (1969); Crone and Bond (1976); Drucker (1972); Foerster (1968); Gangmark and Bakkala (1960); Henry (1978); Hunter (1959); Koski (1966); Lister and Walker (1966); Major and Mighell (1969); Parker (1962, 1968); Pritchard (1947); Ricker (1976); Shapovalov and Taft (1954); Wales and Coots (1954); Walters et al. (1982).

tween populations. Maturity is clearly size related, since it is the largest members of the younger ages which mature. Nevertheless, the overlap in size of mature fish between ages, and the range of size and age at which some of the species mature, indicate that maturity is also strongly age dependent.

Between-population variation in average size of mature fish, within age classes, is generally smaller than the between-age variation within populations. Differences in age specific fork length between populations are about 7 cm for sockeye, 15 cm for chum, 9.5 cm for pink, 11.5 cm for coho, and 22 cm for chinook (Table 1). The size differences between populations do not increase with age suggesting that these size differences are probably established during the first or second ocean-growing season.

In my view, variation in size and age at maturity of the magnitude described above is likely to be adaptive. To interpret this variation in the context of theories of life history it is necessary also to consider age specific patterns of natality and mortality. These parameters also display considerable variation in Pacific salmon.

Variation in Fecundity, Mortality, and Growth Rates

Variation in fecundity reflects variation in age and size within and between species and populations, yet is also species specific. For example, chum and sockeye salmon with the same number of ocean annuli have a similar fecundity, yet chum are much larger than sockeye. Pinks, which are of similar size but younger than the smallest sockeye, have a relatively low fecundity (Table 1). Coho and sockeye of similar size have similar fecundity, but coho show much greater variation between populations (2×) than do sockeye (1.3×). Chinook, because of their large average size, have high average fecundity. Small chinook are similar in size to large sockeye and coho, however, and have a fecundity similar to these species (Table 1).

Perhaps the least studied life-history trait of Pacific salmon is natural mortality. This is not surprising, considering the cost and logistical difficulty of obtaining reliable estimates, particularly for the marine phase of the salmon's life. Mortality during various life-history stages has been estimated, but the data are inadequate for an examination of interpopulation difference (Table 2).

The rates of mortality shown in Table 2 are simply the high and low values reported in the literature and do not relate to a particular location or population. None of these values should be regarded as very precise and some suffer from uncorrectable biases (e.g. Ricker 1976). It is probably the case that there is no "typical" rate for any life stage of any species. The values in Table 2 are merely intended to demonstrate the level of mortality that may be expected to occur during different life stages.

Typically, greatest mortality is in the freshwater stage. A second period of high mortality occurs during early sea life, but annual mortality rates during the oceanic stage are rather small (Table 2). Fishing mortality of maturing fish (10–95%) is currently large and certainly has the potential to impose strong size selection.

Inter- and intrapopulation variation in growth rate is also apparent. This is evidenced by the range in average size at age among populations (Table 1) and by variation in size at age within populations. Species-specific differences in juvenile growth rate in general reflect the length of freshwater residence for the species, being greatest for the species which spend little time in freshwater. Ricker (1976) reviewed data on marine growth and estimated species-specific instantaneous rates of increase in weight. Pink and coho salmon showed the fastest growth (instantaneous rates 0.26 and 0.27 on a monthly basis). Sockeye and chum grew at about half the rate for pink and coho (0.11 and 0.14 per month respectively), and chinook slower still (<0.10 per month). Thus, within the species subgroupings, older age of maturity and greater variation in age of maturity are associated with slower oceanic growth.

Optimum Age and Size at Maturity

If the variation in life-history traits, which I have outlined above, is adaptive it should be possible to encompass it within a general theory of life-history strategies. Theories of life history based on traditional demographic models have been developed (see reviews by Stearns 1976, 1977), and here I consider whether current theory is adequate for predicting age (and size) at maturity for Pacific salmon. In particular, I shall apply two models of optimum age at maturity to the data on salmon.

Bell (1980) argued that optimum age at maturity was the age at which the instantaneous increase in fecundity with age equalled the mortality rate of mature animals (assuming that fecundity is an appropriate measure of contributions to future generations). Bell's (1980) model predicts both the relationship between fecundity and mean age at maturity among populations and the relationship between fecundity and mean age at maturity within multiaged populations (Healey and Heard 1984). Data from sockeye and chinook salmon are available to test these predictions. Healey and Heard (1984) presented data on mean age and fecundity for chinook populations. Similar data for sockeye come from a variety of sources (Foerster and Pritchard 1941; Foerster 1929; Bilton 1970; Aro and Broadhead 1950; MacDonald 1984 MS; Killick and Clemens 1963; Williams 1977; Hanamura 1966; Hartman and Conkle 1969; Major and Craddock 1962). From these sources I calculated average fecundity at a standard length representative of those populations for which fecundity data were available (740 mm postorbit-hypural length for chinook, 590 mm fork

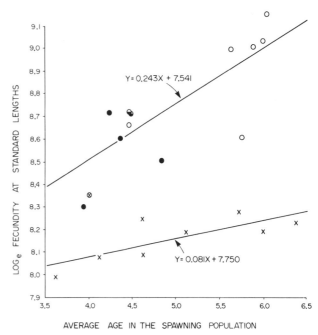

FIG. 1. The relationship between $\log_e$ fecundity at standard length (740 mm post-orbit/hypural length for chinook and 590 mm fork length for sockeye) and average age in the spawning population for chinook (○,●) and sockeye (×). (○) stream-type populations of chinook, (●) ocean-type populations, and (◓) mixed populations. ⊗ is the value for Cultus Lake sockeye, probably an outlier. Regression equations are for all chinook populations and all sockeye populations excluding Cultus Lake.

length for sockeye), and average age for each spawning population. If Bell's (1980) model is correct, the natural logarithm of fecundity at the standard length should be positively correlated with mean age at maturity, and the slope of the regression of ln fecundity on age should equal the instantaneous annual mortality rate of mature fish. For both species, ln fecundity was positively correlated with age of spawners (Fig. 1). In the case of chinook, the slope of the regression of fecundity on age was 0.243, which does not differ significantly from the estimate of natural mortality for mature chinook ($t = 1.242$, $P > 0.05$). In the case of sockeye, the regression on all data, although positive, was not significant. If the data for Cultus Lake, which appears to be an outlier, were removed, the regression was significant (Fig. 1). The slope of the regression was only 0.0184, however, significantly less than the estimates of natural mortality rate for mature sockeye ($t = 5.837$, $P < 0.01$).

Both species, therefore, behave qualitatively as predicted by life-history theory, in that populations which mature at older age have a higher average fecundity at standard size. Only for chinook, however, is the quantitative relationship consistent with theory. For sockeye, populations which mature at an older age (and larger size) do not show an increase in fecundity equivalent to that predicted by theory.

Within populations a similar relationship should hold, with optimum age at maturity being the age at which the gain in fecundity with increasing age just equals losses due to mortality among animals of reproductive age. That is to say, the optimum age at maturity is the age at which a line having slope equal to the instantaneous natural mortality rate is tangent to the curve of ln fecundity on age. Data from five chinook populations and seven sockeye populations are available to test this prediction. Two of the sockeye popu-

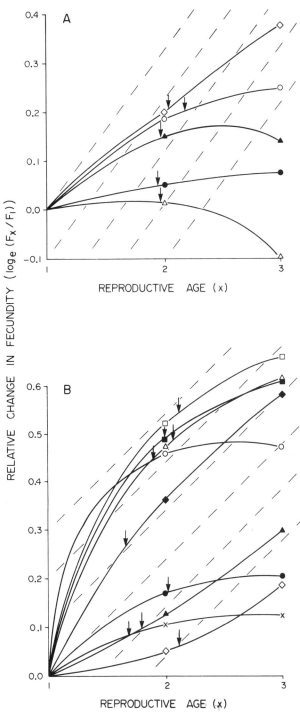

FIG. 2. Relative change in $\log_e$ fecundity with age for chinook (Panel A: $\diamond$ = Nushigak R.; $\bigcirc$ = Columbia R.; $\blacktriangle$ = Big Qualicum R.; $\bullet$ = Quinsam R.; $\triangle$ = Yukon R.) and sockeye (Panel B: $\bigcirc$ = Cultus Lake yearling smolts; $\bullet$ = Cultus Lake 2-year-old smolts; $\triangle$ = Fraser R.; $\blacktriangledown$ = Ozernaia R.; $\square$ = Karluk R. 2-year-old smolts; $\blacksquare$ = Karluk R. 3-year-old smolts; $\diamond$ = Babine R.; $\times$ = Skeena R. fishery; $\blacklozenge$ = Columbia R.). Dashed lines indicate the likely rate of natural mortality of mature-aged fish for each species. Arrows show mean age at maturity in the population.

lations may be further subdivided into fish which spent 1, 2, or 3 years in freshwater before going to sea, giving a total of nine sockeye data sets.

In the case of chinook, four of the five populations matured at an age considerably older (as shown by arrows in Fig. 2) than that predicted by life-history theory (as

shown by comparison of the slopes of the fecundity on age curves with the lines depicting mortality rate in Fig. 2), while for one population (Nushagak), observed and predicted age of maturity were similar. In the case of sockeye, two populations (Ozernaia and Babine River populations) showed a relationship between fecundity and age which was concave upwards, rather than downwards as expected. The curvature for these populations and for the Columbia River population was small, however, so that it is likely that these three populations have a linear relationship between log change in fecundity and age (Fig. 2). A linear relationship indicates that no intermediate age of maturity is optimum. The Ozernaia and Babine populations, for which the slope of the fecundity on age regression was less than the natural mortality rate of sockeye, should all mature at the youngest possible age, while the Columbia River population, for which the slope of the fecundity on age regression was greater than the natural mortality rate, should all mature at the oldest possible age. The remaining six sockeye populations showed the expected relationship between log fecundity and age (concave downwards, Fig. 2), implying that some intermediate age of maturity is optimum. All of these populations matured at an age older than the predicted optimum. For eight of the nine sockeye populations, therefore, the observed age at maturity was older than that predicted by theory, while for one population (the Columbia) the observed age as maturity was considerably younger than that predicted by theory.

The difference between observed and predicted age at maturity for both species was as much as a year, but was generally half a year or less (Fig. 2). Thus, the theory fails in a quantitative prediction of age of maturity within populations of both chinook and sockeye.

Taking a different approach to optimum size, Roff (1981) argued that, in populations where density-dependent effects were small, optimum size at maturity ought to be the size (as defined by the age−growth relationship) that maximizes r in the Euler equation:

(1) $$\sum_t e^{-rt} L_t M_t = 1$$

where: r = the intrinsic rate of increase
L_t = the survival probability to age t
M_t = the surviving female offspring produced by a female of age t.

Roff (1981), working with data on *Drosophila*, expanded this equation to incorporate separate larval and adult growth and mortality rates and time-variant female egg production. He expressed as many parameters as possible in terms of size. By means of this model Roff (1981) was able to predict an optimum size for adult *Drosophila* which agreed closely with the observed size. More recently, Roff (1983) used a similar approach to examine optimum allocation of surplus energy to growth and reproduction in marine fishes. In this case the model failed to predict size and reproductive expenditure correctly for American plaice (*Hippoglossoides platessoides*). Roff (1983) attributed this failure to the presence of density-dependent mortality factors in plaice populations.

A model similar to Roff's (1981) for *Drosophila* may be used to predict optimum age of maturity for different Pacific salmon species from their life-table parameters. The model incorporates separate terms for juvenile and adult mortality and growth. The model equation incorporates a number of simplifying assumptions, which may be relaxed in computer

TABLE 3. Life table values for sockeye chum and pink salmon based on average values from the literature. See text and earlier tables for information sources. Z values are made proportional to size at age rather than constant at age, but total ocean mortality is equivalent to values in Table 2.

Life stage	Age[b]	N	Z[a]	Wt (g)	G[a]	Eggs	Eggs/g
Sockeye							
eggs	0/0	1000.0		0.3			
			4.00		3.510		
smolts	1/0	18.0		10.0			
			1.22		3.910		
ocean 1	1/1	5.4		500.0			
			0.28		1.435		
ocean 2	1/2	4.1		2100.0		1500	0.71
			0.11		0.357		
ocean 3	1/3	3.7		3000.0		1700	0.57
			0.11		0.262		
ocean 4	1/4	3.3		3900.0		1900	0.49
			0.11		0.208		
ocean 5	1/5	2.9		4800.0		2100	0.44
Chum							
eggs	0/0	1000.0		0.4			
			4.5		5.500		
ocean 1	0/1	11.1		100.0			
			1.5		2.995		
ocean 2	0/2	2.5		2000.0			
			0.5		0.811		
ocean 3	0/3	1.5		4500.0		1300	0.29
			0.2		0.320		
ocean 4	0/4	1.2		6200.0		1600	0.26
			0.2		0.136		
ocean 5	0/5	1.0		7200.0		1600	0.22
					0.136		
Pink							
eggs	0/0	1000.0		0.3			
			4.46		6.214		
ocean 1	0/1	11.6		150.0			
			1.20		2.590		
ocean 2	0/2	3.5		2000.0		850	0.42
			0.20		0.406		
ocean 3	0/3	2.8		3000.0		1200	0.40

[a] Z = Instantaneous mortality between life stages. G = Instantaneous growth between life stages.

[b] Age designation refers to growing seasons completed rather than annuli laid down. Freshwater age/marine age.

simulations, provided detailed data are available:

(2) $\sum\limits_{Ta} \exp[GiTi + GaTa - ZiTi - ZaTa - r(Ti + Ta)]$

$W[1 - H(Ta - 1)]F(HTa) = 1$

where: $\exp[-r(Ti + Ta)] = e^{-rt}$ in the Euler equation when Ti is the length of the juvenile period and Ta is the length of the adult period in years.

where: $\exp(-ZiTi - ZaTa)[1 - H(Ta - 1)]$ creates the Lt series for the species. Zi and Za are the annual instantaneous juvenile and adult mortality rates respectively, and H is the incremental proportion of adults maturing each year (i.e., HTa = the proportion maturing at a specific age). The term $[1 - H(Ta - 1)]$ corrects the Lt series for semelparity by eliminating those fish which mature each year from the subsequent year's population.

and

where: $\exp(GiTi + GaTa)W(F)HTa$ creates the Mt series

for the species. Gi and Ga are the juvenile and adult instantaneous annual growth rates, W is the weight of an embryo in grams, F is the production of female eggs per gram of female body weight.

Solving this equation for r using life-table data for sockeye, pink, and chum (Table 3) and a range of maturity schedules (involving 1–3 mature age classes) provides a preliminary prediction of optimum age at maturity (and, by inference, optimum size) for each species (Table 4). Some additional realism was provided in computer calculation of r values by using age-specific rates of growth, mortality and egg production in Table 3 rather than the more restrictive juvenile or adult rates in equation 2.

In terms of their life-table parameters, the three species differ in their early mortality schedules (highest for chum and lowest for sockeye), in their growth rates (highest for pink, lowest for sockeye), and in their egg production rates (highest for sockeye, lowest for chum) (Table 3). Life-table values for pink salmon older than age 2 are merely plausible

TABLE 4. Values of r for the Euler equation for sockeye, chum, and pink salmon based on the life table parameters in Table 3, and various ages as immature and mature fish.

Species	Years as immature	Mature age classes (value of H in eqn 2)		
		1(1)	2(0.5)	3(0.333)
Sockeye	1	0.323	0.480	0.479
	2	0.603	0.539	0.497
	3	0.514	0.463	0.430
Chum	1	0.0435	0.0625	0.0655
	2	0.121	0.106	0.0867
	3	0.121	0.0902	0.0761
Pink	1	0.536	0.465	0.418
	2	0.426	0.372	0.333

TABLE 5. Average landed weight (kg) of all species of Pacific salmon in British Columbia captured by the three commercial gear types in 1974 and 1975. From data in Ricker (1981) and Healey (1982a). Percent of landings attributable to each gear shown in brackets. (from Aro et al. 1977.)

Species	Gear type		
	Seine	Gillnet	Troll
Pink (odd yr)	2.05 (60)	2.20 (23)	2.20 (17)
(even yr)	1.36 (71)	1.70 (21)	1.49 (8)
Chum	5.05 (46)	4.92 (53)	— (1)
Sockeye	2.52 (22)	2.69 (73)	2.92 (5)
Coho	3.22 (20)	3.48 (20)	2.85 (60)
Chinook	4.01 (10)	6.50 (12)	5.15 (78)

values, since no data exist for pinks older than age 2. For all species it should be noted that the life-table values are merely plausible combinations and are not meant to represent any specific populations.

Calculated r values suggest that sockeye will achieve maximum intrinsic rate of increase if they all mature after 2 years as a juvenile and 1 year as an adult (i.e. as a 3-year-old), that chum will achieve maximum r after 2 or 3 years as a juvenile and 1 year as an adult (i.e. as a 3 or 4 year old), and that pink salmon achieve maximum r when they mature after 1 year as an immature and 1 year as an adult (i.e. as a 2 year old). Thus, on the basis of plausible life-table parameter estimates, a model driven by the age-specific patterns of natality and mortality predicts age of maturity in pink and chum well but underestimates age of maturity in sockeye by at least a year. The model fails also to account in any meaningful way for multiple mature-age classes in any species, or for the greater age of maturity among northern populations. This latter consequence is evident by the fact that varying life-table parameters within reasonable bounds does not affect the optimum age for each species.

The application of existing life histories models to salmon is tantalizing in that there is a general qualitative agreement and some quantitative agreement between theoretical prediction and empirical observation. When the models fail quantitatively, they generally predict an optimal age (and consequently a size) at maturity smaller than that observed. This suggests that the models do not capture at least one important component of reproductive success in anadromous salmonids. Density dependent effects may be im-

portant as these have been demonstrated in Pacific salmon (eg. Peterman 1978, 1984a). In my view, however, the most important component ignored by these models is the reproductive value of large size. These include dominance in competition for mates or nest sites, production of larger eggs, and deeper, better protected nests (Healey and Heard 1984; van den Berghe and Gross 1984). In the trade-off among size, egg production and survival, therefore, Pacific salmon appear to have placed more emphasis on older age and larger size.

Size Selection and its Effects in Pacific Salmon Fisheries

Patterns of Size Selectivity in the Fishery

If Pacific salmon species are displaying some optimum age at maturity in which size is one of the values contributing to the optimum, then the consequences of size-selective fisheries could be serious. A change in age or size could reduce fitness to the point of precipitating a population collapse. On the other hand, if size is a highly adaptive trait, there may be strong selective pressure opposing any change in age or size at maturity. In this section I discuss the intensity of size selection operating in the salmon fisheries and what effects this selection may have had in recent years.

Three gear types are employed in the commercial salmon fisheries: gillnet, purse seine, and hook and line (troll). The different gear target on different species: gillnets on sockeye and chum purse seines on pink and chum, and trollers on chinook and coho, as evidenced by the proportion of landings attributable to each gear (Table 5). Purse seines are largely unselective for size, while gillnet and troll are selective for the largest fish. Selectivity by gillnet and troll varies among the species. Gillnet selection is relatively strong for pink, sockeye, coho, and chinook but appears weak for chum; gillnet caught chum being slightly smaller than those taken in seines (Table 5). Measuring size selection by trollers for large coho and chinook is made difficult by the fact that trollers harvest immature fish in mixed stocks which include a high proportion of non-Canadian fish, whereas seines, with which one would like to make comparison, harvest mature fish and relatively few non-Canadian fish. Nevertheless, the differential price per pound paid for large troll-caught fish, particularly chinook, virtually guarantees selection for large size by the fishery.

Selectivity by terminal gillnet fisheries depends on choice of mesh size by the fishermen (Fig. 3). When runs by species or ages of different sizes overlap, as they frequently do (eg. Healey 1982a), the choice of mesh size to capture one species or age class efficiently can influence selectivity for another. Thus, depending on the run, the species, and the gear in use, selection could be great or small, could be directed at the larger or smaller members of the run, or could even select for fish of intermediate size. This kind of variable effect is clear from a comparison of mesh selectivity for sockeye with the size composition of the sockeye run to the Skeena and Fraser rivers (Fig. 3). The mesh sizes used to determine mesh selection span the range of mesh size normally used in these rivers. Nevertheless, overall selection for all species but chum appears to be for the larger fish (Table 5).

In a series of reports (Ricker et al. 1978; Ricker 1980a,b, 1981, 1982; Ricker and Wickett 1980) Ricker and his co-

TABLE 6. Changes in mean weight (kg) of seine caught salmon (except chinook which are troll caught) in northern and southern British Columbia between 1951 and 1975 (except even-year pink salmon which are between 1952 and 1974). From data in Ricker (1981).

Species	Northern B.C.			Southern B.C.		
	1951	1975	% change	1951	1975	% change
Pink						
(even)	2.08	1.37	−34	2.07	1.35	−35
(odd)	2.41	1.72	−29	2.64	2.30	−13
Chum	6.10	5.19	−15	5.26	4.90	−7
Sockeye	2.48	2.38	−4	2.83	2.58	−9
Coho	3.76	2.96	−21	4.47	3.39	−24
Chinook	8.61	5.67	−34	6.73	4.63	−31

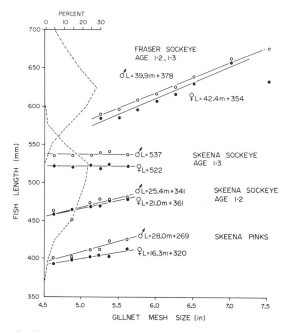

FIG. 3. The relationship between average length of salmon captured (post-orbit/hypural length for Skeena and fork length for Fraser) and gillnet mesh size (stretched measure) for Skeena River pink and sockeye (data from Todd and Larkin 1971) and Fraser River sockeye (data from Peterson 1954). The size frequency (percent) composition of sockeye runs to the two rivers are shown in dashed outline at the left of the diagram.

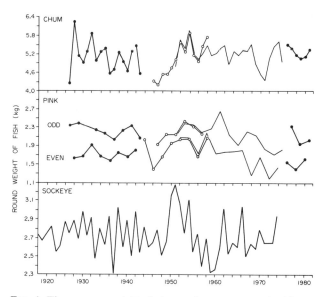

FIG. 4. The average weight of chum salmon, even- and odd-year pink salmon landed along the coast of B.C. and of sockeye salmon in the Fraser River from 1920 to 1981. (●) 1925−42 = data from Hoar (1951); (○) = data from Godfrey (1959a,b); (—) = data from Ricker (1980a) and Ricker et al. (1978); (●) 1976−81 = data from Can. Dep. Fish. Oceans Unpubl. Data. Data source for Fraser sockeye is Ricker (1982).

workers examined historic data on size and age of Pacific salmon caught in British Columbia. They concluded that, between 1951 and 1975, the average size of all species had declined. Changes in size occurred throughout the coast and were large for pink, coho, and chinook (13−35% decline in weight, Table 6). Chum also increased in mean age by about 0.38 yr over the same time period. Except for sockeye, for which there was a negative correlation between variation in size and water temperature in the central Gulf of Alaska, Richer and his co-workers found no consistent relationships between measured environmental factors and fish size. They concluded that trends in size over the period 1951−75 were most likely a consequence of size-selective fishing mortality.

Pink and coho mature mainly at a single age and, therefore, permit a fairly straightforward interpretation of the observed changes in size. If all the change in size of these two species were due to genetic selection, heritability of size would have to be on the order of 0.25−0.35. This is in the

range of observed values of heritability for size in other species (Ricker et al. 1978). Interpretation of changes in size of chinook, chum and sockeye, which mature at more than one age, is complicated by potential selection for fast growth of older fish and slow growth of younger fish, which will occur when selective gear take the larger members of the younger age and the smaller members of the older age. Furthermore, several factors could be contributing to changes in size among these species. Ricker (1981) listed eight possible causes of the change in size of chinook salmon.

Long-Term Fluctuations in the Size of Chum, Pink, and Sockeye

Data on average size prior to 1951 are available for some species (Fig. 4). Since Ricker (1981) argued that serious size selection in salmon fisheries (except for chinook fisheries) probably did not begin until 1945 when fish companies began buying fish by the pound rather than by the piece, any trends in size prior to this time must be due to other causes. An examination of long term series also permits the more recent changes in size to be viewed in the context of known long-term variation in size for the species.

Weights of pink and chum captured by seine in British Columbia statistical areas 1, 3, 7, 12, 25 are available from 1927 to 1981 (Fig. 4). I estimated weight for the 1927−43 period from the number of fish required to produce a 48 lb case of canned salmon (Hoar 1951). These weights, therefore, may not be strictly comparable to the weights from later years. Data for Fraser River sockeye from 1920 to 1974 are from Ricker (1982) and Killick and Clemens (1963). Chum and pink salmon weights from 1976-1981 are from the annual summaries of B.C. catch statistics published by the Department of Fisheries and Oceans.

Chum salmon show evidence of a decline in weight of about 1 kg from 1928 to 1947 ($r = -0.523$, $P < 0.05$). This is larger than the decline in weight reported by Ricker (1981) for the period 1951−74 (Fig. 4; Table 6). Weight of chums increased again from 1947 to 1954 ($r = 0.819$, $P < 0.05$). Since 1954 chums have fluctuated in weight, with particularly low weights recorded in 1970−71. Recent weights (1976−80) do not suggest any persistent trend in weight of chum salmon.

Pink salmon of the odd-year line average about 500 g heavier than pink salmon of the even-year line. Other than this consistent difference between lines, pink salmon weights showed no significant trends in weight prior to 1951, although mean weights in both lines were low in the mid to late 1940's (Fig. 4). Apparent declines in weight from 1951 to 1975 were significant for both lines, as noted by Ricker (1981). Recent weights (1976−81) are considerably higher than those in the early 1970's, however, and do not continue the apparent downward trend. In particular, the mean weight of the odd-year line in 1977−81 (2.12 kg) is almost as large as the mean weight of this line in 1951−57 (2.27 kg) (Fig. 4).

Fraser sockeye show considerable fluctuation in mean weight, but no clear trends prior to 1950. Mean weight of Fraser sockeye was particularly high in 1950−52, and then declined to very low values in 1959−60. Since 1960, weights of Fraser River sockeye have again fluctuated widely with no apparent trend. Average weight from 1961 to 1974 (2.70 kg) is only slightly less than the average weight during 1930−45 (2.75 kg), prior to the imposition of size-selective fishing (Fig. 4). Ricker (1981) presents other examples of the variable sockeye response to size-selective fisheries.

Recent data for chinook (W. E. Ricker, pers. comm. 1984) also indicate increases in mean weight in some areas, but average weights are still considerably below those in the 1950's.

Some of the historic weight changes in Pacific salmon (presented here and by Ricker and his co-workers) appear contrary to an hypothesis of genetic selection for small size. These include: (1) recent increases in mean weight of pink and chinook salmon in some areas; (2) low average weight, and significant trends in weight, over long periods prior to the onset of size-selective fishing in 1945; and (3) variable behaviour of weight data, particularly sockeye weights, from different populations subject to similar intensity of size selection. My purpose, however, is not to refute the hypothesis that selection has occurred. Rather it is to approach the problem from a different point of view. Two observations seem unassailable. First, since 1951, perhaps earlier, Pacific salmon fisheries have been size selective, imposing

relatively higher mortality on intermediate and large sized sockeye, pink, coho, and chinook, and on intermediate and small sized chum. Second, size has a relatively high heritability. Therefore, one would expect genetic selection to have occurred for small size in pink, sockeye, coho, and chinook and for large size in chum. If we do not observe evidence of such selection, and apparently we don't in many instances, then it is appropriate to ask why.

There are four possible explanations for any failure to observe a change in size of Pacific salmon in the face of strong size selection:

1) The data may be inadequate or inaccurate. Salmon size has not been measured with a view to estimating change in size of defined stocks over long periods of time. Size measurements have been collected for a variety of purposes over the years, and methodology has changed from time to time. In recent years, size has been measured to permit an estimate of numbers of fish captured from the total weight of landings. While the sampling methods employed would probably not disguise any long-term trends for major regions of the coast, the data for individual runs or individual years may be inaccurate or even contradictory.

2) The environmental component of variation in size may be very large. If most of the within-year variation in size of salmon has an environmental cause, then the genetic effects of size-selective fisheries will be small, and a very long time would be required to demonstrate a significant genetic alteration of growth rates from field data. Ricker (1980a,b, 1981, 1982), Ricker et al. (1978), and Ricker and Wickett (1980) looked for correlations between ocean temperature and size for all species of Pacific salmon in British Columbia but found consistent relationships only for sockeye. Because of the absence of correlations between fish size and temperature, and because related species (e.g. pink and chum) or adjacent stocks (e.g. odd- and even-year pinks) did not show corresponding changes in mean size, Ricker and his co-workers rejected an environmental explanation for the downward trends in size they observed from 1951 to 1975.

Ricker and his co-workers first regressed both weight and temperature against time, and then regressed residuals of weight on residuals of temperature in their analysis of the effects of temperature on size. They followed a similar procedure in comparing changes in size and changes in ocean salinity. This was the appropriate technique for discovering temperature and salinity effects independent of coincidental associations over time. The approach is, however, sensitive to potential inaccuracies in mean-weight data which I mentioned above. The temperature data available are also subject to errors of measurement (the data from Ocean Station P (50°N, 145°W) are probably the best, those from the coastal lighthouse stations considerably poorer), so that errors in variables may have masked correlations between fish size and temperature. It may be significant that sea-surface temperature in the central Gulf of Alaska declined about 1°C between 1958 and 1975 and has since increased about 0.5°C (Chelton 1984). This temporal pattern of temperature change matches the temporal pattern of changing size of pink, coho, and chinook salmon.

Other environmental factors may have had an important effect on mean size, both within and between years. Numerous authors have described significant relationships between marine survival of Pacific salmon and ocean conditions (see papers in Pearcy 1984). Similar effects on growth have also been found in a few instances, and it seems likely that events which affect survival may also often affect growth. A thorough analysis of such effects is beyond the scope of this paper, but it is worth mentioning that Peterman (1984a,b) and Rogers (1984) reported significant effects of population density on growth of sockeye, Mathews (1984) reported significant correlation between upwelling off the Oregon coast and survival of hatchery coho, Donnelly and Bevan (1984) found a significant correlation between upwelling in the central Gulf of Alaska and survival of pink salmon from the Kodiak archipelago, and, finally, Peterman (1984b) reported a significant decline in an index of zooplankton production in the central Gulf of Alaska during the period 1957-1977, coincident with the declines in size of Pacific salmon reported by Ricker (1981). All these results point to very important environmental influences on size and survival. It seems reasonable, therefore, not to discount completely an environmental explanation for the observed changes in size of some stocks of salmon.

3) For the species which mature at more than one age, the opposing effects of size selection on different ages may result in a complicated response to selection. By taking fish slightly smaller (for chum) or slightly larger (for sockeye) than the mean size in the run, the fisheries for these species have selectively removed the larger members of the younger age class and the smaller members of the older age class in each run. If we are to interpret the observed changes in size and age of each species as response to this kind of selection, then the effects have been different in the two species.

Chum have increased in mean age but not in mean size. This could be a result of selective removal of the faster-growing members of the younger age class, resulting in slower overall growth and more fish delaying maturation until age 0.3. The selective fishery would, however, also be removing the slower growing members of the older age class of mature fish, and this should have the effect of increasing growth rates. If selection were for larger size at age 0.3, and for more fish delaying maturation until age 0.3 then, on balance, one would expect an increase in mean size of chums. If, on the other hand, environmental conditions were causing reduced marine growth of chum and assuming maturation is partly size dependent, then both the 0.2 and 0.3 mature age classes should have smaller average size, and fewer fish would mature at age 0.2. An increase in mean age at maturity because of slower growth to age 0.2 could, therefore, occur without any apparent increase in mean size in the run because the 0.3 age fish would be smaller as well. It seems to me that an environmental explanation of the observed trends in age and size of chum is simpler than an explanation invoking genetic selection. The intensity of size selection has also been rather weak in chum fisheries, since fishing mortality is lightest for this species and the size differential between seine- and gillnet-caught fish is small. Any genetic consequences of this rather weak selection could easily be masked by some overlying environmental effect.

Among sockeye, there have been no apparent trends in mean age, and variable trends in mean size (Ricker 1982). The difference in mean size between age classes contributing to some runs, however, has tended to increase (Fig. 5). Since fishing for maximum catch as well as maximum weight will impose similar opposing selection on age 1.2 vs age 1.3 fish in these runs, selection for smaller fish in the younger age class and larger fish in the older age class

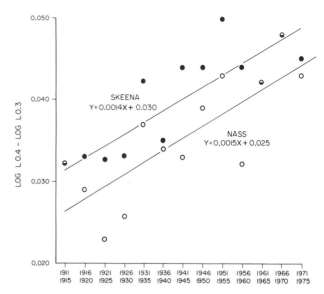

FIG. 5. Difference between the logarithms of length of 5 and 4-year-old sockeye in the Nass and Skeena rivers averaged over 5-year periods from 1911 to 1975. (○) = Nass River, (●) = Skeena River. Least squares regressions for each river as shown.

within sockeye populations has been going on much longer than the selection for small size in species which mature primarily at one age. In 1958, Godfrey (1958) was able to describe significant changes in size at age of sockeye from the Skeena and Owikeno rivers. Ricker (1982) has extended these time series to 1972 and provided comparable data for the Nass River. All three populations show the same pattern of change in size at age (e.g. Fig. 5), but not the same pattern of change in mean size in the run, which has increased in the Skeena and Owikeno, but decreased in the Nass. Average age of sockeye in the runs to these three rivers has shown no consistent pattern of change. Any trends may, however, have been masked by occasional periods of cyclic dominance of broodlines. Also, maturation may be more strongly age dependent in sockeye than in chum.

Overall, sockeye present a confusing array of historic changes in age composition, mean size at age, and mean size in the run (Ricker 1982). The large array of factors potentially contributing to the variation mitigates against any simple model for assessing genetic consequences of the size-selective fisheries. Genetic selection, nevertheless, remains the most attractive explanation for the divergence in mean size of ages 1.2 and 1.3 in northern rivers (Godfrey 1958; Ricker 1982) (Fig. 5). In the Fraser River, however, by far the majority of mature fish are aged 1.2. The complicating effects of multiple age classes cannot be invoked to explain why Fraser sockeye have not shown a persistent decline in average size since 1951 (Fig. 4).

4) Counteracting selective forces may be strong. If size and age at maturity are highly adaptive, then selection opposing any change in growth rate may be suffient to counteract the effects of size-selective fishing. I have already presented an analysis which suggests that size at maturity may be an important component of fitness in some species of salmon. The rather large differences between populations in average age at maturity, in the number of age categories present in the mature population, and in the size at age of mature fish further suggests that both age and size at maturity are adaptive traits. Other observations consistent with this hypothesis include the fact that larger salmon lay rela-

tively fewer, but larger, eggs (Rounsefell 1957; Bilton and Jenkinson 1966). This implies some point at which the trade-off between egg size and egg number is optimal for fitness. Larger coho (and presumably the other species as well) bury their eggs deeper in the spawning gravel (van den Berghe and Gross 1984), thus providing them greater protection against scouring due to floods or redd superimposition and against freezing or dewatering, but making them more vulnerable to low flows and low oxygen. Again, an optimum size of spawning fish for any given stream hydrology or spawning environment is implied. Size (growth rate) and survival are positively correlated in Pacific salmon, at least among juveniles (Ricker 1962; Parker 1971; Healey 1982b; Bilton et al. 1982). Increases in adult mortality due to fishing are not sufficient to change the optimum age of maturity among sockeye, chum, or pink salmon predicted by the model I outlined earlier, so that fundamental change in relative fitness of different life-history strategies may not result from the intensive and size-selective fisheries. Any genetic adjustment to selective fishing, therefore, should take place within the context of the present strategies. Fishing mortality, although large relative to natural mortality of fish of mature age, is not large relative to the total egg-to-adult mortality for each species (Table 2), and the size-selective component of this mortality is smaller still. It seems reasonable to suppose that selection favouring smaller size in the fishery could be counteracted by selection favouring larger size elsewhere in the fish's life.

Acknowledgments

I would like to acknowledge the assistance of my colleagues at the Biological Station in Nanaimo with whom I discussed the ideas in this paper. Bill Ricker, Randall Peterman, and J. Dempson critised a draft of the paper.

References

ANAS, R. E. 1959. Three-year-old pink salmon. J. Fish. Res. Board Can. 16: 91–92.

ARO, K. V., AND G. C. BROADHEAD. 1950. Differences between egg counts of sockeye salmon at Lakelse and Babine Lakes. Fish. Res. Board Can., Prog. Rep. Pacific 82: 17–19.

ARO, K. V., P. L. MILLER, AND J. MCDONALD. 1977. Catches and escapements of Pacific salmon in British Columbia, 1965-1975. Fish. Environ. Can. Fish. Mar. Serv. Data Rep. 39: 1–67.

BAKKALA, R. G. 1970. Synopsis of biological data on the chum salmon, Oncorhynchus keta (Walbaum) 1972. U.S. Fish Wildl. Serv. Circ. 315: 1–89.

BEACHAM, T. D. 1982. Fecundity of coho salmon (Oncorhynchus kisutch) and chum salmon (O. keta) in the northeast Pacific Ocean. Can. J. Zool. 60: 1463–1469.

BELL, G. 1980. The cost of reproduction and their consequences. Am. Nat. 116: 45–76.

BILTON, H. T. 1970. Comparison of the fecundity of sockeye salmon (Oncorhynchus nerka) in the Skeena River catch with the fecundity of those in the escapement. Fish. Res. Board Can. MS Rep. 1096: 8 p.

BILTON, H. T., AND D. W. JENKINSON. 1966. Relationship between egg size and fish size in sockeye salmon (Oncorhynchus nerka). Fish. Res. Board Can. MS Rep. 848: 8 p.

BILTON, H. T., D. F. ALDERDICE, AND J. T. SCHNUTE. Influence of time and size at release of juvenile coho salmon (Oncorhynchus kisutch) on returns at maturity. Can. J. Fish. Aquat. Sci. 39: 426–447.

BIRD, F. 1982. Preliminary forecast model for Kotzebue Sound, Alaska, chum salmon (Oncorhynchus keta). AK. Dep. Fish and Game, Juneau, AK. Information Leaflet 203: 1–27.

CALAPRICE, J. R. 1969. Production and genetic factors in managed salmon populations, p. 377–388 In T. G. Northcote [ed.] Salmon and trout in streams. H. R. McMillan Lectures in Fisheries. Univ. British Columbia, Vancouver, B.C.

CHELTON, D. B. 1984. Commentary: short-term climatic variability in the northeast Pacific Ocean, p. 87–99 In W. G. Pearcy [ed.] The influence of ocean conditions on the production of salmonids in the North Pacific. Oregon State University Sea Grant Program. Corvallis, OR.

CLEAVER, F. E. 1969. Effects of fishing on 1961-brood fall chinook salmon from Columbia River hatcheries. Fish. Commission OR, Res. Rep. 1: 76 p.

CRONE, R. A., AND C. E. BOND. 1976. Life history of coho salmon (Oncorhynchus kisutch) in Sashin Creek, S.E. Alaska. U.S. Fish. Wildl. Serv. Fish. Bull. 74: 879–923.

DONNELLY, R. F., AND D. E. BEVAN. 1984. Environmental factors and the abundance of Kodiak archipelago pink salmon (Oncorhynchus gorbuscha), p. 228–236 In W. G. Pearcy [ed.] The influence of ocean conditions on the production of salmonids in the North Pacific. Oregon State University Sea Grant Program. Corvallis, OR.

DRUCKER, B. 1972. Some life-history characteristics of coho salmon of the Karluk River system, Kodiak Island, Alaska. U.S. Fish Wildl. Serv. Fish. Bull. 70: 79–94.

FOERSTER, R. E. 1929. An investigation of the life history and propagation of the sockeye salmon (Oncorhynchus nerka) at Cultus Lake, British Columbia. No. 2. The run of 1926. Contr. Can. Biol. Fish. Vol. IV: 39–53.

FOERSTER, R. E., AND A. L. PRITCHARD. 1941. Observations on the relation of egg content to total length and weight in the sockeye salmon (Oncorhynchus nerka) and the pink salmon (O. gorbuscha). Trans. Roy. Soc. Can. Section V: 51–60.

GALBREATH, J. L., AND R. L. RIDENHOUR. 1964. Fecundity of Columbia River chinook salmon. OR. Fish Comm. Res. Brief 10: 16–27.

GANGMARK, H. A., AND R. G. BAKKALA. 1960. A comparative study of unstable and stable (Artificial channel) spawning streams for incubating king salmon at Mill Creek. CA. Fish Game 46: 151–164.

GODFREY, H. 1958. A comparison of sockeye catches at Rivers Inlet and Skeena River, B.C., with particular reference to age at maturity. J. Fish. Res. Board Can. 15: 331–354.

1959a. Variation in the annual average weight of chum salmon in British Columbia waters, 1946–1958. J. Fish. Res. Board Can. 16: 553–554.

1959b. Variations in annual average weights of British Columbia pink salmon 1944–1958. J. Fish. Res. Board Can. 16: 329–337.

1965. Coho salmon, p. 1–40. In Salmon of the North Pacific, Part 9. Coho, chinook, and masu salmon in offshore waters. Int. N. Pac. Fish. Comm. Bull. 16, Vancouver, B.C.

HAMILTON, J. A. R., L. O. ROTHFUS, M. W. ERHO, AND J. D. REMINGTON. 1970. Use of a hydroelectric reservoir for the rearing of coho salmon (Oncorhynchus kisutch). WA. Dep. Fish. Res. Bull. 9: 1–65.

HANAMURA, N. 1966. Sockeye salmon in the far east. pp. 1–28. In: Salmon of the North Pacific Ocean Part II. A Review of the life history of North Pacific salmon. Int. N. Pac. Fish. Comm. Bull. 18, Vancouver, B.C.

HART, J. L. 1973. Pacific fishes of Canada. Bull. Fish. Res. Board Can. 1980: 740 p.

HARTMAN, W. L., AND C. Y. CONKLE. 1969. Fecundity of red salmon at Brooks and Karluk Lakes, Alaska. U.S. Fish Wildl. Serv. Fish. Bull. 61: 53–60.

HEALEY, M. C. 1982a. Multispecies, multistock aspects of Pacific salmon management, p. 119–126 In M. C. Mercer [ed.] Multispecies approaches to fisheries management advice.

Can. Spec. Publ. Fish. Aquat. Sci. 59.

1982b. Timing and relative intensity of size selective mortality of juvenile chum salmon (*Oncorhynchus keta*) during early sea life. Can. J. Fish. Aquat. Sci. 39: 952−957.

1983. Coastwide distribution and ocean migration patterns of stream- and ocean-type chinook salmon, *Oncorhynchus tshawytscha*. Can. Field-Nat. 97: 427−433.

HEALEY, M. C., AND W. R. HEARD. 1984. Inter- and intra-population variation in the fecundity of chinook salmon (*Oncorhynchus tshawytscha* and its relevance to life history theory. Can. J. Fish. Aquat. Sci. 41: 476−483.

HENRY, K.A. 1978. Estimating natural and fishing mortalities of chinook salmon, *Onchrhynchus tshawytscha*, in the ocean based on recoveries of marked fish. Fish. Bull. 76: 45−57.

HOAR, W. S. 1951. The chum and pink salmon fisheries of British Columbia 1917−1947. Bull. Fish. Res. Board Can. 90: 46 p.

HUNTER, J. G. 1959. Survival and production of pink and chum salmon in a coastal stream. J. Fish. Res. Board Can. 16: 835−886.

ISHIDA, T. 1966. Pink salmon in the far east, p. 29−40. *In* Salmon of the North Pacific Ocean, Part II. A Review of the life history of North Pacific salmon. Int. N. Pac. Fish. Comm. Bull. 18, Vancouver, B.C.

IHSSEN, P. E., H. E. BROOKE, J. M. CASSELMAN, J. M. McGLADE, N. R. PAYNE, AND F. M. UTTER. 1981. Stock identification: materials and methods. Can. J. Fish. Aquat. Sci. 38: 1835−1855.

KILLICK, S. R., AND W. A. CLEMENS . 1963. The age, sex ratio, and size of Fraser River sockeye salmon 1915−1960. Int. Pac. Salmon Fish. Comm. Bull. XIV: 1−140.

KNUDSEN, C. M., C. K. HARRIS, AND N. D. DAVIS. 1983. Origins of chinook salmon in the area of the Japanese mortherhip and land-based drift-net fisheries in 1980. Document submitted to annual meeting of INPFC, Anchorage, USA, November, 1983. 71 p. U. WA. Fish. Res. Inst., FRI − UW − 83125, Seattle.

KOSKI, K. V. 1966. The survival of coho salmon (*Oncorhynchus kisutch*) from egg deposition to emergence in three Oregon streams, M.Sc. thesis, Oregon State University, Corvallis, OR. 84 p.

KWAIN, W., AND J. A. CHAPPEL. 1978. First evidence for even-year spawning pink salmon, *Oncorhynchus gorbuscha*, in Lake Superior. J. Fish. Res. Board Can. 35: 1373−1376.

LARKIN, P. A. 1981. A perspective on population genetics and salmon management. Can. J. Fish. Aquat. Sci. 38: 1469−1475.

LISTER, D. B., AND C. E. WALKER. 1966. The effect of flow control on freshwater survival of chum, coho, and chinook salmon in the Big Qualicum River. Can. Fish Cult. 37: 3−25.

LOEFFEL, R. E., AND H. O. WENDLER. 1969. Review of the Pacific coast chinook and coho salmon resources with special emphasis on the troll fishery. Informal Committee on chinook and coho, reports by the United States and Canada on the status, ocean migrations, and exploitation of northeast Pacific stocks of chinook and coho salmon to 1964. Vol. 1: report of the United Station Section: 1−107.

McBRIDE, D. N., H. H. HAMNER, AND L. S. BUKLIS. 1983. Age, sex, and size of Yukon River salmon catch and escapement, 1982. AK. Dep. Fish Game Juneau, AK., Tech. Data Rep. 90: 1−141.

MacDONALD, J. 1984. Summary of biological knowledge of populations of B.C. and Yukon salmonids. Unpub. MS Dep. Fish. Oceans. Pacific Region Salmonid Enhancement Program. Vancouver, B.C.

MacLEAN, J. A., AND D. O. EVANS. 1981. The stock concept, discreetness of fish stocks, and fisheries management. Can. J. Fish. Aquat. Sci. 38: 1889−1898.

MAJOR, R. L., AND D. R. CRADDOCK. 1962. Influence of early maturing females on reproductive potential of Columbia River blueback salmon (*Oncorhynchus nerka*). U.S. Fish Wildl. Ser. Fish. Bull. 61: 429−437.

MATHEWS, S. B. 1984. Variability of marine survival of Pacific salmonids: a review, p. 161−182 *In* W. G. Pearcy [ed.] The influence of ocean conditions on the production of salmonids in the North Pacific. Oregon State University Sea Grant Program, Corvallis, OR.

MESIAR, D. C. 1984. Abundance, age, sex, and size of coho salmon (*Oncorhynchus kisutch*) (Walbaum) catches and escapements in southeastern Alaska, 1982. AK. Dep. Fish Game, Juneau, AK. Tech. Rep. 104: 1−97.

NEAVE, F. 1958. The origin and speciation of *Oncorhynchus*. Trans Roy. Soc. Can. Ser. 3, Sec. 5, Vol. 52: 25−39.

NICOLETTE, J. P. 1984. A 3-year-old pink salmon in an-odd year run in Lake Superior. N. Am. J. Fish. Manage. 4: 130−132.

PARKER, R. R. 1962. Estimations of ocean mortality rates for Pacific salmon (*Oncorhynchus*). J. Fish. Res. Board Can. 19: 561−589.

1968. Marine mortality schedules of pink salmon of the Bella Coola River, central British Columbia. J. Fish. Res. Board Can. 25: 757−794.

1971. Size-selective predation among juvenile salmonid fishes in a British Columbia inlet. J. Fish. Res. Board Can. 28: 1503−1510.

PEARCY, W. G. [ed.]. 1984. The influence of ocean conditions on the production of salmonids in the North Pacific. Oregon State University Sea Grant Program, Corvallis, OR: 1−327.

PETERMAN, R. M. 1978. Testing for density-dependent marine survival in Pacific salmonids. J. Fish. Res. Board Can. 35: 1434−1450.

1984a. Density-dependent growth in early ocean life of sockeye salmon (*Oncorhynchus nerka*). Can. J. Fish. Aquat. Sci. 41: 1825−1829.

1984b. Interaction among sockeye salmon in the Gulf of Alaska, p. 187−199. *In* W. G. Pearcy [ed.] The influence of ocean conditions on the production of salmonids in the North Pacific. Oregon State University Sera Grant Program. Corvallis, OR.

PETERSON, A. E. 1954. The selective action of gillnets on Fraser River sockeye salmon. Int. Pac. Salmon Fish. Comm. Bull. 5: 1−101.

PRITCHARD, A. L. 1937. Variation in the time of run, sex proportions, size, and egg content of adult pink salmon (*Oncorhynchus gorbuscha*) at McClinton Creek, Masset Inlet, B.C. J. Biol. Board Can. 3: 403−416.

1943. The age of chum salmon taken in the commercial catches in British Columbia. Fish. Res. Prog. Rep. Pacific 54: 9−11.

1947. Efficiency of natural propagation of Pacific salmon. Can. Fish. Cult. 1: 22−26.

RICH, W. H. 1925. Growth and degree of maturity of chinook salmon in the ocean. U.S. Bureau Fish. Bull. 41: 14−90.

RICKER, W. E. 1962. Comparison of ocean growth and mortality of sockeye salmon during their last two years. J. Fish. Res. Board Can. 19: 531−560.

1976. Review of the rate of growth and mortality of Pacific salmon in salt water and non-catch mortality caused by fishing. J. Fish. Res. Board Can. 33: 1483−1524.

1980a. Changes in the age and size of chum salmon (*Oncorhynchus keta*). Can. Tech. Rep. Fish. Aquat. Sci. 930: 99 p.

1980b. Causes of the decrease in age and size of chinook salmon (*Oncorhynchus tshawytscha*). Can. Tech. Rep. Fish. Aquat. Sci. 944: 25 p.

1981. Changes in the average size and average age of Pacific salmon. Can. J. Fish. Aquat. Sci. 38: 1636−1656.

1982. Size and age of British Columbia sockeye salmon (*Oncorhynchus nerka*) in relation to environmental factors and the fishery., Can. Tech. Rep. Fish. Aquat. Sci. 1115: 117 p.

RICKER, W. E., H. T. BILTON, AND K. V. ARO. 1978. Causes of

the decrease in size of pink salmon (*Oncorhynchus gorbuscha*). Can. Tech. Rep. Fish. Aquat. Sci. 820: 93 p.

RICKER, W. E., AND W. P. WICKETT. 1980. Causes of the decrease in size of coho salmon (*Oncorhynchus kisutch*). Can. Tech. Rep. Fish. Aquat. Sci. 971: 63 p.

ROGERS, D. E. 1984. Trends in abundance of northeastern Pacific stocks of salmon, p. 100−127 *In* W. G. Pearcy [ed.] The influence of ocean conditions on the production of salmonids in the North Pacific. Oregon State University Sea Grant Program. Corvallis, OR.

ROFF, D. A. 1981. On being the right size. Am. Nat. 118: 405−422.

1983. An allocation model of growth and reproduction in fish. Can. J. Fish. Aquat. Sci. 40: 1395−1404.

ROUNSEFELL, G. A. 1957. Fecundity of North American salmonidae. U.S. Fish Wildl. Serv. Fish. Bull. 57: 450−468.

1958. Factors causing decline in sockeye salmon of Kaluk River, Alaska. U.S. Fish Wildl. Serv. Fish. Bull. 58: 79−169.

SANO, S. 1966. Chum salmon in the far east, p. 41−58 *In* Salmon of the North Pacific Ocean Part II. A Review of the life history of North Pacific salmon. Int. N. Pac. Fish. Comm. Bull. 18, Vancouver, B.C.

SHAPAVALOV, L., AND A. C. TAFT. The life history of the steelhead rainbow trout (*Salmo gairdneri gairdneri*) and silver salmon (*Oncorhynchus kisutch*) with special reference to Wadell Creek, California, and recommendations regarding their management. CA. Dep. Fish Game, Fish. Bull. 98: 375 p.

STEARNS, S. C. 1976. Life-history tactics: a review of the ideas. Quart. Rev. Biol. 51: 2−47.

1977. The evolution of life-history traits: a critique of the theory and a review of the data. Ann. Rev. Ecol. Syst. 8: 145−171.

THORSTEINSON, F. V., W. H. NOERENBERG, AND H. D. SMITH. 1963. The length, age, and sex ration of chum salmon in the Alaska peninsula, Kodiak Island, and Prince William Sound areas of Alaska. U.S. Fish Wild. Serv. Spec. Sci. Rep. Fish. 430: 84 p.

TODD, I. S., AND P. A. LARKIN. 1971. Gillnet selectivity in sockeye (*Oncorhynchus nerka*) and pink salmon (*O. gorbuscha*) of the Skeena River system, British Columbia. J. Fish. Res. Board Can. 28: 821−842.

TSUYUKI, H., AND E. ROBERTS. 1966. Inter-species relationships within the genus *Oncorhynchus* based on biochemical systematics. J. Fish. Res. Board Can. 23: 101−107.

TSUYUKI, H., E. ROBERTS, AND W. E. VANSTONE. 1965. Comparative zone electropherograms of muscle myogens and blood hemoglobins of marine and freshwater vetebrates and their application to biochemical systematics. J. Fish. Res. Board Can. 22: 203−213.

TURNER, C. E., AND H. T. BILTON. 1968. Another pink salmon in its third year. J. Fish. Res. Board Can. 25: 1993−1996.

VAN DEN BERGHE, E. P., AND M. R. GROSS. 1984. Female size and nest depth in coho salmon (*Oncorhynchus kisutch*). Can. J. Fish. Aquat. Sci. 41: 204−206.

WAGNER, W. C., AND T. M. STAUFFER. 1980. Three-year-old pink salmon in Lake Superior tributaries. Trans. Am. Fish. Soc. 109: 458−460.

WALES, J. H., AND M. COOTS. 1954. Efficiency of chinook salmon spawning in Fall Creek, California. Trans. Am. Fish. Soc. 834: 137−149.

WALTERS, C., R. HILBORN, M. STALEY, AND F. WONG. 1982. An assessment of major commercial fish and invertebrate stocks on the west coast of Canada; with recommendations for management. Report to the Commission on Pacific Fisheries Policy. Available from Environmental and Social Systems Analysis Ltd., Vancouver, B.C.

WILLIAMS, I. V. 1977. Investigation of the prespawning mortality of sockeye in Chilko River in 1971. Int. Pac. Salmon Fish. Comm. Prog. Rep. 35(Part 1): 22 p.

YANCEY, R. M., AND F. V. THORSTEINSON. 1963. The king salmon of Cook Inlet, Alaska. U.S. Fish Wildl. Serv. Spec. Sci. Rep. Fish. 440: 18 p.

Game Theory and the Evolution of Atlantic Salmon (*Salmo salar*) Age at Maturation

Ransom A. Myers

Fisheries Research Branch, Department of Fisheries and Oceans, P.O. Box 5667, St. John's, Nfld. A1C 5X1

Abstract

MYERS, R. A. 1986. Game theory and the evolution of Atlantic salmon (*Salmo salar*) age at maturation, p. 53−61. *In* D. J. Meerburg [ed.] Salmonid age at maturity. Can. Spec. Publ. Fish. Aquat. Sci. 89.

This paper deals with the evolutionary dynamics of the age at maturation of Atlantic salmon (*Salmo salar*) in a game theoretic context. It is shown that female age at maturation cannot be treated as an optimization process if there is competition for spawning substrate and concomitant redd superimposition. A mixed evolutionarily stable strategy for female age at maturation may result because of deeper redd depth for larger females.

Male sea age, anadromous age at maturation, and precocious maturation of male parr are shown to be evolutionarily linked by their effects on sex ratio and the number of matings possible for anadromous males. Multiple evolutionarily stable equilibria may exist between the proportion of males maturing as parr and the proportion maturing as 1-sea-winter or multi-sea-winter salmon.

Résumé

MYERS, R. A. 1986. Game theory and the evolution of Atlantic salmon (*Salmo salar*) age at maturation, p. 53−61. *In* D. J. Meerburg [ed.] Salmonid age at maturity. Can. Spec. Publ. Fish. Aquat. Sci. 89.

L'étude porte sur la dynamique évolutive de l'âge à maturité du saumon de l'Atlantique (*Salmo salar*) dans un contexte théorique basé sur le jeu. L'auteur explique que l'âge des femelles à maturité ne peut être traité comme un processus d'optimisation s'il existe une compétition pour le substrat de fraie et une superposition des sillons concomitants. Le processus peut conduire à une stratégie mixte et évolutivement stable pour l'âge des femelles à maturité en raison de la plus grande profondeur des sillons pour les femelles plus grosses.

L'auteur montre que l'âge-mer des mâles, l'âge anadrome à maturité et le cheminement précoce vers la maturité du tacon mâle sont évolutivement liés par leurs effets sur le sexe-ratio et le nombre d'accouplements possibles pour les mâles anadromes. De multiples équilibres évolutivement stables existent probablement entre la proportion des mâles qui atteignent la maturité en tant que tacons et la proportion qui atteint la maturité en tant que saumon unibermarin ou polybermarin.

Introduction

Anadromous Atlantic salmon, *Salmo salar*, display enormous variability in age at maturation both within and among populations. Adults may mature after 1, 2, 3, or 4 years at sea (Jones 1959). As many as 80% of the males may mature precociously as parr and then migrate to the sea (Myers 1984). In other populations precocious males do not appear to become anadromous adults (Gibson 1983).

In spite of this great within-population variability, optimal life-history theory has been applied to the Atlantic salmon (Schaffer and Elson 1975; Schaffer 1979). Optimization theory is a useful approximation for the evolution of age at maturation if an individual's fitness does not depend upon the maturation phenotypes of other members of the population (except through the population's growth rate or equilibrium density, see Charlesworth 1980). The coexistence of alternative maturation phenotypes, e.g. precocious and non-precocious maturation of male parr in many populations of Atlantic salmon (Myers et al. 1985), suggests that precocious maturation is not a single frequency-independent optimum (Myers 1984; Gross 1984). Here I treat the evolution of salmon age at maturation using Maynard Smith's (1982) game theoretic notion of an Evolutionarily Stable Strategy (ESS). A strategy is an ESS if rare individuals using a different strategy cannot invade the population under the influence of natural selection. In many situations, no single maturation strategy is evolutionarily stable, rather a mixture of different maturation strategies will be evolutionarily stable (a mixed ESS).

My goal here is to illustrate various factors that are important for the evolution of salmon age at maturation. I shall discuss two models: one for the evolution of male age at maturation for a given female pattern of maturation, and the other describing the role that competition for spawning substrate possibly plays in the evolution of anadromous female age at maturation.

In any model, verbal or mathematical, assumptions are made about the behavior of the system. These assumptions belong to the following categories. First, there are assumptions which accurately describe empirical observations, e.g. in the models that follow males will be assumed to be able to mate more than once. Second, there are assumptions made for heuristic reasons; they result in a simplified model that is more understandable but is only a rough approximation of reality. For example, I will assume that all anadromous adults die after spawning. While this assumption is clearly not true (an average of 10% of males survive to spawn again in North America; Ducharme 1969), it does not affect the main points I shall be making. Finally, there are assumptions made out of ignorance; insufficient empirical observations exist to precisely describe real behavior. In this case a range of feasible behaviors can be analyzed, and the sensitivity of the results to the assumptions tested.

One purpose of this presentation is to identify experimental studies that are important for understanding the evolution of age at maturation. This understanding is crucial to the proper management of Atlantic salmon.

Definition of the Evolutionarily Stable Strategy

A strategy here means the pattern of sexual maturation for males or females. For example, two alternative types of maturation for females are:

(i) mature after 1 year at sea (as a grilse[1]),
(ii) mature after 2 years at sea (as a 2-sea-winter [2SW] salmon).

If the only biologically feasible strategies are that the female progeny of every female grilse mature only as grilse, and the female progeny of every 2SW female salmon mature only as 2SW salmon, then these alternative strategies constitute the "feasible set" of strategies. A biologically more realistic set of feasible strategies for females is the set such that a female zygote from a female grilse becomes a grilse with probability r and a 2SW salmon with probability $1 - r$, where $0 \leq r \leq 1$. Same for offspring of 2SW females. In this case there would be an infinite number of feasible strategies instead of just two. A more complex and realistic set would consist of a set of strategies that are partially environmentally determined.

The formal definition of an ESS for salmon age at maturation will now be given (see Maynard Smith 1982 for more details). Let the fitness of a single individual using maturation strategy A in a population employing a second maturation strategy B be $W(A,B)$. A maturation strategy I (e.g. maturation as a grilse) will be an ESS if $W(J,I) < W(I,I)$ for any other feasible maturation strategy $J \neq I$. The case where $W(J,I) = W(I,I)$ is more complex and requires additional notation. Let $W(J,Q_{q,J,I})$ be the fitness of a maturation strategy J in a population, Q, in which a proportion q matures using strategy J and a proportion $(1 - q)$ matures using strategy I. The conditions for I to be an ESS, for all $J \neq I$, are

$$\text{either } W(J,I) < W(I,I)$$

$$\text{or } \quad W(J,I) = W(I,I)$$

and, for small q,

$$W(J,Q_{q,J,I}) < W(I,Q_{q,J,I}),$$

(Maynard Smith 1982).

Often no single strategy is an ESS (Maynard Smith 1982). That is, $W(J,I) > W(I,I)$ and $W(I,J) > W(J,J)$ which implies that neither J nor I are an ESS. The ESS is a mixture of maturation strategies I and J.

The Role of Precocious Maturation as Parr in Determining Male Sea Age at Maturation

The Basic Model

In this section I investigate the evolutionary consequences of precocious maturation of male parr for male maturation after migration to the sea.

I consider two alternative male life histories: precocious sexual maturation as parr followed by maturation after one or more years at sea, and maturation only after migration to the sea. Define $N_F(t)$, $N_{Aj}(t)$, and $N_p(t)$ to be the number of anadromous females, anadromous males that have spent

---

[1]Grilse are salmon which have matured or are about to mature after one winter in the sea. Salmon which spend more than one winter at sea are called multi-sea-winter salmon.

TABLE 1. Description of principal parameters and variables used in the male age-at-maturation model. The variable t refers to the year.

α_p	Maximum number of matings possible for precocious male parr
α_A	Maximum number of matings possible for anadromous adult males
β_j	Average number of matings for a male of sea age j
γ_j	Proportion of females mated by males of sea age j
E	Egg number of adult females
G_{Aj}	Gonad weight of an adult male that has spent j winters at sea
G_p	Gonad weight of a precocious parr
M_p	Conditional mortality rate due to precocity
$m_{Aj}(t)$	Number of eggs fertilized by an adult male which has spent j winters at sea
$m_p(t)$	Number of eggs fertilized by a precocious parr
$N_{Aj}(t)$	Number of adult males which have spent j winters at sea
$N_F(t)$	Number of adult females
$N_p(t)$	Number of precocious male parr
q	Proportion of males programmed to mature precociously as parr
P_0	Survival to the first year
P_{Aj}	Survival from sea year j-1 to j for females and non-precocious males
P_p	$1 - M_p$
r	Proportion of males programmed to mature as grilse
θ	See Eq. 11

j years at sea, and precocious parr on the spawning grounds in year t, respectively. Model parameters and variables are listed in Table 1.

In the basic model I make the following simplifying assumptions: (i) there is no limit to the number of precocious male parr that can participate in a mating, (ii) male parr mature precociously at only one age and size, (iii) all surviving precocious parr migrate to the sea, (iv) all females are the same size and age, (v) only one male which has migrated to the sea is present at each mating, and (vi) the reproductive schedules for all anadromous males, whether originally precociously mature or not, are the same. Assumption (i) is evaluated by Myers (1983). Assumptions (ii–iv) are made so that one age class of parr and only one age class of anadromous females would have to be considered. The full evaluations of these assumptions would require the development of more complex numerical models. Assumptions (v) and (vi) are evaluated after the basic model is analyzed.

Initially I am interested in calculating the number of eggs fertilized by an individual precocious parr, m_p, and those fertilized by an individual adult male of sea age j, m_{Aj}. In general, both will depend upon the gonad weight of a precocious parr, G_p, the gonad weight of an adult male after j years at sea, G_{Aj}, the abundance of each sex class, and the behavioral interactions, between males. A precocious parr's sperm is assumed to be as viable as an adult male's (Alm 1943).

Adult males and precocious parr can produce more than one batch of milt and may mate more than once (Alm 1943; Jones 1959). Here I assume that: (i) precocious male parr can fertilize eggs from α_p females, (ii) anadromous adults can fertilize eggs from α_A females, and (iii) the amount of milt produced at a mating is proportional to the wet weight of the gonad. If precocious parr are rare, the number of eggs fertilized by a parr during one female's spawning while accompanying a male of sea age j will then be

$$\frac{EG_p}{G_{Aj} + G_p},$$

where E is the number of eggs per adult female.

Since male parr may mate several times, and there may be anadromous males of different sizes, then the number of eggs fertilized by a rare precocious male parr is the number of matings possible for a precocious male, α_p, times the number of eggs per female, E, times the proportion of eggs fertilized by precocious males per mating. That is

$$m_p = \alpha_p E \sum_j \gamma_j \frac{G_p}{G_{Aj} + G_p},$$

where γ_j is the proportion of females mated by males of sea age j. As the number of precocious parr increases the above equation no longer remains valid because of competition between parr. This would be expected to become important if there is more than one precocious male at each mating. In the case where there is more than one parr per mating we must consider the number of eggs fertilized by other precocious parr. The average number of precocious parr that any given precocious parr must compete with at a mating is the number of competing precocious parr in the population $(N_p - 1)$ times the number of matings a male parr participates in, α_p, divided by the number of anadromous females laying eggs, N_F. Thus, the average number of precocious male parr any given precocious parr must compete with at a mating is

$$\frac{\alpha_p (N_p - 1)}{N_F}.$$

Each of these precocious males will shed sperm, G_p, in competition with the other mates. Thus, for a population with N_p precocious males, we have

$$(1) \qquad m_p = \alpha_p E \sum_j \gamma_j \frac{G_p}{G_{Aj} + G_p \left(1 + \frac{\alpha_p (N_p - 1)}{N_F}\right)}.$$

The number of eggs fertilized by an anadromous male at sea age j is

$$(2) \qquad m_{Aj} = \frac{\beta_j E G_{Aj}}{G_{Aj} + G_p \left(1 + \frac{\alpha_p (N_p - 1)}{N_F}\right)}$$

where β_j is the average number of matings for a male of sea age j. Thus, $\gamma_j = \beta_j N_{Aj}/N_F$. If all males have equal access to females then

$$(3) \qquad \beta_j = \frac{N_F}{\sum_j N_{Aj}} \qquad \text{if } \sum_j N_{Aj} < \alpha_A N_F$$

$$\qquad = \alpha_A \qquad \text{if } \sum_j N_{Aj} \geq \alpha_A N_F.$$

More complex functional forms of β_j will be discussed later. Equation (3) assumes there is an upper limit to the number of females an anadromous male can spawn with. Myers and Hutchings (1985) showed that precocious male parr will stimulate females to spawn in the absence of anadromous males. However, in the situations considered here in which precocious males migrate to the sea after spawning, there will always be anadromous males present at any spawning.

If a stable equilibrium exists in a constant environment between two male life histories in a steady-state population, then the number of eggs fertilized by males over their lifespan using these two strategies will be the same. For males that mature precociously at river age 1 and for non-precocious males, this implies that,

$$(4) \qquad P_0 m_p + P_0 P_p \sum_j \left(\prod_{k=1}^{j} P_{Ak}\right) m_{Aj}$$

$$= P_0 \sum_j \left(\prod_{k=1}^{j} P_{Ak}\right) m_{Aj}$$

where P_0 is 1st year survival is fresh water for a male or female fry, P_{Ak} is the survival at sea for an adult male of sea-age k, and the mortality due to precocious maturation is $M_p = 1 - P_p$.

Application of the Basic Model

If a mixture of precocious and non-precocious males is evolutionarily stable then some frequency dependent mechanism must be in operation (Maynard Smith 1982). The simplest of these is the effect of precocious maturation on anadromous adult sex ratio. For example, as the number of precocious parr increase, the sex ratio of the smolt run becomes biased towards females because of mortality associated with precocious maturation (Myers 1984). Thus, for an all-grilse population the number of matings per anadromous male increases with frequency of precocious maturation. This would create a frequency-dependent factor that could make precocious maturation a component of a mixed strategy.

In order to apply (4) it is necessary to specify the mechanisms that give rise to males of different ages. Two special cases are considered below: (i) an all grilse population, and (ii) a population consisting of all 2SW females, and a mixture of grilse and 2SW males. For the following models the small proportion of repeat spawners will be ignored.

A Grilse Population

It is useful to calculate the conditions when precocious maturation will persist in a population, i.e. when a rare precocious male will fertilize more eggs over his lifetime than a male that does not mature as a parr. I consider the case in which anadromous males return from the sea after one year, die after spawning, and the initial sex ratio is 1:1. Males using the precocious maturation strategy can invade a population if the number of eggs fertilized by males that mature precociously is greater than those fertilized by males that mature only after anadromous migration when precocious males are rare. The number of eggs fertilized by precocious males is the sum of the number fertilized as a parr, $P_0 m_p$, plus the number fertilized after anadromous migration, $P_0 P_p P_{A1} m_{A1}$. Thus, males that mature precociously can be expected to invade a population if

$$P_0 m_p + P_0 P_p P_{A1} m_{A1} > P_0 P_{A1} m_{A1}$$

or

$$m_p > (1 - P_p) P_{A1} m_{A1},$$

or

(5) $m_p > M_p P_{A1} m_{A1}$.

In a population of grilse $\gamma_1 = 1$ by definition. Substituting (1) and (2) into (5) we have

(6) $\alpha_p G_p > M_p P_{A1} \beta_1 G_{A1}$.

Since there is a 1:1 sex ratio at birth for Atlantic salmon, and mortality has been assumed to be the same for males and females in the absence of maturation, then there should be an approximate 1:1 sex ratio in the anadromous adults if precocity is rare. Thus, the number of matings per anadromous male grilse, β_1, is approximately 1. The condition for males that mature precociously to invade the population is thus

(7) $\dfrac{\alpha_p G_p}{P_{A1} G_{A1}} > M_p$.

Inequality 7 has a simple interpretation: precociously maturing males can invade a population if the ratio of the sperm shed by a precocious male (assumed proportional to $\alpha_p G_p$), to that shed by an anadromous male times adult survival (assumed proportional to $P_{A1} G_{A1}$) is greater than the mortality due to precocious maturation (M_p). Thus, the cost of precocious maturation, M_p, can be simply compared with the relative gain in the number of eggs fertilized, the left-hand side of (7). Caswell et al. (1984) obtained a result similar to inequality (7) for a population in which precocious males did not migrate to the sea.

We now calculate the evolutionarily stable proportions of precocious males. Let q be the proportion of males that mature precociously in the population and let evolutionarily stable values of q be denoted by q^*. It may occur that it is evolutionarily stable for no males to mature precociously, $q^* = 0$, or that all males mature precociously, $q^* = 1$, or that a mixed ESS occurs, $0 < q^* < 1$. The condition for $q^* = 0$ is simple, the inequality in (7) is reversed. A mixed ESS will occur if the number of eggs fertilized by precocious and non precocious males is the same, i.e. an equilibrium point occurs, and this equilibrium is stable. The conditions for precocious and non precocious males to fertilize the same number of eggs is

(8) $m_p = M_p P_{A1} m_{A1}$.

The derivation for (8) is the same as for (5).

In a population consisting only of grilse, anadromous males will be of one size and (3) would apply. Thus, the average number of matings per male grilse is

$$\beta_1 = \frac{N_{F1}}{N_{A1}}, \text{ if } N_{A1} < \alpha_A N_{F1}.$$

That is, the average number of matings a male grilse participates in is the ratio of female grilse to male grilse, unless males are very rare. If the initial sex ratio is 1:1 and anadromous males can mate with many females, i.e. α_A is large, then the ration of N_{F1} to N_{A1} at demographic equilibrium can easily be calculated. The ratio of the number of anadromous males that had not matured precociously to the number of anadromous females, N_F, is $(1 - q)$ because the mortality rates of females and non-precocious males are assumed to be equal. The ratio of the number of anadromous males that had matured as parr to the number of anadromous females is q times the reduction in survival caused by precocious maturation, P_p. Thus, the average number of matings per grilse at demographic equilibrium is

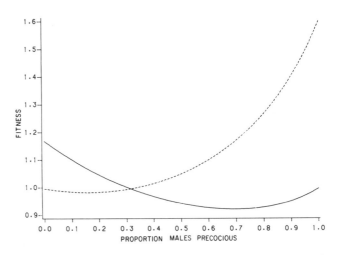

FIG. 1. Fitnesses of males that mature precociously as parr (—) and those that mature only after migration to the sea as grilse (---) as a function of the proportion of males that mature precociously, q. For this example $\alpha_p = 2$, $G_p = 4$ g, $G_{A1} = 160$ g, $P_p = 0.34$, and $P_{A1} = 0.06$. Fitness is defined as the average number of eggs fertilized over a lifetime, and is calculated from eq. 11 for precocious males and eq. 12 for non-precocious males.

$$\beta_1 = \frac{N_{F1}}{(1 - q) N_{F1} + q P_p (N_{F1})},$$

or

(9) $\beta_1 = \dfrac{1}{(1 - q) + q P_p}$.

The evolutionarily stable values of q, q^*, are obtained by substituting (9) into (8) and (6). Thus,

(10a) $q^*, = 0$ if $\dfrac{1}{M_p} \le \dfrac{G_{A1} P_{A1}}{\alpha_p G_p}$

(10b) $= \dfrac{1}{M_p} - \dfrac{G_{A1} P_{A1}}{\alpha_p G_p}$ if $\dfrac{G_{A1} P_{A1}}{\alpha_p G_p} < \dfrac{1}{M_p} < 1$

$$+ \frac{G_{A1} P_{A1}}{\alpha_p G_p}$$

(10c) $= 1$ if $\dfrac{1}{M_p} \ge 1 + \dfrac{G_{A1} P_{A1}}{\alpha_p G_p}$.

Equation (10b) specifies an equilibrium q^*. I demonstrate graphically how to determine if this q^* is evolutionarily stable. The fitness of a precocious male for fixed q is the number of eggs fertilized over his lifetime, i.e.

(11) $P_0 m_p + P_0 P_p P_{A1} M_{A1}$.

Similarly, the fitness of a non-precocious male is

(12) $P_0 P_{A1} m_{A1}$.

Consider a population in which a mixed ESS exists if the proportion of precociously maturing males is q^* (Fig. 1). If $q = q^*$, then the number of eggs fertilized over the lifetime of a male that matures precociously is equal to the number of eggs fertilized by a male that matures after anadromous migration. If a greater proportion of males mature precociously, i.e. $q > q^*$, then the fitness of precociously maturing males, given by (11), is less than males that matured after migration to the sea, given by (12) (Fig. 1). Similarly, if more males were non-precocious, then they would fertilize proportionally fewer eggs.

As the adult survival decreases (i.e. mortality at sea increases), the precociously maturing male parr becomes evolutionarily stable, first as a mixed ESS, and then as the only type of pattern of maturation that is evolutionarily stable.

A Population With Only 2SW Females

Consider a population in which all females mature after two winters at sea and there can be both grilse and 2SW males. Let r be the proportion of males that are "programmed" to become grilse. Initially assume that the probability of becoming a grilse is independent of the probability of becoming a procious male, i.e. there is no genetic covariation between these two traits. The number of adults in each age and sex class can be calculated given the number of 1-year-old parr, N. That is, if the initial sex ratio is 1:1 at demographic equilibrium we have

$$(13) \quad N_{F2} = .5 N P_{A1} P_{A2}$$

$$N_{A1} = .5N \, r \, ((1 - q) + q P_p) \, P_{A1}$$

$$N_{A2} = .5N \, (1 - r) \, ((1 - q) + q P_p) \, P_{A1} P_{A2}.$$

We now need to specify the number of matings in which males of each age class will participate. The following behaviour is assumed in formulating a functional form for γ_1, the proportion of females mated by grilse.

1) γ_1 is zero if N_{A1} is zero and 1 if N_{A2} is zero (that is, if no grilse are present they will fertilize no eggs).

2) γ_1 is a smooth increasing function of $\dfrac{N_{A1}}{N_{A1} + N_{A2}}$.

3) Males which have migrated to the sea are capable of fertilizing eggs from a large number of females in the absence of competition, i.e. α_A is large. Sockeye salmon can successfully fertilize at a male:female ratio of 1:15 (Mathisen 1962). Similar results have been obtained in Newfoundland for Atlantic salmon under semi-natural spawning conditions at sex ratios of 1:7 (Pratt 1968).

4) Older, larger males may competitively displace younger, smaller males (Mathisen 1962; Myers and Hutchings 1986; Hutchings and Myers 1985). Thus γ_1 is a convex function of $\dfrac{N_{A1}}{N_{A1} + N_{A2}}$.

I propose the following functional form:

$$(14) \quad \gamma_1 = \left(\frac{N_{A1}}{N_{A1} + N_{A2}} \right)^{\theta},$$

where $\theta > 1$. Substituting (13) into (14) we have

$$(15) \quad \gamma_1 = \left(\frac{r}{r + (1 - r) P_{A2}} \right)^{\theta}.$$

This function has the desired properties of the above four conditions but has not been verified experimentally. The average number of matings performed by grilse males at demographic equilibrium is now

$$(16) \quad \beta_1 = \gamma_1 \frac{N_F}{N_{A1}}$$

$$= \left(\frac{r}{r + (1 - r) P_{A2}} \right)^{\theta} \frac{P_{A2}}{(1 - q) + q P_p}.$$

The proportion of matings in which male 2SW salmon participate is $\gamma_2 = 1 - \gamma_1$, and $\beta_1 = \gamma_1 N_F / N_{A1}$. The resulting form of β_1 and β_2 as functions of r and p appear biologically reasonable and are consistent with behavioral observations on other salmonids (Fig. 2; Matheson 1962; Hanson and Smith 1967). That is, as the proportion of males that mature precociously, q, increases the number of matings per grilse, β_1, and 2SW salmon, β_2, increases (Fig. 2). This is caused by the female biased sex ratio associated with precocious maturation. As the proportion of male grilse increases in the population, β_1 increases and then levels out (Fig. 2a). This initial greater access to females is caused by the reduction in competition from 2SW salmon, while the leveling off is caused by competition among male grilse for matings with females. The number of mating per 2SW salmon, β_2, first increases and then decreases with increasing r for $\theta = 2$ (Fig. 2b). There are unfortunately no empirical observations to verify this behavior.

Changes in the relationship between r and q are linked by the effect both have on the number and ages of competing anadromous males. As q increases, the proportion of males to females in the smolt run decreases making access to females more possible for grilse males. Similarly, as r increases, the competition among males for matings will be keener since the ratio of adult males to females will

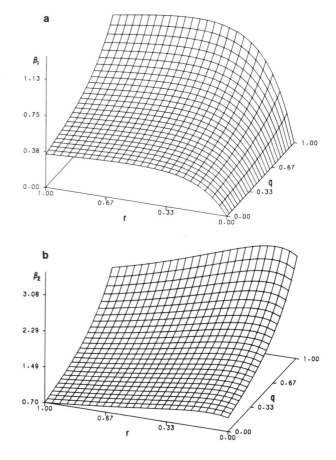

FIG. 2(a). Hypothesized relationship between the average number of matings of a male grilse, β_1, the proportion of males maturing precociously as parr, q, and the proportion of males programmed to return as grilse, r (see eq. 16). Theta is equal to two. (b) Hypothesized average number of matings of 2SW males, β_2.

57

increase, and the advantage of foregoing precocious maturation for a greater probability of matings as an anadromous adult is decreased.

To determine possible equilibrium points, we plot the equilibrium values of r for fixed q, i.e. the $\Delta r = 0$ isocline, and the equilibrium values of q for fixed r, i.e. the $\Delta q = 0$ isocline. That is, for a population in which the proportion of precociously maturing males, q, is held artificially constant, I determine the resulting equilibrium proportion of males that are programmed to mature as grilse, i.e. $\Delta r = 0$. There are three conditions under which $\Delta r = 0$. First, if $\Delta r = 0$ at $r = 1$, then the fitness of 2SW males is greater than the fitness of grilse males if grilse males are rare. Second, if $\Delta r = 0$ at $r = 0$, then the fitness of grilse males is greater than the fitness of 2SW males when 2SW males are rare. Third, if $\Delta r = 0$ for some r^* such that $0 < r^* < 1$, then the fitness of males that mature as grilse is equal to the fitness of males that mature as 2SW salmon at $r = r^*$.

In the first case, i.e. $r = 0$, we have

$$q(P_0 m_p + P_0 P_p P_{A1} m_{A1}) + (1 - q)(P_0 P_{A1} m_{A1})$$
$$< q(P_0 m_p + P_0 P_p P_{A1} P_{A2} m_{A2})$$
$$+ (1 - q)(P_0 P_{A1} P_{A2} m_{A2}).$$

That is

(17a) $r^* = 0$ if $m_{A1} < P_{A2} m_{A2}.$

Similarly,

(17b) $0 < r^* < 1$ if $m_{A1} = P_{A2} m_{A2}$

and

(17c) $r^* = 1$ if $m_{A1} > P_{A2} m_{A2}.$

The $\Delta r = 0$ isoclines are determined using m_{A1} and m_{A2} from Eq. 2 where the β_j's are determined from Eq. 16 and the N_p's and N_F's are determined from Eq. 13. Although the resulting algebraic expressions are complex, the $\Delta r = 0$ isoclines are easily calculated and plotted (Fig. 3).

Similarly, the proportion of precociously maturing males that does not change, $\Delta q = 0$, is determined for each fixed r. The intersection of these two lines are equilibrium points (possibly unstable).

This process is illustrated in Fig. 3 with the following parameter values:

(18) α_p = 2 (Alm 1943) P_p = 0.34 (Myers 1984)
   G_{A1} = 160 g (Robitaille et al. 1982) P_{A1} = 0.1
   G_{A2} = 340 g (Robitaille et al. 1982) P_{A2} = 0.35 (Horsted 1980)
   G_p = 4 g (Alm 1943) θ = 2.

There are no biological data available to estimate θ, other than that it must be greater than 1. $\theta = 2$ is used here only as an example. There is considerable uncertainty in these parameter estimates, e.g. P_{A2} and α_p may be too low. In particular, the value of P_{A2} used here is much lower than that estimated by Doubleday et al. (1979). A lower estimate was used because (i) the value of P_{A2} proposed by Doubleday et al. (1979) was much too high to be consistent with evolutionary theory (Myers and Doyle 1983), and (ii) a lower value was needed to compensate for the assumption that only one anadromous male was present at each mating. The $\Delta r = 0$ isocline for these parameter values is typical of that seen for biologically realistic parameters.

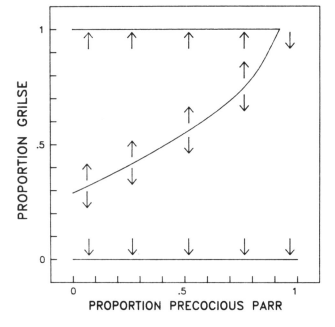

FIG. 3. Equilibrium proportions of males maturing as grilse ($\Delta r = 0$) in relationship to the proportion of males maturing precociously (q). The grilse zero-isocline is the locus of points for which r is in equilibrium ($\Delta r = 0$) at the given value of q. The arrows show the change in r for fixed p. Parameter values given in (18). The $\Delta r = 0$ isoclines are calculated from eq. 17.

There is a stable line of equilibria at $r = 0$, and another line of equilibria that contains both stable and unstable points (Fig. 3). The $\Delta q = 0$ isocline is considerably simpler (Fig. 4). The isoclines combined yield three equilibrium points, one of which is unstable (Fig. 5). In such a system a change from a population containing few precocious male parr and 2SW salmon males can change very rapidly to a population containing many precocious parr and male grilse.

Thus far we have considered only life-histories at equilibrium. The actual dynamics of the system will depend upon the heritabilities and the genetic covariation between the two traits (precocious maturation as parr and maturation as a grilse). The dynamical changes in q and r have been simulated for a simple system in which each trait controlled by single unlinked sex-linked loci (the dotted lines in Fig. 5). The final evolutionarily stable mixed strategy depends upon the initial conditions, i.e. the original q and r. Thus, a sudden increase or decrease in q or r might change the system from one ESS to another.

Varying the model parameters leads to two main changes in the relative positions of the isoclines. Increasing G_{A1} or P_{A1} can result in the elimination of the stable equilibrium at low precocity and low proportion grilse. Similarly an increase in θ, G_{A2}, or P_{A2} may result in elimination of the equilibrium point at high proportions of precocious male parr and a high proportion of grilse. Similarly, if multiple anadromous males at each mating are included in the model the line of equilibria at $r = 0$ will tend to become unstable.

I have discussed here one mechanism that can lead to a mixed ESS for precocious maturation, i.e. the frequency dependent advantage of multiple matings accruing to anadromous males as the sex ratio of males to females

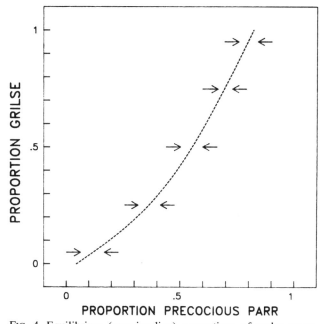

FIG. 4. Equilibrium (zero-isocline) proportions of males precocious ($\Delta q = 0$) in relationship to the proportion of males maturing as grilse (r). Arrows show the change in q for fixed r. This graph is the counterpart of Fig. 3.

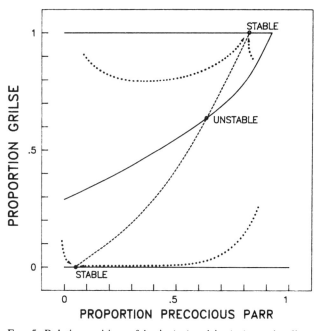

FIG. 5. Relative positions of the Δr (—) and Δq (---) zero-isoclines (locus of points of equilibrium) in relation to the proportion of precociously maturing male parr, and the proportion of anadromous males maturing as grilse. There are two stable and one unstable equilibria. The stable equilibria are separated by an unstable equilibrium, or saddle point. The dotted lines represent the changes in the proportions under the assumption that each trait is controlled by a sex-linked locus.

decreases due to precocious maturation of male parr. An alternative theory was put forward by Myers (1983) for Atlantic salmon, and Gross (1984) for Pacific salmon (*Oncorhynchus* spp.). They suggested that the frequency dependent mechanisms leading to a mixed ESS are the behavioral interactions among parr at the spawning site and limitations due to space, which effectively limit the number of precocious males that can shed their sperm in competition with anadromous males. A complete theory would include both types of frequency dependence.

The primary purpose of these models for male age at maturity is to identify the information that must be collected before evolutionary theories of male age at maturation can be tested. Nevertheless, there are some conclusions that can be drawn from the information at hand. In particular, the theory proposes an important link between male sea age at maturation and the proportion of males that mature precociously. That is, the sea age of males and females should be similar in rivers with a low incidence of precocious maturation, but if a large proportion of males mature precociously then male sea age should be less. However, it is not a simple matter to estimate age-specific rates of precocious maturation because of the confounding effect of maturation on smolting. A census of the parr and smolt population is necessary to estimate the rates of precocious maturation for all parr age classes; these data are available for only one river, the Little Codroy in Newfoundland (Myers 1984). The available data on rates of precocious maturation have been compiled by Myers et al. (1985). From these data it is clear that two rivers, the St. Jean and Moisie in Quebec, have a lower rate of precocious maturation than all others surveyed; the proportion of males maturing precociously is less than 15% for 1-, 2-, and 3-year-old parr. Furthermore, there is little difference in the sea age at maturation for males and females for these two populations (mean sea ages: Moisie males — 2.50, Moisie females — 2.88; St. Jean males — 2.14, St. Jean females — 2.19; data from Schieffer (1971)). In most other rivers in North America approxi-

mately 60–80% of males mature precociously (Myers et al. 1985), and the difference between mean sea age of males and females is much greater (e.g. the mean sea age of males from the Little Codroy River is 1.1 while it is 1.9 for females). These preliminary results need to be verified by more intensive surveys.

The Matamek River population has recently shown an apparent rapid increase in the proportion of males maturing precociously as parr (Gibson 1978); this might be considered evidence of a population shifting between stable equilibria. However, Myers et al. (1985) showed that changes in the proportion of mature male parr in the Matamek River can be accounted for by changes in growth alone.

Competition for Spawning Substrate and Female Age At Maturation

The game-theoretic notion of ESS corresponds to an optimization solution if the fitness of an individual strategy depends only upon the other strategies in the population insofar as they affect the population growth rate, in the density independent case, or the carrying capacity, for the density dependent case (Charlesworth 1980). While this is clearly not the case for males, it may be the case for females.

Redd superimposition, and the associated egg mortality, can lead to situations where an optimization approach is invalid. Consider two alternative strategies for females: maturation as grilse and maturation as 2SW salmon. Larger 2SW females bury their eggs deeper than grilse, and thus are less susceptible to egg mortality due to redd superimposition (Jones 1959: p. 106). Thus, the maturation strategy of a female will depend upon the maturation strategies of her competitors. That is, a female that matures as a grilse in a population in which females mature after 2SW, may stand a good chance of having her eggs destroyed by redd superimposition. On the other hand, the eggs of a 2SW female in a population of grilse females will be relatively protected from redd superimposition. A mixed ESS in which some females mature as grilse, and some mature as 2SW females may result. In the absence of redd superimposition, the fitness of a grilse female would have been greater (Myers 1986). Thus, the evolution of age at maturation of female salmon may not be adequately approximated as a game against nature (i.e. an optimization process) if size-dependent redd superimposition is potentially an important source of egg mortality.

Redd superimposition can be mitigated either by the use of post-spawning defense of redds, delaying spawning, or by the use of alternative spawning substrate. Post-spawning redd defense may reduce redd superimposition in chinook salmon (*Oncorhynchus tshawytscha*; Nielson and Banford 1983), but does not appear to significantly reduce redd superimposition in pink salmon (*O. gorbuscha*; McNeil 1967). All three alternative strategies probably involve costs, i.e. energy expended defending redds could be expended on eggs, late spawning may mean delayed fry emergence, and egg mortality could be higher in alternative substrates.

If smaller females may use inferior spawning substrate in the presence of larger females, the choice of spawning substrate can be viewed as a habitat selection problem, i.e. selection of habitat for eggs. There is a simple, and testable ESS theory of habitat selection, which predicts that the density of individuals in habitats should be such that individuals in all habitats should have the same fitness (Maynard Smith 1982). There is unfortunately no information on the size-dependent choice of spawning substrate and subsequent egg survival for Atlantic salmon.

General Discussion

The great within-population variability in male life histories implies that the game-theoretic approach to the evolution of male life histories is needed for Atlantic salmon (Myers 1983; Gross 1984). If substrate competition and redd superimposition are important, then a game-theoretic approach is needed for females as well. However, in fish species which do not compete for spawning substrate the optimization and game-theoretic solutions are the same, and the simpler optimization methods can readily be applied to the study of age at maturation for females. For example, Myers and Doyle (1983) used optimal life history theory to estimate mortality rates of several fish species based on age at maturation and other life-history traits.

The evolution of Atlantic salmon is of more than academic interest. The precocious maturation of male parr is responsible for at least 60% of the male salmon production in Newfoundland (Myers 1984). It is feasible to artificially select against anadromous males that have matured as parr using scale analysis (Myers and Hutchings 1986). Artificial selection against precocious maturation could be carried out in a hatchery or in natural populations as males pass through a fishway or counting fence. It is necessary to have a good understanding of the evolution of Atlantic salmon age at maturation before such a scheme should be carried out in natural populations. If early- and late-maturing males are maintained as an evolutionarily-stable mixture of maturation phenotypes, then any artificial alteration in the phenotype

ratio could result in a compensatory response by the population to re-establish a stable equilibrium. For example, instead of selecting against maturation as parr, the realized selection might be for males to forego smoltification altogether and mature only in the river.

For all the many studies on Atlantic salmon it is remarkable what we do not know about the basic biology of the species. Prime among these unknowns is the process whereby males of different sizes and ages compete for females. Exceedingly few matings of Atlantic salmon have been observed under natural conditions and published (Belding 1934; Ouellet 1977; Myers and Hutchings 1985; Hutchings and Myers 1985); there is no quantitative information. Without such information it is impossible to test fully quantitative theories of the evolution of age at maturation of Atlantic salmon. There is a similar lack of information on the numbers of precocious male parr taking part in matings. Although it is known that precocious male parr can mate several times (Alm 1943) and can stimulate females to spawn in the absence of anadromous males (Myers and Hutchings 1985), there are no estimates of how many times males mate under natural conditions.

Even when such quantitative observations are made, there is still a need to assess the relative contribution males of different age and size make in the fertilization of eggs. It is not necessary to carry these experiments out under the conditions previously mentioned, but it is necessary to reflect the combinations and relative placement of females that occur under natural conditions. The relative contributions can be assessed through electrophoretic analyses of allozymes (Schroder 1982).

In conclusion, the analysis of the evolution of age at maturation of Atlantic salmon must be viewed in a game-theoretic context. Furthermore, the analysis of any genetic effects of fishing pressure must be considered in a similar manner. Changes in the size structure of populations by altering fishing patterns may have profound indirect effects on the selection intensity due to the types of behavioral patterns discussed here. Predictions of the effects of changes in the salmon fishing regulations cannot be made unless the demographic consequences of spawning behaviour are considered.

Acknowledgments

I thank E. Dalley, B. Dempson, G. Evans, J. Gibson, M. Healey, C. Herbinger, J. Hutchings, R. Peterman, R. Porter, and D. Reddin for helpful comments and discussion.

References

ALM, G. 1943. Fertilization experiments with salmon parr. Inst. Freshwat. Res. Drottningholm Rep. 22: 1–40.

BELDING, D. 1934. The spawning habits of the Atlantic salmon. Am. Fish. Soc. Trans. 34: 211–216.

CASWELL, H., R. J. NAIMAN, AND R. MORIN. 1984. Evaluating the consequences of reproduction in complex salmonid life cycles. Aquaculture 43: 123–134.

CHARLESWORTH, B. 1980. Evolution in age-structured populations. Cambridge University Press, Cambridge.

DALLEY, E. L., C. W. ANDREWS, AND J. M. GREEN. 1983. Precocious male Atlantic salmon parr (*Salmo salar*) in insular Newfoundland. Can. J. Fish. Aquat. Sci. 40: 647–652.

DOUBLEDAY, W. G., D. R. RIVARD, J. A. RITTER, AND K. U. VICKERS. 1979. Natural mortality rate estimates for North Atlantic salmon in the Sea. ICES C.M.1979/M:26, 15 p.

DUCHARME, L. J. A. 1969. Atlantic salmon returning for their fifth and sixth consecutive spawning trips. J. Fish. Res. Board Can. 26: 1661–1664.

GIBSON, R. J. 1978. Recent changes in the population of juvenile Atlantic salmon in the Matamek River, Québec, Canada. J. Cons. Int. Exp. Mer 38: 201–207.

GROSS, M. 1984. Sunfish, salmon, and the evolution of alternative reproduction strategies and tactics in fishes, p. 55–75. *In* R. Wooton and G. Potts [ed.] Fish reproduction: strategies and tactics. Academic Press, London.

HANSON, A. J., AND H. D. SMITH. 1967. Mate selection in a population of sockeye salmon (*Oncorhnychus nerka*) of mixed age-groups. J. Fish. Res. Board Can. 24: 1955–1977.

HORSTED, SV. AA. 1980. Simulation of home-water catches of salmon surviving the West Greenland fisheries as a method for estimating the effects of the West Greenland fishery on home-water stocks and fisheries. Rapp. P.-V. Réun. Cons. Int. Explor. Mer 176: 142–146.

HUTCHINGS, J. A., AND R. A. MYERS. 1985. Mating between anadromous and non-anadromous Atlantic salmon, *Salmo salar*. Can. J. Zool. 63: 2219–2221.

JONES, J. W. 1959. The Salmon. Collins, London, 192 p.

MATHISEN, O. A. 1962. The effect of altered sex ratios on the spawning of red salmon. Univ. Wash. Pub. Fish. 1: 139–245.

MAYNARD SMITH, J. 1982. Evolution and the theory of games. Cambridge Univ. Press, London.

MCNEIL, W. J. 1967. Randomness in distribution of pink salmon redds. J. Fish. Res. Board Can. 24: 1629–1634.

MYERS, R. A. 1983. Evolutionary change in the proportion of precocious parr and its effect on yield in Atlantic salmon. ICES C.M.1983/M:14.

    1984. Demographic consequences of precocious maturation of Atlantic salmon (*Salmo salar*). Can. J. Fish. Aquat. Sci. 41: 1349–1353.

    1986. Competition for spawning space: effects on age at first reproduction and on coexistence of salmonids. Oikos. (in press)

MYERS, R. A., AND R. W. DOYLE. 1983. Predicting natural mortality rates and reproduction–mortality trade-offs from life history data. Can. J. Fish. Aquat. Sci. 40: 612–620.

    1986. Selection against parr maturation in Atlantic salmon. Aquaculture. (in press)

MYERS, R. A., AND J. A. HUTCHINGS. 1985. Mating of anadromous Atlantic salmon, *Salmo salar* L., with mature male parr. ICES C.M.1985/M:8 Anadromous and Catadromous Fish Committee (Ref. F Mariculture Committee).

MYERS, R. A., J. A. HUTCHINGS, AND R. J. GIBSON.1985. Variation in precocious maturation within and among populations of Atlantic salmon. ICES C.M.1985/M:9.

NEILSON, J. D., AND C. E. BANFORD. 1983. Chinook salmon (*Oncorhynchus tshawytscha*) spawner characteristics in relation to redd physical features. Can. J. Zool. 61: 1524–1531.

OUELLET, G. 1977. Group spawning of four Atlantic salmon on Anticosti Island. Nat. Can. 104: 507–510.

PRATT, J. D. 1968. Spawning distribution of Atlantic salmon (*Salmo salar* L.) in controlled flow channels. M.Sc. thesis, Dep. of Biology, Memorial University of Newfoundland, Nfld. 143 p.

ROBITAILLE, J. A., I. BABOS, Y. CÔTÉ, M. BRETON-PROVENCHER, G. SCHOONER ET G. HAYEUR. 1982. Biologie du saumon dans les eaux du fleuve Koksoak, en Ungava. Rapport conjoint de SAGE Ltée, du M.L.C.P. et de Gilles Shooner Inc. présenté à Hydro-Québec, Direction Environnement. 160 p., 21 tableaux, 33 fig.

SCHAFFER, W. M. 1979. The theory of life-history evolution and its application to Atlantic salmon. Symp. Zool. Soc. Lond. 44: 307–326.

SCHAFFER, W. M., AND P. F. ELSON. 1975. The adaptive significance of variations in life history among local populations of Atlantic salmon in North America. Ecology 56: 577–590.

SCHIEFFER, K. 1971. Ecology of Atlantic salmon, with specific reference to occurrence and abundance of grilse in North Shore Gulf of St. Lawrence River. Ph.D. thesis, Univ. Waterloo, Ont. xvi + 129 p.

SCHRODER, S. L. 1982. The influence of intrasexual competition on the distribution of chum salmon in an experimental stream, p. 275–285. *In* E. L. Brannon and E. O. Salo [ed.] Salmon and Trout Migratory Behavior Symposium. Published by School of Fisheries, University of Washington, Seattle, WA.

Growth and Maturation Patterns of Atlantic Salmon, *Salmo salar*, in the Koksoak River, Ungava, Quebec

Jean A. Robitaille[1]

352-A, rue Saint-Laurent, Lévis, Qué. G6V 3W5

Yvon Côté

Ministère du Loisir, de la Chasse et de la Pêche, 150 est, boul. Saint-Cyrille, Québec, Qué. G1R 4Y1

Gilles Shooner

Gilles Shooner Inc., 40, rue Racine, Loretteville, Qué. G2B 1C6

and Gaétan Hayeur

Hydro-Québec, 870 est, boul. Maisonneuve, Montréal, Qué. H2L 1Y1

Abstract

ROBITAILLE, J. A., Y. CÔTÉ, G. SHOONER, AND G. HAYEUR. 1986. Growth and maturation patterns of Atlantic salmon, *Salmo salar*, in the Koksoak River, Ungava, Quebec, p. 62–69. *In* D. J. Meerburg [ed.] Salmonid age at maturity. Can. Spec. Publ. Fish. Aquat. Sci. 89.

Salmon smolts from the Koksoak River, Ungava, Québec, can reach adult size and maturity either by growing at sea or in the estuary, or both. Smolt age was not found to be related to the duration of post-smolt life, either directly or indirectly through a predetermination of the place where growth is achieved. The most obvious feature of the smolt age distribution was the strength of one year-class, which made the mean smolt age fluctuate from year to year. It is thought that low sea temperatures in Ungava bay restrict movements in and out of the estuary and contribute to trapping some smolts. The double-spawning and freshwater feeding of some salmon are believed to be adaptations to harsh winter conditions within the river. The high productivity of the Koksoak estuary, the absence of anadromous Arctic char in this system and some reproductive advantages related to an estuarine life are factors suggested to explain how entrapped smolts can grow and become functional spawners instead of being lost from the population.

Résumé

ROBITAILLE, J. A., Y. CÔTÉ, G. SHOONER, AND G. HAYEUR. 1986. Growth and maturation patterns of Atlantic salmon, *Salmo salar*, in the Koksoak River, Ungava, Quebec, p. 62–69. *In* D. J. Meerburg [ed.] Salmonid age at maturity. Can. Spec. Publ. Fish. Aquat. Sci. 89.

Les smolts de saumon produits dans le bassin du fleuve Koksoak, en Ungava (Québec), peuvent atteindre la taille adulte et la maturité en réalisant leur croissance en estuaire, en mer ou encore partiellement aux deux endroits. Dans ce réseau hydrographique, l'âge à la smoltification ne semble pas affecter le temps mis pour atteindre la maturité, que ce soit de façon directe ou par l'intermédiaire d'une détermination du lieu de croissance après la smoltification. La principale caractéristique des distributions d'âge à la smoltification est la prédominance d'une classe d'âge, qui explique les changements importants dans l'âge moyen à la smoltification, d'une année à l'autre. Il semble que les basses températures des eaux de la baie d'Ungava restreignent les possibilités, pour les saumons, de quitter l'estuaire et d'y revenir, ce qui pourrait expliquer l'emprisonnement accidentel de certains smolts. Les conditions hivernales rigoureuses à l'intérieur même du réseau auraient causé l'apparition, chez certains saumons, d'un phénomène de double fraie, accompagné d'une reprise de l'alimentation active en eau douce. La forte productivité de l'estuaire du Koksoak, l'absence d'omble chevalier anadrome dans ce bassin et certains avantages reproducteurs découlant de la croissance estuarienne permettent d'expliquer comment des smolts confinés à ce fleuve peuvent y croître et devenir des géniteurs fonctionnels, plutôt que de représenter une perte pour la population.

Introduction

On the western side of the Atlantic, the northernmost populations of Atlantic salmon (*Salmo salar*) are found in some of the rivers flowing into Ungava Bay (Québec, Canada). In the Koksoak River, sea-run salmon was first reported by McLean (1849), while landlocked salmon (or ouananiche) was found by Low (1895) in the same system,

above the impassable Chute du Calcaire on the Caniapiscau River. Distributions of sea-run salmon and ouananiche are known to overlap in some areas in this system. Robitaille et al. (1982) reported catches of both types of fish in the same net, 480 km upstream from the Koksoak estuary, in Lake Mortier, along Delay River. Some of the biological characteristics of the species in the Koksoak River system have been described by Power (1969) for sea-run fish, and by Dubois and Le Jeune (1975), and Leclerc and Power (1980) for ouananiche.

From 1867 until the end of the 1930's, a commercial

---

[1]Present address: Department of Fisheries and Oceans, 901 Cap Diamant, C.P. 15 500, Québec, Qué. G1K 7Y7.

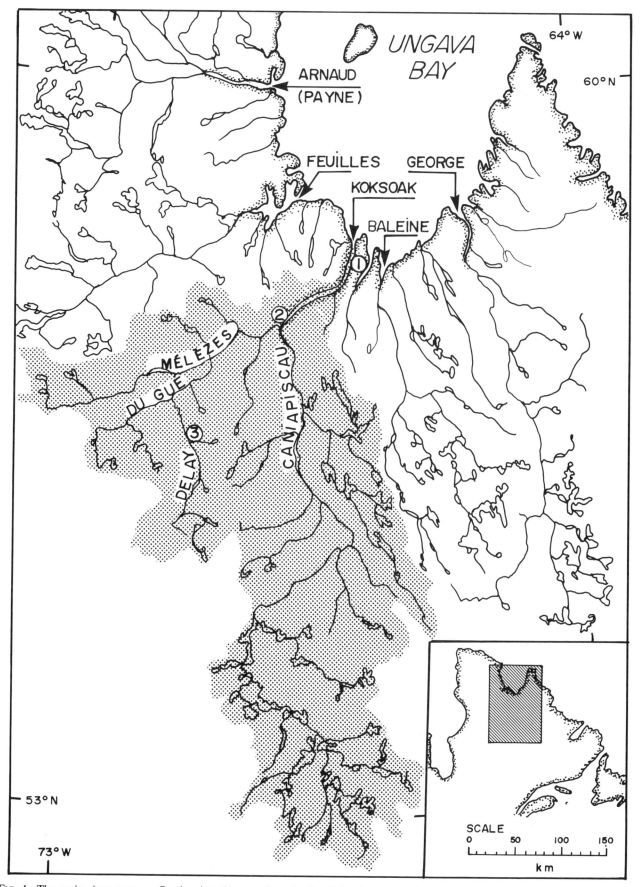

FIG. 1. The main river systems flowing into Ungava Bay. In the Koksoak system (shaded catchment), the Caniapiscau branch is inaccessible to anadromous salmon, except for the first 25 km, where no adequate spawning bed can be found. Most spawning areas are in the Mélèzes River and its tributaries. Sampling sites and years: (1) Estuary, 1980 and 1981; (2) Mélèzes−Caniapiscau confluence, 1979 and 1980; (3) Delay River sportfishing camp, 1979, 1980, and 1981.

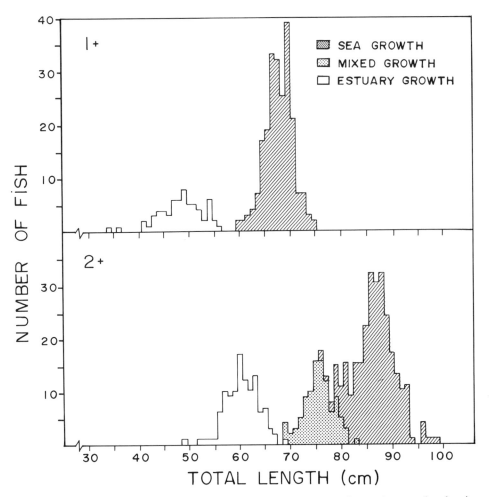

FIG. 2. Length distribution of maiden salmon by post-smolt age and growth type. Overlapping distributions are shown one on top of the other. Sample from the estuary, 1980.

fishery for salmon in the Koksoak estuary was operated by the Hudson's Bay Company (Power 1976). At the present time, salmon is harvested by Inuit natives from Kuujjuaq, setting gillnets in the estuary in a partially subsistance, partially commercial fishery. There is only one sportfishing camp in the part of the upper river accessible to sea-run fish.

Among the catch of Inuit fishermen in the Koksoak estuary, Power (1962) mentioned the presence of a few fish "with apparently aberrant life histories. Many of these seem to have spent their sea life in the estuary and have consequently grown only slowly. (...) biologically of great interest but of no importance from the point of view of the fishery." Recent samples from this estuary and from the sport fishery in the upper river have indicated however that the status of these "aberrant" salmon may have changed from that prevailing in the 1960's (Breton-Provencher and Robitaille 1982).

This paper deals with growth types of the Koksoak salmon and addresses some aspects of growth and maturation after smolting, as related to river life, in the harsh climatic and hydrological conditions (Power 1969, 1981) met by salmon at the northern limit of its range.

Materials and Methods

The data in this paper come from a set of seven samples totalling over 3200 fish taken in the Koksoak River and its tributaries from 1979 to 1981 (Fig. 1). Two samples were obtained in 1979 and 1980 by experimental fishing with gillnets or trap-nets at Mélèzes−Caniapiscau confluence. Examination of all catches at the sportfishing camp in the upper river in 1979, 1980, and 1981 provided three samples. The last two samples were collected during surveys of the harvest by Inuit fishermen in the estuary, in 1980 and 1981. Details on methodologies are available in manuscript reports (Robitaille et al. 1980, 1982; Breton-Provencher and Robitaille 1982; Gillis and Dumas 1982).

All smolt ages presented are derived from scales of fish caught one year or more after their downstream migration as smolts. No extensive study of smolts has yet been done in any Ungava river.

Scale readings were performed under the supervision of the same person, ensuring consistency over the 3 years. In this paper, post-smolt life and post-smolt age refer to the entire period following smolt migration. Sea age is taken from the scales as the number of winter bands laid down at sea; estuary age is the equivalent for fish which never go beyond the estuary after smolting.

Results

Post-smolt Growth and Reproduction

Koksoak smolts can reach adult size and maturity by growing either at sea or in the estuary. In each of the seven samples from this river, at least 20% of the scales showed

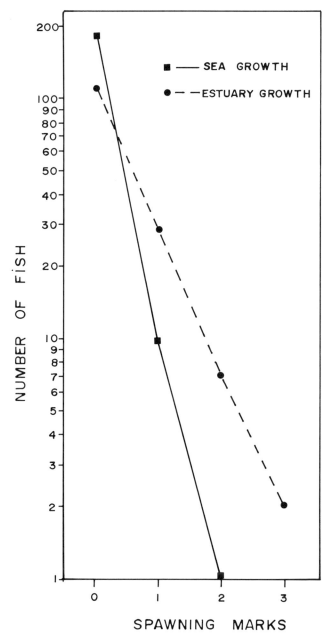

FIG. 3. Number of fish in relation to the number of spawning marks. Sample from Mélèzes–Caniapiscau confluence, 1979.

are regarded as marine or sea-growing salmon.

The time needed for a Koksoak salmon to reach maturity is related to its sex and growth type (Robitaille et al. 1984b). In sea-run salmon, one sea-year fish are mostly males and two sea-year fish are mostly females (Table 1). Marine and mixed-growth males are immature when they return to the river. Three weeks prior to spawning time, they still have a gonado-somatic index (GSI) smaller than 1%. They must spend about fourteen months in fresh water before they can spawn for the first time. No evidence of a delayed maturation was found for females with the same growth types: these fish spawn the same year they enter the river. However, some of them stay in fresh water afterwards and spawn again in the second year, without migrating back to sea in the interim. Evidence of this phenomenon was the presence of residual eggs in the body cavity of maturing females caught on the spawning grounds a few weeks before fresh fish entered the Koksoak estuary, 380 km downstream.

Estuary males usually mature sooner after smoltification than estuary females, 1 or 2 years for the former, 2 or 3 years for the latter (Robitaille et al. 1982). When estuary males and females reach a GSI higher than 3 or 4%, they migrate from the estuary towards the spawning areas and spawn in the same year. Estuary males do not have to spend over a year in fresh water before spawning, as sea or mixed-growth males do. Estuary fish of both sexes can recondition either in fresh water or in the estuary and spawn in consecutive years.

Fish of both sexes and of any type of post-smolt growth survive and regain condition in fresh water by reverting to active feeding in June and July. Circuli laid down in fresh water are seen on the scale margin of many salmon caught from June to September on the spawning areas. However, when two spawnings occur in consecutive years, these few circuli, when present, are obliterated the second autumn, leaving only one spawning mark instead of two. Recapture of a tagged estuary female has confirmed that scale reading can underestimate the true number of spawnings. The number of spawning marks seen on the scales is nevertheless thought to be somewhat indicative of how many times fish have migrated from the feeding areas, in the sea or the estuary, to the spawning grounds. Figure 3 shows that survival between spawning migrations is three to four times higher for estuary than for marine salmon. Up to five distinct spawning marks have been recorded on the scales of estuary fish.

Duration and Location of Post-Smolt Growth in Relation to Smolt Age

The most striking feature of smolt age distributions is the dominance of one year-class over more than one smolt run (Fig. 4). Our data show that the 1974 year-class was dominant in the 1+ post-smolt age-group sampled in both 1979 and 1980 and in the 2+ age-group sampled in 1980 and 1981, for each post-smolt growth type. This means that fish from the 1974 hatching have dominated both the 1978 and 1979 smolt runs. The strength of the 1974 year-class reduced the mean smolt age in 1978, compared to the previous year. Then, as fish from the same year-class contributed to the 1979 smolt run, the mean smolt age increased again. Statistically significant differences were found between age distributions of consecutive sampling years within the same post-smolt age-group or in comparisons between post-smolt

one or more atypical winter bands during post-smolt life. The irregular band measures less than 0.24 mm, while the typical one associated with sea-run salmon is more than 0.24 mm wide. The compact winter band has been shown to be formed on the scales of fish which spend the winter in fresh water, where growth ceases (Robitaille et al. 1984a). Salmon with only this type of winter mark on their scales spend the summer in the Koksoak estuary, growing at a rate of about 2 mm per day from mid-July to mid-September. For each year of residence in the Koksoak, these fish are smaller than their sea-going counterparts by about 12 cm (Fig. 2). Some salmon never migrate beyond the estuary before reaching maturity. They are referred to as estuary salmon. Others leave the Koksoak estuary one year after smolting and spend the rest of their pre-reproductive life at sea: these are mixed-growth salmon. Finally, at least half of the scales in each of the seven samples showed a growth pattern typical of the ordinary sea-going salmon. These fish

TABLE 1. Sex-ratio of maiden salmon by post-smolt age-group and growth type. Sample from the estuary, 1980.

Growth Type	Age-Group	Sex Ratio (%♂ : %♀)	Sample size
Sea	1+	82:18	50
	2+	18:82	56
Estuary	1+	45:55	22
	2+	24:76	45
Mixed	2+	13:87	23

age-groups 1+ and 2+ for the same sampling years (Chi-square test, $P < 0,05$). However, smolt age distributions are similar when compared between salmon groups from the same smolt runs and growth types (as indicated by arrows on Fig. 4).

No relation was found between smolt age and post-smolt growth type. Significant differences in smolt age distributions were found, in some cases, between fish of two post-smolt growth types within the same sample year and the same post-smolt age-group, but no definite trend emerged from these comparisons.

Discussion

Smolt age is high in Ungava rivers due to the short growing season for parr (Power 1969), and to the larger smolt size which may be necessary for better survival during the seaward migration into the cold waters of Ungava Bay.

In a sample of adults from the Mélèzes−Caniapiscau confluence, no difference in smolt size was found between post-smolt growth types nor between post-smolt age-groups (Robitaille et al. 1980). However, these results should be considered preliminary because the comparisons were made with back-calculated lengths, a method which may not be precise enough in this case.

In the analysis of the Koksoak River data sets, the time spent on the feeding grounds prior to the first spawning was not found to be related to river age. However, as growth type was known to affect age at maturity in males, an indirect effect of river age on maturity was still possible if growth types were related to smolt age. As the comparisons of the smolt age distributions between growth types (within post-smolt age-groups and within sampling years) showed no trends, this indirect effect can be rejected.

In the sample years 1979, 1980 and 1981, the predominant feature of the smolt age distributions was the strength of the 1974 year-class. This phenomenon made smolt-age distributions quite different between post-smolt age-groups from the same sample year or between years within the same post-smolt age-group. But the smolt age distribution of the 1+ post-smolt age-group sampled one year is similar to the distribution for fish of the 2+ age-group caught the next year.

Selection of feeding area and thus growth type for an individual smolt seems to be a matter of chance, not predetermined by river life. When the water temperature of Ungava Bay allows it, smolts present in the estuary can leave for the sea. However, it seems that conditions are favourable for only a short period of time and some smolts remain trapped inside the estuary, as Power (1981) sug-

gested. Depending upon the conditions prevailing each year, one might expect changes in the relative size of the groups of fish which stay in the estuary and of those which leave. As the smolt age distribution is expected to change throughout a run (Osterdahl 1969), a subset of smolts that go to sea within a short period of time may not be representative of the age distribution for the whole run. This would explain the differences in smolt age between growth types which sometimes occur in some samples, without showing any definite trend.

The temperature barrier of Ungava Bay and the severe hydrological conditions within the Koksoak River system are thought to have led to the double spawning of some females and to the freshwater feeding of most fish spending over one year in the upper part of the river. Both adaptations also occur in salmon populations of the George River (Y. Côté, unpublished data). In the years when ice stays late in the bay, sometimes until the beginning of September, the fishing is poor; this is a well known fact both to the present day Inuit fishermen and to the Hudson's Bay Company fishermen of the late 1800's and early 1900's (Power 1976). Because of the presumably small number of smolts which could have gone out to sea during those years of rigorous ice conditions in the bay, it could be expected that returns of sea-run fish one and two years later would also be low. "In 1948 there was an almost complete failure of the salmon run in both the Koksoak and the George Rivers" (Dunbar and Hildebrand 1952). In such disastrous years, there is no doubt that double spawning ensures that at least a minimum number of eggs are deposited on the spawning beds. This behaviour and the physiological adaptations sustaining it are likely to have been selected for because of the advantage they give to the individual spawner on risky spawning and incubating grounds. Carter (1978) and Power (1981) described the severe hydrological conditions in some parts of the Koksoak system. Low winter water levels, frasil and anchor ice, and scraping of the river bed by ice blocks in the spring may cause heavy mortalities of eggs or alevins in some years. Some females have the opportunity to contribute to recruitment in two consecutive years and, by spreading the risks of incubation over two winters, some progeny are likely to survive. These females might have a better chance to spawn twice by staying close to the spawning grounds rather than returning to sea for reconditioning, especially with the difficulties encountered both when leaving and reentering the river.

The estuary growth of some fish and the delayed maturation of male mixed or sea-growth salmon are not likely to be caused solely by the temperature constraints on movement. Both phenomena seem to be absent from the Baleine and George Rivers, where the effects of a thermal barrier should be similar to those observed in the Koksoak.

We suggest that a combination of three factors have allowed the survival of those smolts trapped in the estuary and their growth into functional spawners. These factors are a highly productive estuary, the absence of spawning populations of Arctic char, *Salvelinus alpinus*, and some reproductive advantages of estuary life.

The high production of fish larvae on which salmon feed may contribute to delay smolt migration. The Koksoak River probably has the most productive estuary of all rivers flowing into Ungava Bay. Although no extensive study of the biological productivity of these estuaries has as yet been undertaken, there are some indications that the greater flow

SAMPLING YEAR

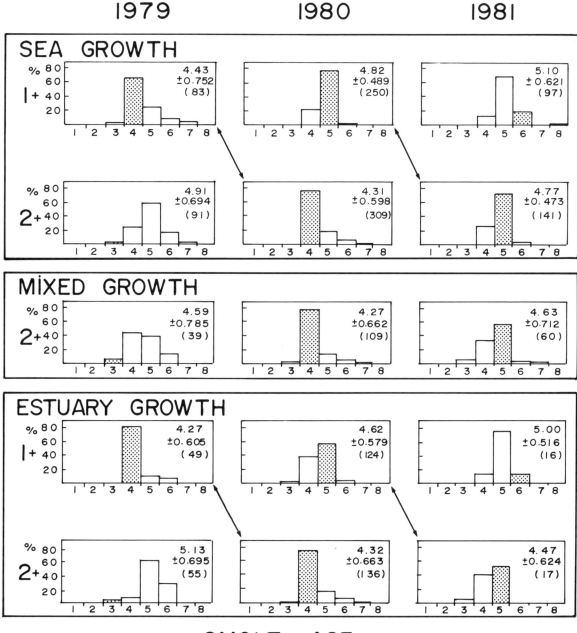

FIG. 4. Smolt age distribution of maiden salmon by post-smolt age-group and growth type. The 1974 year-class is shaded. The mean, standard deviation and sample size (in parentheses) are given for each group. Arrows show groups compared within smolt runs and growth types.

and warmer water drawn from the Caniapiscau lake systems, the long mixing zone of the estuary itself, and the high tides have resulted in a higher production of small fish on which salmon can feed. At some places within the estuary, salmon and brook char (*Salvelinus fontinalis*) can be seen frantically feeding on schools of sculpin fry (Shorthorn and Arctic sculpins, *Myoxocephalus scorpius* and *M. scorpioides*). This food item has been mentioned as the most important for estuary salmon during August (Robitaille et al. 1984a). It seems possible that this abundance of food diverts smolts from their seaward migration long enough to contribute to their being stranded in the estuary. It also allows enough growth for estuary salmon to survive and reach

maturity.

We also suggest that the absence of spawning populations of anadromous Arctic char in the Koksoak might have allowed the occurrence of the estuary growth form in salmon. Although Arctic char seem to have been present in substantial numbers in the Koksoak system in past years (Dunbar and Hildebrand 1952), catches of this species in fresh water, upstream from the estuary, are now very incidental and no runs have been reported in recent years. Some catches of Arctic char are reported in the outer part of the Koksoak estuary, but, as the annual harvest for this species is quite low, these fish are believed to come from neighboring rivers which do have spawning runs. Insofar as the migration patterns of immature estuary salmon from fresh to salt water and back (Robitaille et al. 1984a) are so similar to that of the anadromous Arctic char, we believe that the absence of the latter might be somehow related to the presence of the former.

Although sea-growing salmon are by far the most valuable group in the harvest and the most important egg depositors in this river system, there are some indications that mature estuary salmon help stabilize recruitment over the years.

For male smolts, the advantages of an estuary life are a lower age at maturity, a probable higher survival between smolting and first spawning, a shorter reconditioning period and better survival between subsequent spawnings. After a first post-smolt winter in the Koksoak River, some males become mature during the second summer (at estuary age 1+) and spawn the same year.

The earlier maturation of males explains the unbalanced sex-ratio in mixed-growth fish. Stimuli for seaward migration may be already waning for many estuary males nearing maturity at estuary age 1+ and only a small proportion of these fish would take advantage of a second chance to migrate out of the estuary. However, most females are immature at estuary age 1+ and to them it may still be worth migrating to sea.

For those fish which do go out to sea, a year's growth in the estuary results in a larger size at migration and reduces the average duration of sea life by one year, both factors possibly allowing a higher survival than for smolts leaving the estuary for two years at sea. The average number of eggs for a mixed-growth female is equivalent to about 80% of what is produced by a typical 2-sea-year fish in the Koksoak (Robitaille et al. 1984b). However, if comparisons of total eggs produced could be made between two equally sized groups of smolts, one spending two years at sea, the other achieving mixed growth, it seems possible that the drawback of a lower fecundity for mixed-growth females might be partially or totally offset by their higher survival.

Even for female fish which never migrate beyond the estuary, this type of habitat provides a shorter reconditioning period and better survival between spawnings. These fish spawn three times more often than sea-growing salmon during their lifetime, and this may more than compensate for the lower number of eggs spawned each time.

The abundance of estuary salmon in the Koksoak seems to have been higher in recent years (1979–81) than it had been in the early 1960's. However, the evidence for this trend cannot be derived directly from harvest records of estuary fish for several reasons. Whereas the earlier samples (Power 1970) were taken at the Inuit Cooperative in Kuujjuaq, those of 1980 and 1981 were obtained by visiting the fishing camps along the estuary. During these visits, it was noted that the fishermen ate the smaller fish (mostly estuary) and kept the larger, more valuable salmon (mostly sea or mixed-growth maiden fish) for sale at the Cooperative. Another factor is the date of sampling: samples from the 1960's were taken during the peak of the run and thus the number of estuary fish, predominant in the harvest both before and after this peak, may have been underestimated. Finally, over these years there have been changes in the type of fishing gears and in the fishing sites, which are thought to have increased the proportion of estuary fish in the annual harvest. As these objections do not hold for mixed-growth fish, the proportion of these salmon is thought to be a better,

though indirect, indicator of changes in the abundance of estuary fish. The percentage of this category among maiden fish coming back from the sea is reported by Power (1980) to have risen from about 1 to 6% (maximum 9% in 1966) in the 1960's to about 15% in 1979 and 19% in 1980.

The greater occurrence of estuary salmon may have been caused by a lower survival of the larger sea-growing fish or by deteriorating conditions for migrations in and out of the estuary. The latter might be related to a downward trend of sea water temperatures in the Northwest Atlantic ocean since 1960 (Dunbar 1982).

The occurrence of four distinct patterns of pre-reproductive growth (ouananiche, sea, estuary and mixed growth) shows that salmon are quite flexible and can shunt from the typical sea growth in response to environmental constraints to migrations in and out of the river. This plasticity, together with reproductive adaptations to harsh climatic and hydrological conditions, have allowed Koksoak salmon to maintain substantial numbers in this river at the northern limit of the species range.

Acknowledgments

We would like to address our special thanks to Imre Babos who performed most of the scale readings and supervised other readers. We also acknowledge the James Bay Energy Corporation for allowing us to use some data collected for this organization. Dr A. T. Bielak, Dr G. Power and I. McQuinn provided useful comments.

References

BRETON-PROVENCHER, M., AND J. A. ROBITAILLE. 1982. Analyse de la récolte de saumons effectuée par les Inuit de Kuujjuaq en 1980. Rapport de SAGE Ltée présenté au Groupe d'étude conjoint Caniapiscau-Koksoak (SEBJ). 30 p.

CARTER, D. 1978. Tronçon inférieur de la rivière Caniapiscau. Hydrologie, hydraulique, glaces, transport solide. Société d'Energie de la Baie James. 104 p.

DUBOIS, A., AND R. LE JEUNE. 1975. Etude de l'ouananiche de la rivière Caniapiscau (1973–1975). Centre d'études nordiques, Université Laval. 59 p.

DUNBAR, M. J. 1982. Twentieth century marine climatic change in the Northwest Atlantic and subarctic regions. NAFO Sci. Coun. Stud. 5: 8–15.

DUNBAR, M. J., AND H. H. HILDEBRAND. 1952. Contribution to the study of the fishes of Ungava Bay. J. Fish. Res. Board Can. 9: 83–128.

GILLIS, D., AND R. DUMAS. 1982. Koksoak River Fish Study 1981. MS report prepared for Caniapiscau–Koksoak Joint Study Group by Makivik Corporation Research Department. 63 p.

LECLERC, J., AND G. POWER. 1980. Production of brook char and ouananiche in a large rapid, tributary of the Caniapiscau river, northern Quebec. Environ. Biol. Fish. 5(1): 27–32.

LOW, S. P. 1895. Report on exploration in the Labrador Peninsula along East Main, Koksoak, Hamilton and other rivers. Annu. Rep. Geol. Surv. Can. N.S. 8(L): 387 p.

MCLEAN, J. 1849. Twenty-five year's service in the Hudson's Bay territory. London, R. Bentley, 1849, 2 volumes. Champlain Soc., Toronto, Ont. 1932.

OSTERDAHL, L. 1969. The smolt run of a small Swedish river. In: Symposium on salmon and trout in streams. Swed. Salmon Res. Inst. Report LF1, MEDD 8: 205–215.

POWER, G. 1962. A report on the 1961 fishery for Atlantic salmon in Ungava. MS report, approx. date 1962. University of Waterloo, Waterloo, Ont. 20 p.

　　　　1969. The salmon of Ungava Bay. Arctic Inst. North

Am. Tech. Pap. 22: 72 p.

    1970. Studies on the salmon of Ungava. Min. Tourisme, Chasse et Pêche, Québec. Travaux en cours en 1965. 1970: 69−70.

    1976. History of the Hudson's Bay Company salmon fisheries in the Ungava Bay region. Polar Record, 18(113): 151−161.

    1980. A Report on the 1979 Fishery for Atlantic salmon in Ungava. MS report, approx. date 1980. University of Waterloo, Waterloo, Ont. 17 p.

    1981. Stock characteristics and catches of Atlantic salmon (*Salmo salar*) in Quebec, and Newfoundland and Labrador in relation to environmental variables. Can. J. Fish. Aquat. Sci. 38: 1601−1611.

ROBITAILLE, J. A., Y. CÔTÉ, G. OUELLET, R. LE JEUNE, AND G. SHOONER. 1980. Etude des populations de saumons du fleuve Koksoak I. Caractéristiques biologiques et évaluation des effectifs. Rapport conjoint MLCP−SAGE, présenté au Groupe d'étude conjoint Caniapiscau-Koksoak, SEBJ. 84 p.

ROBITAILLE, J. A., I. BABOS, Y. CÔTÉ, M. BRETON-PROVENCHER, G. SHOONER AND G. HAYEUR. 1982. Biologie du saumon dans les eaux du fleuve Koksoak, en Ungava. Rapport conjoint de SAGE Ltée, Gilles Shooner Inc. et du MLCP présenté à Hydro-Québec, Direction Environment. 169 p.

ROBITAILLE, J. A., Y. CÔTÉ, G. SHOONER, AND G. HAYEUR. 1984a. Croissance estuarienne du saumon atlantique (*Salmo salar*) dans le fleuve Koksoak, en Ungava. Rapp. tech. can. sci. halieut. aquat. 1314: vii + 23 p.

ROBITAILLE, J. A., Y. CÔTÉ, G. HAYEUR, AND G. SHOONER. 1984b. Particularités de la reproduction du saumon atlantique (*Salmo salar*) dans une partie du réseau Koksoak, en Ungava. Rapp. tech. can. sci. halieut. aquat. 1313: vii + 33 p.

Independence of Sea Age and River Age in Atlantic Salmon (*Salmo salar*) from Quebec North Shore Rivers

Alex T. Bielak

Atlantic Salmon Federation, Suite 1030, 1435 St-Alexandre, Montreal, Qué H3A 2G4

and Geoffrey Power

Department of Biology, University of Waterloo, Waterloo, Ont. N2L 3G1

Abstract

BIELAK, A. T., AND G. POWER. 1986. Independence of sea age and river age in Atlantic salmon (*Salmo salar*) from Quebec North Shore rivers, p. 70–78. *In* D. J. Meerburg [ed.] Salmonid age at maturity. Can. Spec. Publ. Fish. Aquat. Sci. 89.

Examination of sex, river age, and sea age data for angled Atlantic salmon (*Salmo salar*) from 20 Quebec North Shore rivers provided strong evidence for the independence of sex and river age, and of river age and sea age. Examination of mean smolt age data supported conclusions drawn from R×C tests of independence both accounting and not accounting for year of smolt migration. Future studies should not focus on river age per se as a determinant of sea age.

Résumé

BIELAK, A. T., AND G. POWER. 1986. Independence of sea age and river age in Atlantic salmon (*Salmo salar*) from Quebec North Shore rivers, p. 70–78. *In* D. J. Meerburg [ed.] Salmonid age at maturity. Can. Spec. Publ. Fish. Aquat. Sci. 89.

L'examen de données sur le sexe, sur l'âge-rivière et sur l'âge-mer pour du saumon de l'Atlantique (*Salmo salar*) pêché à la ligne dans 20 rivières de la Côte Nord québécoise a fourni de bonnes raisons de croire à l'indépendance du sexe et de l'âge-rivière d'une part et de l'âge-rivière et de l'âge-mer d'autre part. L'examen des données concernant l'âge moyen des smolts est venu confirmer les conclusions faisant suite à des essais de R×C d'indépendance tenant compte ou ne tenant pas compte des années de migration des smolts. Les études à venir ne devraient pas porter sur l'âge-rivière en soi, comme déterminant de l'âge-mer.

The question of the influence exerted by the freshwater stage of a salmon's life on its age of first return is still largely unresolved. Gardner (1976), in his substantial and thorough review of factors which may influence the sea age and maturation of Atlantic salmon, concluded that no single factor could be identified as regulating maturation and the age at which salmon return to freshwater. Although individual studies had indicated that there was a relationship between fast growth in freshwater and an early return from the sea, other experiments had shown the converse. He concluded, "it is certain there is no causal or universal relationship between growth rate in freshwater (. . .) and the age at eventual return to freshwater."

Subsequent studies have confirmed this conflicting state of affairs. For example, Hansen and Lea (1982), Khalturin (1978), and Chadwick et al. (1978, 1986) report a relationship, while Robitaille et al. (1986), Kazakov (1981), and Fontenelle et al. (1980) find no evidence for any relationship in their investigations. For British sea trout (*Salmo trutta*), Fahy (1978) showed the duration of the parr cycle, and size of smolt, to be independent of the length of returning fish, and to have little influence on the age at spawning. Additionally very few of the studies addressed the potential relationship between sex and river age.

In this study, evidence is presented of the independence of sex and age at smoltification (river age), and of river age and age at first return (sea age) in salmon from twenty Quebec North Shore rivers. The Quebec North Shore is an area where there is a near-absence of human factors likely to affect the results of analyses, or to confuse their interpretation, and where a simple river-entry migration pattern ensures no analytical complications arise with respect to early/late or spring/autumn spawning runs (Bielak 1983, 1984). Schiefer's (1971) hypothesis regarding the influence of the freshwater phase on the occurrence of grilse was taken as the point of departure for a more complete examination of the relationship between river age and sea age.

Materials and Methods

River age and sea age, and thus year of smolt migration, were determined from scale readings of two collections of representative samples of salmon populations from 20 North Shore rivers. All samples prior to 1972 were obtained by Schiefer (1971 and unpublished), the second collection being made by Bielak (1984). Samples were collected almost exclusively from sports fishing camps where guides determined weight and fork length and took scale samples. Information on sex was also obtained for most fish. Sampling was undertaken according to a standardised protocol, and frequent field visits indicated the data were reliable, and the two collections compatible. Scale readings were verified in each instance by G. Power. Previous spawners were excluded from the study. Relationships among sex, river age, and sea age were tested to determine the influence of (1) sex on length of freshwater life and (2) length of freshwater life on age at first return for all the study rivers.

Data Analysis

Three methods of analysis were adopted for every year and sampling period. Even with the substantial data sets

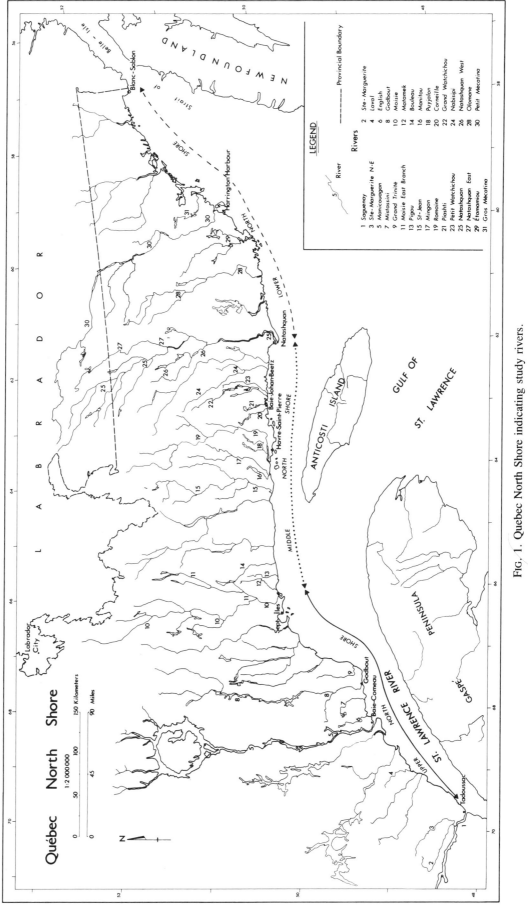

FIG. 1. Quebec North Shore indicating study rivers.

71

TABLE 1. Relationship between sea age, smolt age, and sex of salmon for Quebec North Shore rivers, 1969−83. All pre-1972 samples reworked after Schiefer (1971 and unpublished). All post-1972 samples after this study. M = Male; F = Female; T = Total number. Numbers in parentheses indicate means based on small sample size.

River (Sample period)	Sea age (yr)	2+			3+			4+			5+			6+			Mean smolt age (yr)		
		M	F	T	M	F	T	M	F	T	M	F	T	M	F	T	M	F	T
Ste-Marguerite (1970−71)	1+	3	0	6	43	0	58	12	0	17	0	0	0	0	0	0	(3.2)	—	3.1
	2+	1	1	2	21	45	68	22	43	65	1	4	5	1	0	1	3.6	3.5	3.5
	3+	0	1	1	13	32	46	9	30	39	1	5	6	0	0	0	3.5	3.6	3.5
Ste-Marguerite (1980−82)	1+	6	0	8	42	14	227	20	3	75	0	0	1	—	—	—	3.2	3.2	3.2
	2+	1	1	3	77	94	263	33	45	124	0	1	1	—	—	—	3.3	3.3	3.3
	3+	0	0	0	10	20	92	11	14	38	1	0	1	—	—	—	3.6	3.4	3.3
Ste-Marguerite North-East (1982)	1+	1	0	4	0	0	6	0	0	1	—	—	—	—	—	—	(2.0)	—	2.6
	2+	0	3	3	1	12	14	0	8	8	—	—	—	—	—	—	(3.0)	(3.2)	3.2
	3+	0	1	1	2	3	5	1	1	2	—	—	—	—	—	—	(3.3)	(3.0)	3.1
Laval (1981−83)	2+	—	—	2	—	—	11	—	—	1	—	—	—	—	—	—	—	—	2.9
	3+	—	—	8	—	—	21	—	—	2	—	—	—	—	—	—	—	—	2.8
	4+	—	—	0	—	—	2	—	—	1	—	—	—	—	—	—	—	—	(3.3)
Mistassini (1970−71)	1+	4	1	6	11	3	18	3	0	4	—	—	—	—	—	—	2.9	2.8	2.9
	2+	1	10	11	3	42	46	1	5	6	—	—	—	—	—	—	3.0	2.9	2.9
Godbout (1970−71)	2+	—	—	—	27	23	50	4	14	18	0	1	1	—	—	—	(3.1)	(3.4)	(3.3)
	3+	—	—	—	0	1	1	0	0	0	0	0	0	—	—	—	—	—	—
Godbout (1980-81)	1+	0	0	0	49	1	50	27	0	27	3	0	3	—	—	—	3.4	(3.0)	3.4
	2+	0	1	1	17	37	54	13	21	34	0	0	0	—	—	—	3.4	3.3	3.4
Grand Trinité (1978−82)	1+	95	7	112	807	42	911	177	8	202	7	0	8	—	—	—	3.1	3.0	3.1
	2+	6	21	27	17	73	92	3	17	21	0	1	1	—	—	—	2.9	3.0	3.0
Moisie (1969−71)	1+	1	0	1	11	0	12	16	0	17	2	0	2	—	—	—	3.6	—	3.6
	2+	1	1	2	37	12	68	93	39	160	10	2	15	—	—	—	3.8	3.8	3.8
	3+	1	1	2	65	125	194	150	229	388	9	24	33	—	—	—	3.7	3.7	3.7
Moisie (1980−82)	1+	—	—	0	—	—	3	—	—	1	—	—	0	—	—	—	—	—	(3.3)
	2+	—	—	4	14	12	172	21	15	159	2	1	5	—	—	—	3.7	3.6	3.5
	3+	—	—	8	17	53	287	5	20	107	0	1	1	—	—	—	3.2	3.3	3.3
Matamek (1969−71)	1+	11	1	12	125	11	137	26	0	26	2	0	2	1	0	1	3.1	2.9	3.1
	2+	1	1	2	10	30	40	5	2	7	0	0	0	0	0	0	3.3	3.0	3.1
St-Jean (1970)	1+	—	—	—	1	0	1	1	0	1	0	0	0	0	0	0	(3.5)	—	(3.5)
	2+	—	—	—	3	2	5	13	8	23	27	11	40	2	3	5	4.5	4.6	4.6
	3+	—	—	—	0	0	0	5	4	9	4	1	5	0	0	0	4.4	4.2	4.4
St-Jean (1980−82)	1+	—	—	1	19	0	22	37	1	44	2	0	3	—	—	—	(3.7)	(4.0)	3.7
	2+	—	—	0	25	39	70	69	117	198	8	14	22	—	—	—	3.8	3.9	3.8
	3+	—	—	0	3	2	5	2	2	4	0	0	0	—	—	—	3.4	3.5	3.4
Mingan (1970−71)	1+	—	—	—	10	0	10	4	0	4	0	0	0	0	0	0	3.3	—	3.3
	2+	—	—	—	12	60	72	13	30	43	4	4	8	0	1	1	3.7	3.4	3.5
	3+	—	—	—	1	2	3	0	1	1	0	0	0	0	0	0	(3.0)	(3.3)	(3.3)
Mingan (1980−82)	1+	2	0	2	78	2	80	55	3	58	4	0	4	—	—	—	3.4	3.6	3.4
	2+	0	0	0	22	53	75	19	41	60	3	5	8	—	—	—	3.6	3.5	3.5
Romaine (1970−71)	1+	0	0	0	3	0	3	0	0	0	0	0	0	—	—	—	(3.0)	—	(3.0)
	2+	9	5	14	44	15	59	13	4	17	1	1	2	—	—	—	3.1	3.0	3.1
	3+	1	0	1	3	2	5	4	1	5	0	0	0	—	—	—	(3.4)	(3.3)	3.4
Corneille (1970−71)	1+	6	0	6	35	1	36	4	0	4	—	—	—	—	—	—	3.0	(3.0)	3.0
	2+	2	7	9	42	93	136	0	5	5	—	—	—	—	—	—	3.0	3.0	3.0
Corneille (1980−82)	1+	2	0	2	69	12	81	7	3	10	1	0	1	1	0	1	3.1	3.2	3.1
	2+	2	7	9	55	113	168	2	8	11	0	0	0	0	0	0	3.0	3.0	3.0
Piashti (1983)	1+	3	0	3	5	2	7	—	—	—	—	—	—	—	—	—	(2.6)	—	2.7
	2+	0	2	2	0	6	6	—	—	—	—	—	—	—	—	—	(3.0)	(2.8)	2.8
Grand Watchichou (1981−83)	1+	—	—	—	31	4	102	26	9	90	3	3	22	—	—	—	3.5	3.9	3.6
	2+	—	—	—	26	63	108	43	65	134	13	4	25	—	—	—	3.8	3.6	3.7
Petit Watchichou (1983)	1+	—	—	—	1	0	1	0	0	0	1	0	1	—	—	—	(4.0)	—	(4.0)
	2+	—	—	—	2	5	7	2	1	3	0	0	0	—	—	—	3.5	3.2	3.3

TABLE 1. (*Continued*)

River (Sample period)	Sea age (yr)	2+			3+			4+			5+			6+			Mean smolt age (yr)		
		M	F	T	M	F	T	M	F	T	M	F	T	M	F	T	M	F	T
Nabisipi[a] (1980, 1982)	1+	—	—	—	1	0	1	1	0	1	0	0	0	0	0	0	(3.5)	—	(3.5)
	2+	—	—	—	1	10	11	18	42	60	4	8	12	3	0	3	4.3	4.0	4.1
Natashquan (1980−82)	1+	—	—	—	16	9	96	27	31	278	5	9	69	0	0	0	3.8	4.0	3.9
	2+	—	—	—	5	8	38	17	44	151	3	12	30	1	1	2	4.0	4.1	4.0
Olomane (1972)	1+	0	0	0	0	0	0	1	0	1	0	0	0	0	0	0	—	—	—
	2+	1	0	1	17	14	31	38	30	69	8	5	15	1	0	1	3.9	3.8	3.9
	3+	0	0	0	2	2	4	0	0	0	0	0	0	0	0	0	(3.0)	(3.0)	(3.0)
Olomane (1980−82)	1+	0	0	0	14	0	14	8	2	10	1	0	1	—	—	—	3.4	(4.0)	3.5
	2+	0	1	1	31	46	78	27	40	70	1	0	1	—	—	—	3.5	3.5	3.5
Etamamiou (1980-82)	1+	2	0	2	167	32	207	253	83	323	19	4	23	1	2	3	3.6	3.8	3.7
	2+	0	0	0	8	47	55	17	90	108	2	6	8	0	0	0	3.8	3.7	3.7
Gros Mecatina (1980−82)	1+	—	—	—	48	67	175	20	39	123	1	1	5	—	—	—	3.3	3.4	3.4
	2+	—	—	—	1	8	17	2	3	7	0	0	1	—	—	—	(3.7)	3.3	3.4

[a]Sample from commercial net near mouth of river

TABLE 2. Smolt age distribution by sex for grilse, Natashquan River, 1980−82.

Smolt age (yr)	Sea age 1+	
	Males	Females
3+	16	9
4+	27	31
5+	5	9

G-Williams for total set = 3.3131.
$\chi^2_{0.05(2)} = 5.991$; $P = 0.19$.

TABLE 3. Smolt age distribution by sex for 2+ salmon, Natashquan River, 1980−82.

Smolt age (yr)	Sea age 2+	
	Males	Females
3+	5	8
4+	17	44
5+	3	12
6+	(1)	(1)

G-Williams = 1.1177 (not including 6+ group).
$\chi^2_{0.05(2)} = 5.991$; $P = 0.57$.

TABLE 4. Smolt age distribution by sea age, Natashquan River, 1980−82.

Smolt age (yr)	Sea age (yr)	
	1+	2+
3+	96	38
4+	278	151
5+	69	30
6+	(0)	(2)

G-Williams = 2.2963 (non including 6+ group).
$\chi^2_{0.05(2)} = 5.991$; $P = 0.27$.

involved, the preferred analysis could not always be applied because of small numbers of fish in some of the test categories.

First, mean smolt ages were compared for each sea age-class. Statistical tests were not applied at this stage given the inherent problems of dealing with a discrete variable such as smolt age. Rather it was hoped that trends and patterns revealed in the complete data set would provide support for possible conclusions derived from other analyses.

Second, where the data allowed, the R×C test of independence (including tests of all subsets) was carried out between sexes for each sea age-class and among sea age-classes without attempting to account for smolt-year, i.e., the data for all the years in a sample period were analysed together. Only the major age-classes prevalent in each river and sample were considered, and Williams correction to estimates of *G* was applied to account for small sample sizes in some years (Sokal and Rohlf 1981). The level of significance was chosen at the 5% probability.

The third, and preferred, analysis used the *G*-test as previously described, but it took into account the year of smolt migration by creating layers of two-way contingency tables of sex and river age, and/or river age and sea age. A similar approach using the chi-square test was used by Fontenelle et al. (1980) in the analysis of salmon data from Brittany and lower-Normandy.

Results

The sheer volume of test results precluded the inclusion of all here. However, a type example where all three analyses could be carried out for a single river and sampling period is given below.

Analysis of Results for Natashquan River Samples, 1980−82.

First analysis — mean smolt ages: Although male smolt

TABLE 5. Smolt age distribution by sex, for grilse and 2+ salmon, Natashquan River for smolt years 1978–81. (m = male, f = female, GW = G-Williams).

Smolt year	Sea age	Brood year 1974 m/f	1975 m/f	1976 m/f	1977 m/f	1978 m/f
1978	1+					
	2+	2/5	3/5			
1979	1+					
	2+	3/3	8/10	1/1} GW = 0.0586		
1980	1+		1/8	9/31	3/9} GW = 0.7145	
	2+	(1/1)	0/9	7/29	1/2} GW = 2.8150	
1981	1+		0/0	4/1	18/0	13/0

$\chi^2_{0.05(2)} = 5.991$.

TABLE 6. Smolt age distribution by sea age, Natashquan River for smolt years 1978–81. (GW = G-Williams).

Smolt year	Sea age	Brood year 1974	1975	1976	1977	1978
1978	1+					
	2+	11	10			
1979	1+	2	18	6} GW = 1.7681		
	2+	6	22	2}		
1980	1+	(0)	11	54	15} GW = 0.4100	
	2+	(2)	24	118	26}	
1981	1+		0	56	206	75
	2+					

$\chi^2_{0.05(2)} = 5.991$.

age (Table 1) for both grilse and salmon is lower than female smolt age, the differences are minimal, as are those between 1+ and 2+ sea age-classes.

Second analysis — (a) differences between males and females: Grilse: G-Williams is not significant at the 5% level (Table 2) and the null hypothesis that river age is independent of sex cannot therefore be rejected. Two sea-year salmon: The question arises whether or not to include infrequently occurring age-classes in the analyses. They have been excluded in most cases because their inclusion in the tests may have a disproportionate effect on the results of the analysis. In any case, their rare appearance in the samples indicates their minor biological importance. As an example, results obtained by including and excluding the rare 6+ smolt group (2 fish out of 664 = 0.3%) in the analyses of the Natashquan River sample are: where 6+ smolts are included, $\chi^2_{0.05(2)} = 5.991$. Therefore, we cannot reject the null hypothesis that river age is independent of sex for 2+ salmon ($P = 0.57$) (Table 3). Where all smolt ages are included $\chi^2_{0.05(3)} = 7.815$. The same conclusion is reached ($P = 0.70$).

Second analysis — (b) differences between 1+ and 2+ salmon: for all age-classes (Table 4): Excluding 6+ smolts, we cannot reject the null hypothesis that sea age is independent of river age ($P = 0.27$). If 6+ smolts are included in the analysis, the same conclusion is reached ($P = 0.10$).

Third analysis — (a) differences between males and females by year of smolt migration: In the three cells tested (Table 5), and excluding 6+ smolts, the null hypothesis that age at smolt migration is independent of sex cannot be rejected ($P = 0.97$, 0.7, and 0.2, respectively). When 6+ smolts are included in the analysis for the 1980 smolt year, $\chi^2_{0.05(3)} = 7.815$ and the null hypothesis is also not rejected ($P = 0.27$).

Third analysis — (b) differences between sea ages accounting for smolt year: Exclusion of 6+ smolts for the 1979 and 1980 smolt years (Table 6) does not allow rejection of the null hypothesis that sea age is independent of river age ($P = 0.13$ and 0.81, respectively). In 1980, if 6+ smolts are included in the analysis the null hypothesis is still accepted, with a highly non-significant probability ($P = 0.62$).

Summary of analyses of Natashquan River data, 1980–82: Results of G-test analyses indicate that river age is independent of sex, and that river age does not have an effect on sea age. Inspection of smolt ages supports these conclusions. In essence, for the Natashquan River samples obtained between 1980 and 1982, proportions of salmon and grilse are the same whatever the age at smolt migration.

Analysis of Mean Smolt Age Data

Mean smolt ages are shown by sex for each river and sample period, as well as number of fish of each smolt age and sex sampled (Table 1). Since not all fish were sexed, totals may differ from the sums of numbers of males and females. That table includes Schiefer's (1971) original data, together with some supplementary samples, and this mixture accounts for most of the discrepancies between his original values and the reworked ones in Table 1. The results suggest that minor differences in mean smolt age between males and females are not consistent within or

74

TABLE 7. Results of R × C G-tests for independence of river age and sex using total samples.

River	Sampling period	Sea age of males and females tested	Probability
Not significant at the 5% level			
Corneille	70/71	2+	0.17
	80-82	1+	0.47
	80-82	2+	0.58
Etamamiou	80-82	2+	0.79
Godbout	70/71	2+	0.07
	81/82	2+	0.62
Olomane	1972	2+	0.92
	80-82	2+	0.87
Gros Mecatina	80-82	1+	0.61
	80-82	2+	0.26
Matamek	69-71	1+	0.17
	69-71	2+	0.09
Mingan	70/71	2+	0.07
	80-82	1+	0.75
	80-82	2+	0.88
Mistassini	70/71	1+	0.60
	70/71	2+	0.79
Moisie	69-71	2+	0.68
	69-71	3+	0.40
	80-82	2+	0.89
	80-82	3+	0.77
Natashquan	80-82	1+	0.19
	80-82	2+	0.57
Petit Watchichou	1983	2+	0.67
Romaine	70/71	2+	0.80
	70/71	3+	0.67
St-Jean	1970	2+	0.59
	1970	3+	0.74
	80-82	2+	0.96
	80-82	3+	0.71
Ste-Marguerite	70/71	2+	0.89
	70/71	3+	0.81
	80-82	1+	0.14
	80-82	2+	0.78
	80-82	3+	0.37
Trinité	78-82	1+	0.72
	78-82	2+	0.89
Grand Watchichou	81-83	1+	0.10
Significant at the 5% level			
Etamamiou	80-82	1+	0.02
Nabisipi	80/82	2+	0.03
Grand Watchichou	81-83	2+	0.001

TABLE 8. Results of R × C G-tests for independence of river age and sex by smolt year.

River	Smolt year	Sea age of males and females tested	Probability
Not significant at the 5% level			
Etamamiou	1978	2+	0.31
	1979	1+	0.61
	1979	2+	0.63
	1980	1+	0.05
	1980	2+	0.56
Gros Mecatina	1979	1+	0.25
Mingan	1978	2+	0.46
	1979	2+	0.56
	1980	1+	0.95
	1980	2+	0.50
Moisie	1967	2+	0.85
	1967	3+	0.35
	1968	2+	0.33
Natashquan	1979	2+	0.97
	1980	1+	0.70
	1980	2+	0.27
Ste-Marguerite	1967	3+	0.80
	1968	2+	0.28
	1968	3+	0.88
	1969	2+	0.57
	1977	3+	0.38
	1978	2+	0.64
	1979	1+	0.60
	1980	2+	0.68
	1981	1+	0.25
Trinité	1977	1+	0.96
	1978	1+	0.73
	1978	2+	0.73
	1979	1+	0.62
	1980	1+	0.73
	1980	2+	0.18
Grand Watchichou	1981	1+	0.15
	1981	2+	0.05
	1982	2+	0.88
Significant at the 5% level			
Moisie	1966	3+	0.006
Ste-Marguerite	1979	3+	0.03
Grand Watchichou	1980	2+	0.03

between any age-class. Of the total comparisons between sexes, 7 mean smolt ages are equal, 18 show males slightly older than females and 13 females slightly older than males. In general, there are no noticeable differences, irrespective of sex, between sea ages. In fact, the uniformity within most river samples is remarkable.

Analysis of R×C G-Tests; Differences Between Sexes

Results of tests of independence of river age and sex for the total data sets (Table 7) can be contrasted with the results of tests for the same relationship whilst accounting for smolt year (Table 8). Probability values are shown in each instance; they clearly show that, in 92% of the cases, sex has

no influence on the number of years a salmon spends in freshwater, regardless of the test used. All the common sea age classes (1+ — 21, 2+ — 40, and 3+ — 11) are well represented in the non-significant results (Tables 7 and 8).

Even in the six cases where the tests were significant at the 5% level, probability values are generally marginal. In contrast, most non-significant results are highly so. Given the large number of tests made ($n = 78$) one may expect that four wrong classifications might occur by chance alone. The sheer number of independent data sets revealing the same trend, when considered together, minimizes the probability of existence of any relationship between river age and sex.

Analysis of R×C G-Tests; Differences Between Sea Ages

Results of tests of independence of sea age and river age, accounting and not accounting for smolt-year, respectively,

TABLE 9. Results of R × C G-tests for independence of sea age and river age using total samples.

River	Sampling period	Sea ages tested	Probability
Not significant at the 5% level			
Corneille	70/71	1+ vs 2+	0.12
	80-82	1+ vs 2+	0.22
Etamamiou	80-82	1+ vs 2+	0.46
Godbout	81/82	1+ vs 2+	0.75
Olomane	80-82	1+ vs 2+	0.52
Gros Mecatina	80-82	1+ vs 2+	0.44
Laval	81-83	1+ vs 2+ vs 3+	0.61
Matamek	69-71	1+ vs 2+	0.76
Mingan	70/71	1+ vs 2+ vs 3+	0.66
	80-82	1+ vs 2+	0.27
Mistassini	70/71	1+ vs 2+	0.70
Moisie	69-71	1+ vs 2+ vs 3+	0.66
Natashquan	80-82	1+ vs 2+	0.27
Piashti	1983	1+ vs 2+	0.77
Romaine	70/71	2+ vs 3+	0.39
St-Jean	1970	2+ vs 3+	0.10
	80-82	1+ vs 2+ vs 3+	0.20
Ste-Marguerite	80-82	1+ vs 2+ vs 3+	0.09
Ste-Marguerite (N.E.)	1982	1+ vs 2+ vs 3+	0.42
Grand Watchichou	81-83	1+ vs 2+	0.20
Significant at the 5% level			
Moisie	80-82	2+ vs 3+	<0.001
Ste-Marguerite	70/71	1+ vs 2+ vs 3+	<0.001
Trinité		1+ vs 2+	0.01

appear in Tables 9 and 10. The great majority (86%) of tests were highly non-significant at the 5% level leading to the conclusion that age at first return of North Shore salmon is independent of the number of years spent in freshwater. (For the purposes of this analysis generalized independence of sex and river age was assumed.) Again, most of the eight significant results are only marginally so. Where significance levels are high, this can be explained by the prominence of a particular river age in one sea age-class; tests of subsets excluding that river age are highly non-significant.

The ratios of significant to non-significant results for both R×C procedures are statistically the same, which in itself, provides further evidence for the lack of effect of river age on sea age. If such an effect existed, but had been masked by the lumping of several years' data, one would have expected the ratios to differ.

Discussion

It is clear from the results presented here that, for Quebec North Shore salmon stocks, no relationship can be determined between (1) sex and river age and (2) river age and sea age. The few instances where a significant relationship appears may either be due to chance or perhaps to peculiar local circumstances (Bielak 1984). The fact that changes in mean smolt age have occurred since Schiefer's (1971) study (Bielak and Power 1985) does not seem to be important, since the lack of any relationships is also evident in the earlier samples. In fact, if there were a relationship between river age and sea age, decreased smolt age should entail concomitant increases in the proportions of younger sea age-classes, and especially of grilse. Analysis of historical records (Bielak 1984) does not support such a conclusion as regards the proportions of North Shore grilse.

It seems, therefore, that Schiefer's (1971) hypothesis relating the occurrence of grilse to juvenile growth rate in freshwater does not hold. Central to his theory was the idea that fast-growing male parr became precociously mature, and subsequently returned after spending a minimal time at sea (i.e., 1 yr). Recent studies (Dalley et al. 1983; Myers 1984) describe the substantial reduction in overwinter survival of precocious parr. The conclusion of Dalley et al. (1983) is that in insular Newfoundland "too few precocious parr migrate as smolt to contribute to the grilse population." In view of (1) the heavy investment by precocious North Shore parr in gonadal tissue (up to 20% by weight — pers obs.) and (2) severe and prolonged North Shore winters, examination of smolt runs of various North Shore rivers would probably confirm their conclusion.

The contradictory results of previous studies on the nature of any relationship between smolt age and age at first return may be due to a variety of potentially confusing elements which are generally absent in North Shore rivers. These may include the presence of unsampled early or late spawning runs or the effects of using hatchery reared fish. For instance, Fontenelle et al. (1980) strongly suspected the existence of a late run of fish, but due to local fishing season constraints were unable to sample it. Similarly, the survival of precocious parr in fish hatcheries (Saunders et al. 1982; Thorpe and Morgan (1980) could severely bias the results of investigations in some areas but not others, depending on the survivorship of such individuals in nature.

Various factors may act to modify age at first return; Ricker (1972, for Pacific salmon), Schaffer and Elson

TABLE 10. Results of R × C G-tests for independence of sea age and river age by smolt year.

River	Smolt year	Sea ages tested	Probability
Not significant at the 5% level			
Corneille	1979	1+ vs 2+	0.65
Etamamiou	1980	1+ vs 2+	0.94
Godbout	1980	1+ vs 2+	0.35
Olomane	1980	1+ vs 2+	0.63
Gros Mecatina	1979	1+ vs 2+	0.40
	1980	1+ vs 2+	0.67
Laval	1980	2+ vs 3+	0.92
Matamek	1968	1+ vs 2+	0.66
Mingan	1969	1+ vs 2+	0.53
	1979	1+ vs 2+	0.46
Mistassini	1969	1+ vs 2+	0.93
Moisie	1967	2+ vs 3+	0.91
	1968	1+ vs 2+ vs 3+	0.38
	1979	2+ vs 3+	0.09
Natashquan	1979	1+ vs 2+	0.13
	1980	1+ vs 2+	0.81
Romaine	1968	2+ vs 3+	0.86
St-Jean	1978	2+ vs 3+	0.84
	1979	1+ vs 2+	0.41
	1980	1+ vs 2+	0.13
Ste-Marguerite	1968	2+ vs 3+	0.55
	1969	1+ vs 2+	0.15
	1979	1+ vs 2+ vs 3+	0.59
	1980	1+ vs 2+	0.11
Trinité	1977	1+ vs 2+	0.05
	1978	1+ vs 2+	0.31
	1979	1+ vs 2+	0.36
	1980	1+ vs 2+	0.14
Grand Watchichou	1980	1+ vs 2+	0.25
	1981	1+ vs 2+	0.64
Significant at the 5% level			
Corneille	1980	1+ vs 2+	0.01
Etamamiou	1979	1+ vs 2+	0.02
Mingan	1980	1+ vs 2+	0.04
Moisie	1978	2+ vs 3+	<0.001
Ste-Marguerite	1978	2+ vs 3+	0.01

(1975), and Gardner (1976) have comprehensively discussed the possibility of both environmental and genetic control of age at first maturity. The results of this study strongly suggest that, for the North Shore at least, growth in freshwater (and thus freshwater environment) does not dictate age at first return to a major extent, although in certain isolated instances, there may be a correlation between smolt age and sea age. Although the possibility that marine environment plays a role in determining age at first return cannot be discounted (see Saunders et al. 1983), a number of recent publications underline the importance of genetic factors in this respect (e.g., Thorpe and Morgan 1978; Bailey et al. 1980a,b; Glebe et al. 1980). However, none of these studies should be considered in isolation, since no one of them can provide a clear explanation to the phenomenon.

The results of our study lend support to the conclusion of Naedval et al.(1978) that "the variation in age at first maturity of Atlantic salmon is largely attributed to a genetic base, probably originating as an adaptation to different river conditions (but that) environment may have some influence on age at which salmon first mature, since fish of the same river origin, reared under different environmental conditions, give similar but not identical results." We suggest that the focus of future investigations shift from river age per se as an important regulator of age at first return. Integrated studies of genetic factors, effects of freshwater and marine environments on growth rates, and of the interactions between them, are more likely to contribute to our understanding of how age at first maturity is controlled.

Acknowledgments

This work was supported by grants from the Atlantic Salmon Association and Woods Hole Oceanographic Institution and a NATO studentship to A.T.B. We thank E. M. P. Chadwick and R. E. Cutting whose suggestions improved the manuscript; K. Schiefer and the Québec Ministère du Loisir, de la Chasse et de la Pêche for the use of unpublished data.

References

BAILEY, J. K., M. I. BUZETA, AND R. L. SAUNDERS. 1980a. Returns of three year-classes of sea ranched Atlantic salmon of various river strains and their hybrids. I.C.E.S. CM 1980/M:9, Anad. Cat. Committee. 10 p.

BAILEY, J. K., R. L. SAUNDERS, AND M. I. BUZETA. 1980b. Influence of parental smolt age and sea age on growth and smolting of hatchery-reared Atlantic salmon (*Salmo salar*). Can. J. Fish. Aquat. Sci. 37: 1379–1386.

BIELAK, A. T. 1983. Salmon studies on the Quebec North Shore. 1982 Northeast Atlantic Salmon Workshop, Moncton, N.B. Atlantic Salmon Federation Special Publications Series 11: 54–55.

 1984. Quebec North Shore Atlantic salmon stocks. Ph.D. dissertation, University of Waterloo, Waterloo, Ont. 235 p.

BIELAK, A. T., AND G. POWER. 1985. Changes in mean smolt age of Atlantic salmon in Quebec North Shore rivers. Naturaliste Can. 112(4).

CHADWICK, E. M. P., T. R. PORTER, AND P. DOWNTON. 1978. Analysis of growth of Atlantic salmon (*Salmo salar*) in a small Newfoundland river. J. Fish. Res. Board Can. 35: 60–68.

CHADWICK, E. M. P., R. G. RANDALL, AND C. LÉGER. 1986. Ovarian development of Atlantic salmon (*Salmo salar*) smolts and age at first maturity, p. 15–28. *In* D. J. Meerburg [ed.] Salmonid age at maturity. Can. Spec. Publ. Fish. Aquat. Sci. 89.

DALLEY, E. L., C. W. ANDREWS, AND J. M. GREEN. 1983. Precocious male Atlantic salmon parr (*Salmo salar*) in insular Newfoundland. Can. J. Fish. Aquat. Sci. 40: 647–652.

FAHY, E. 1978. Variation in some biological characteristics of British sea trout, *Salmo trutta* L. J. Fish. Biol. 13: 123–138.

FONTENELLE, G., G. DOUAIRE, J. L. BAGLINIÈRE, P. PROUZET, AND Y. HARACHE. 1980. Atlantic salmon (*Salmo salar* L.) in Brittany and Lower-Normandy: Preliminary observations on the general characteristics of adults. Fish. Mgmt. 11: 87–100.

GARDNER, M. L. G. 1976. A review of factors which may influence the sea-age and maturation of Atlantic salmon (*Salmo salar* L.). J. Fish. Biol. 9: 289–327.

GLEBE, B. D., W. EDDY, AND R. L. SAUNDERS. 1980. The influence of parental age at maturity and rearing practice on precocious maturation of hatchery-reared Atlantic salmon parr. I.C.E.S. CM 1980/F:8 Mariculture Committee. 5 p.

HANSEN, L. P., AND T. B. LEA. 1982. Tagging and release of Atlantic salmon smolts (*Salmo salar* L.) in the River Rana, Northern Norway. Rep. Inst. Freshw. Res., Drottningholm. 60: 31–38.

KAZAKOV, R. V. 1981. Relation between sizes of adult Atlantic salmon (*Salmo salar* L.) and duration of river and sea-life periods. Aquaculture 24: 327−340.

KHALTURIN, D. K. 1978. Smolt age and the duration of the marine period in the life of anadromous salmonids (Salmonidae). J. Ichthyol. 18(6): 871−885.

MYERS, R. A. 1984. The role of precocious maturation in the demography of Atlantic salmon (*Salmo salar*). Can. J. Fish. Aquat. Sci. 41: 1349−1353.

NAEDVAL, G., M. HOLM, O. INGEBRIGTSEN, AND D. MØLLER. 1978. Variation in age at first spawning in Atlantic salmon (*Salmo salar*). J. Fish. Res. Board Can. 35: 145−147.

RICKER, W. E. 1972. Hereditary and environmental factors affecting certain salmonid populations, p. 19−160. *In* R. C. Simon and P. A. Larkin [ed.] The Stock Concept in Pacific Salmon. H. R. MacMillan Lectures in Fisheries. University of British Columbia.

ROBITAILLE, J. A., Y. CÔTÉ, G. SHOONER, AND G. HAYEUR. 1986. Growth and maturation patterns of Atlantic salmon, *Salmo salar*, in the Koksoak River, Ungava, Quebec, p. 62−69. *In* D. J. Meerburg [ed.] Salmonid age at maturity. Can. Spec. Publ. Fish. Aquat. Sci. 89.

SAUNDERS, R. L., E. B. HENDERSON, AND B. D. GLEBE. 1982. Precocious sexual maturation and smoltification in male Atlantic salmon (*Salmo salar*). Aquaculture 28: 211−229.

SAUNDERS, R. L., E. B. HENDERSON, B. D. GLEBE, AND E. J. LOUDENSLAGER. 1983. Evidence of a major environmental component in determination of the grilse: larger salmon ratio in Atlantic salmon (*Salmo salar*). Aquaculture 33: 107−118.

SCHAFFER, W. M., AND P. F. ELSON. 1975. The adaptive significance of variations in life history among local populations of Atlantic salmon in North America. Ecology 56: 577−590.

SCHIEFER, K. 1971. Ecology of Atlantic salmon, with special reference to occurrence and abundance of grilse, in North Shore Gulf of St. Lawrence rivers. Ph.D. dissertation, University of Waterloo, Waterloo, Ont. 129 p.

SOKAL, R. R. AND F. J. ROHLF. 1981. Biometry, 2nd ed. Publ. W. H. Freeman and Co., CA. 859 p.

THORPE, J. E., AND R. I. G. MORGAN. 1978. Parental influence on growth rate, smolting rate and survival in hatchery-reared juvenile Atlantic salmon (*Salmo salar*). J. Fish. Biol. 13: 549−556.

1980. Growth-rate and smolting-rate of progeny of male Atlantic salmon parr (*Salmo salar* L.). J. Fish. Biol. 17: 451−459.

Age at First Maturity of Atlantic Salmon (*Salmo salar*) — Influences of the Marine Environment

J. B. Dempson, R. A. Myers, and D. G. Reddin[1]

Department of Fisheries and Oceans, Fisheries Research Branch, P. O. Box 5667, St. John's, Nfld. A1C 5X1

Abstract

DEMPSON, J. B., R. A. MYERS, AND D. G. REDDIN. 1986. Age at first maturity of Atlantic salmon (*Salmo salar*) — influences of the marine environment, p. 79–89. *In* D. J. Meerburg [ed.] Salmonid age at maturity. Can. Spec. Publ. Fish. Aquat. Sci. 89.

This paper examines several aspects of influences of the marine environment on the sea age at maturity of Atlantic salmon (*Salmo salar*), recognizing three possible types of variation. (1) Variation among populations (geographic variation) was examined from grilse:MSW salmon records, sea growth rates, and sea temperature data. Analyses of several historical catch records provided no consistent evidence for a temporal change in grilse:MSW salmon ratios. There was no evidence for a link between post-grilse growth rate and sea age at maturity in North American rivers. In addition, we found no evidence that ocean temperature influences sea age at maturity in North American salmon stocks. (2) Within-population variation among smolt classes was examined by testing the hypothesis that sea temperature affects the grilse:MSW salmon ratio between cohorts using a time series model. Data from Moisie and Matapedia rivers, Quebec, and sea surface temperatures from Boothbay Harbour, Maine; St. Andrews, New Brunswick; and Grimsey Island, Iceland, showed no detectable effect on grilse:MSW salmon ratios. Similarly we found no evidence that heavy ice concentrations affected sea age at maturity through a change in distribution and subsequent delay in migration. (3) Within-population variation within smolt classes was examined using circuli counts during the first year of sea life as an index of ocean growth to test the hypothesis that sea growth rate influences sea age at maturity. Information from the literature indicated contradictory results between sea-cage and wild salmon studies. In sea-cage studies, faster-growing fish have a greater tendency to mature earliest. For samples of salmon from Miramichi River, New Brunswick, 1971–80, and Sand Hill River, Labrador, 1974, there were no consistent significant differences in growth rates of grilse and 2SW salmon within a smolt class even when separated by sex. Different marine migration routes for grilse and multi-sea-winter salmon may have caused the contradictory results observed between sea-caged and wild studies.

Résumé

DEMPSON, J. B., R. A. MYERS, AND D. G. REDDIN. 1986. Age at first maturity of Atlantic salmon (*Salmo salar*) — influences of the marine environment, p. 79–89. *In* D. J. Meerburg [ed.] Salmonid age at maturity. Can. Spec. Publ. Fish. Aquat. Sci. 89.

Les auteurs examinent plusieurs aspects des influences du milieu marin sur l'âge du saumon de l'Atlantique (*Salmo salar*) mature à son arrivée en mer et reconnaissent trois types possibles de variations. (1) La variation parmi les populations (variation géographique) a été examinée à partir de relevés de madeleineaux:saumons polybermarins, de vitesses de croissance en mer et de données concernant la température de la mer. Les analyses de plusieurs relevés de prises historiques n'ont fourni aucune preuve systématique pour un changement temporel dans les rapports madeleineaux:saumons polybermarins. Les auteurs n'ont trouvé aucune corrélation entre la vitesse de croissance après le stade de madeleineau et le temps d'arrivée à maturité dans les cours d'eau d'Amérique du Nord. En outre, les auteurs n'ont trouvé aucune preuve que la température de l'océan pouvait influencer l'âge du madeleineau à son arrivée en mer dans les peuplements de saumons nord-américains. (2) La variation dans la population parmi les classes de smolts a été examinée par l'essai de l'hypothèse voulant que la température de la mer influe sur le rapport madeleineau:saumons polybermarins entre les cohortes en faisant appel à un modèle de séries chronologiques. Les données provenant des rivières Moisie et Matapédia (Québec) et les températures à la surface de la mer prises à Boothbay Harbour (Maine), à St. Andrews (Nouveau-Brunswick) et dans l'île Grimsey (Islande) n'ont révélé aucun effet décelable sur les rapports madeleineaux:saumons polybermarins. Dans un même temps, les auteurs n'ont trouvé aucune preuve que de fortes concentrations de glace pouvaient influer sur le temps d'arrivée à maturité en suscitant un changement dans la répartition et un retard subséquent dans la migration. (3) La variation dans la population à l'intérieur des classes de smolts a été examinée au moyen de dénombrements d'anneaux de croissance au cours de la première année de vie en mer à titre d'indices de croissance en mer pour vérifier l'hypothèse voulant que la vitesse de croissance en mer influe sur le temps d'arrivée à maturité. Les informations tirées de la documentation ont donné des résultats contradictoires entre les études sur le saumon en cage marine et celles sur le saumon à l'état sauvage. Dans les études sur le saumon en cage, les poissons à croissance plus rapide ont une tendance plus forte à atteindre la maturité les premiers. Pour certains échantillons de saumons pris dans la rivière Miramichi (Nouveau-Brunswick) de 1971 à 1980 et dans la rivière Sand Hill (Labrador) en 1974, il n'existait aucune différence significative et systématique dans les vitesses de croissance du madeleineau et du saumon dibermarin à l'intérieur d'une classe de smolts même lorsque les poissons ont été séparés par sexe. Différentes routes de migration marine pour le madeleineau et le saumon polybermarin pourraient avoir donné ces résultats contradictoires observés entre les études sur les poissons en cage marine et les poissons sauvages ainsi que l'absence de résultats cohérents dans la présente étude.

Introduction

The purpose of this paper is to examine several aspects of marine influences on sea age at first maturity of Atlantic salmon (*Salmo salar*). An understanding of factors influencing maturation has practical applications for the management of the Atlantic salmon resource. The ratio of grilse (maturing after one winter at sea — 1SW) to multi-sea-

---

[1] Authorship in alphabetical order.

winter (MSW) salmon show variations both within stocks (Elson 1974) and among stocks (Berg 1964; Power 1981; Thorpe and Mitchell 1981). Although some of this variation can be attributed to differing age at first maturity (Gardner 1976), errors in catch records and annual variations in fishing and natural mortality may also contribute to observed differences in maturity ratios.

Considerable information exists on the influence of environmental and genetic factors on age at first maturity of Atlantic salmon (White and Huntsman 1938; Elson 1973; Piggins 1973; Gardner 1976; Naevdal 1983; Gjerde 1984). Few studies, however, have specifically addressed the effect of the marine environment. Consequently, knowledge of the influence of the marine environment on age at first maturity of Atlantic salmon is often speculative, rather than based on information we do know with certainty. In this paper we shall discuss how the marine environment influences both geographical variation in sea age at first maturity, and temporal variation within populations. Also, we examine data to determine if there is a relationship between growth in the marine environment and sea age at maturity.

There are three types of covariation between sex-specific age at maturation and marine environmental factors:

1) Variation among populations (geographic variation);
2) Variation among smolt classes in the same population;
3) Variation within a smolt class in the same population.

The evolutionary and physiological processes determining age at maturity of Atlantic salmon may be affected differently by the environment in these three cases and each was treated separately where possible. The term smolt class was used here to refer to those salmon that smoltified in the same year. The life history terminology we used was that of Allen and Ritter (1977). The effects of age and weight of smolts on age at first maturity were also considered in light of their potential importance as suggested by Ritter (1972). Where possible, data were treated separately by sex because of demonstrated variations due to precocity (Dalley et al. 1983; Myers 1984) and differences in adult size (Chadwick 1982).

1. Geographic Variation

The Data for Grilse and Salmon

There are two difficulties with interpreting data presently available on the geographic distribution of sea age at maturity of Atlantic salmon: (i) size-selective fishing mortality alters the apparent distributions of sea age at maturity of stocks measured in rivers, and (ii) the present sea ages at maturity may represent an evolutionary response to fishing pressure and may not be representative of the primordial condition. The first difficulty can be partially mitigated by using records collected before 1965 when the West Greenland fishery began on a large scale. The West Greenland fishery harvests only fish destined to return as MSW salmon. In some rivers, such as the Miramichi in New Brunswick, more complete records are available after the commercial estuarine and river fisheries ended with the 1971 fishery. Nevertheless, only broad geographic patterns can be recognized with the data at hand.

The more serious difficulty is the possible evolutionary response due to fishing pressure. We examine three types of data to detect possible changes in the grilse:MSW salmon composition of stocks: (i) quantitative historical records on

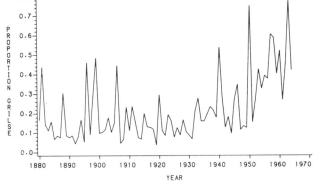

FIG. 1. Ratio of the catch of grilse in year t to the catch of MSW salmon in year $t + 1$ (less the proportion of salmon in year $t + 1$ that weight over 25 lb) from the Restigouche Angling Club.

the ratio of grilse to MSW salmon; (ii) anecdotal historical evidence; and (iii) a spectral analysis of historical catch records from which age at maturity may be inferred.

There are catch records from the 1880–1965 period on the numbers of grilse, MSW salmon, and salmon over 25 pounds from the Restigouche Angling Club on the Matapedia tributary of the Restigouche River in Quebec. Assuming that the angling catch adequately reflects the size composition of fish returning to the river, the data show an apparent increasing trend in the grilse:salmon ratio after the 1930s, but no evidence of this trend before 1930 (Fig. 1). This latter change could be a demographic response to changing fishing patterns; for example, the salmon drift-net fishery at Port aux Basques, Newfoundland, began in the early 1930s (Taylor 1985).

Taylor (1985) has collected and analyzed the available historical records of the salmon fishery in Newfoundland which show substantial exports of salmon from the early 18th century until the present. In the early 1870s a system of river wardens was put into place in Newfoundland. The evidence from their reports, recorded in the *Journals of the Newfoundland House of Assembly*, provided the first estimates of the size of individual salmon on a river-by-river basis. The average weight of a salmon estimated by these wardens between 1871 and 1875 were: Garnish River — 5 lb, Salmonier River — 3 lb, Grandy's Brook — 10 lb, Conne River — 3 lb, Gander River — 5 to 10 lb, Freshwater Bay rivers — 2.5 lb. The reliability of these data is unknown although more current information shows that the approximate mean weights for 1SW and 2SW salmon are 3.8 and 8.8 lb, respectively (data from Sand Hill River, Labrador; Anderson 1985). This would indicate that salmon stocks, at least in some rivers in Newfoundland, were dominated by grilse over 100 years ago. Most rivers in Newfoundland continue to be dominated by 1SW salmon today (Moores et al. 1978).

If this anecdotal evidence is accurate, and no drastic changes have occurred in grilse:MSW salmon ratios, then the life-cycle of the Atlantic salmon in Newfoundland should have been the same 100 years ago as it is today. This hypothesis can be tested by a spectral analysis of the yearly exports of salmon — even though records were not kept on the ages or weights of individual fish. Spectral analysis is used to transform a time series of data, e.g. exports of salmon per year, into its frequency components (Jenkins and Watts 1968). The amplitude to these frequency components, when squared, yields the spectrum of the time series. The

TABLE 1. Distribution of smolt ages from rivers in eastern Newfoundland.

River	Sample size	Smolt age			
		2	3	4	5
Exploits River	952	0.02	0.53	0.41	0.04
Gander River	22	0.00	0.55	0.36	0.09
Indian Bay River	76	0.00	0.79	0.21	0.00
Northwest River	45	0.00	0.31	0.42	0.27
Pipers Hole River	37	0.00	0.62	0.35	0.03
Ragged Harbour River	63	0.05	0.71	0.24	0.00
Riverhead Brook	75	0.05	0.68	0.24	0.03
Salmonier River	54	0.09	0.78	0.07	0.06
Terra Nova River	41	0.00	0.59	0.34	0.07

presence of a large narrow peak at a particular frequency in the spectrum indicates that the time series has periodicity at that frequency. In particular, large peaks occur in the spectrum of Pacific salmon time series data that corresponds to the life cycle of the species (Mysak et al. 1982). The average duration from egg to egg for Atlantic salmon (grilse) from the east coast of Newfoundland is presently 5.4 years, i.e. an average smolt age of 3.4 years (Table 1). If this was also true in the past, a pattern of peaks and troughs should be detectable at 1/5.4 year (0.185) cycles per year for a grilse life history and 1/6.4 year (0.156) cycles per year for a 2SW salmon life history. There is a continuous record of exports from eastern Newfoundland collated by Taylor (1985) from 1803 to 1910., The spectrum of Taylor's data was estimated (see Jenkins and Watts 1968 for an explanation of spectral analysis). There is a clear peak at approximately 0.185 cycles per year, but no peak is apparent at 0.156 cycles per year (Fig. 2). We conclude that eastern Newfoundland was probably dominated by grilse for at least the last 100 years.

Sea Growth Rate

Schaffer and Elson (1975) provided evidence that growth rate at sea is a prime determinant of sea age at maturity. Myers and Hutchings (1985) reanalyzed this proposed relationship, and found that the positive correlation between mean sea age and post-grilse growth rate was spurious. This was due primarily to systematic errors in ageing amplified by use of a highly nonrobust statistic. Since errors were mainly due to misidentification of fish that had spawned previously at virgin sea age i as fish of virgin sea age $i + 1$, the mean lengths of fish spawning for the first time after two or more winters at sea were underestimated. The magnitude of this error increases as the mean sea age decreases because the ratio of fish that are misclassified to those that spend more than one year at sea increases.

We conclude that at present there is no reliable evidence linking post-grilse growth rate and sea age at maturity.

Sea Temperature Data

Huntsman (1938) and Scarnecchia (1983) hypothesized that ocean temperature may have an influence on the sea age at maturity in Atlantic salmon. In areas where warmer marine temperatures were observed, growth rates were faster and salmon matured at an earlier age. This was investigated for North American Atlantic salmon using archived oceanographic data from the Marine Environ-

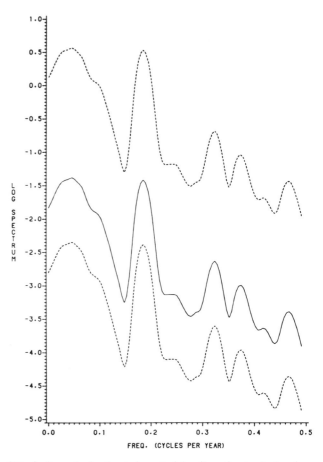

FIG. 2. Smoothed estimated spectral density estimates (—) and approximate 95% confidence intervals (---) for eastern Newfoundland salmon exports from 1803 to 1910 using a frequency bandwidth of 0.018. The linear trend from the data was removed from the data before the analysis.

mental Data Service, Ottawa, Canada. Information on sea temperatures within 10 m of the surface, obtained between 1938 and 1983 in July–August for areas within a 50 km radius of 49 salmon producing rivers in Quebec, New Brunswick, Nova Scotia, and Newfoundland, were used in the analysis. These data were primarily gathered by fisheries and oceanographic research ships from Canada, the United States, Germany, and the Soviet Union. Sea ages were obtained from research captures of salmon (Myers and Hutchings 1986). For the analysis, data were sorted by position into an array of boxes 0.5 degrees latitude by 0.5 degrees longitude. The closest box to the mouth of the river was used if it contained 10 or more observations. Alternatively, observations from those boxes closest to the original box were averaged with the original data to obtain the final value. Since length of river available to salmon has been shown to be an important covariate of sea age at maturity (Power 1981), this variable was included as a covariate in the analysis. Information on river length was obtained from the Atlantic Salmon Association distribution map (Anon. 1983).

For all rivers combined, the variation in mean sea age and ocean temperature was not statistically significant either with ($P = 0.30$) or without ($P = 0.80$) the river length variable included. Although not significant ($P = 0.38$), temperature was inversely related to mean sea age for the Quebec data. Partial correlation was used to remove the effect of river length in examining the influence of ocean temperature. Again there was no significant effect of sea temperature ($P = 0.75$).

2. Within-Population Variation Among Smolt Classes

Sea Temperature and the Grilse–MSW Salmon Ratio

We seek to test the hypothesis that higher sea temperatures increase the ratio of grilse to MSW salmon between cohorts (Saunders et al. 1983). Traditional methods such as simple correlation and regression are completely inadequate to treat such time series problems because of autocorrelations and trends within environmental and biological data. Thus we use a transfer function model (the reader should consult Box and Jenkins (1976) for a full explanation of the methods used here).

Two records of salmon catches and three data series of sea-surface temperature records were used in the analysis. Sea ages of salmon were inferred from size data. Estimates of the numbers of grilse, salmon, and large salmon (greater than 25 lb) were available from the angling records of the Restigouche Salmon Club, on the Matapedia tributary of the Restigouche River, Quebec, from 1880 to 1965 (Fig. 1; Anon. 1966). The ratio of grilse in year i to salmon less than 25 lb in year $i+1$ was used as the index of grilse maturation. Because the year 1965 is before the escalation of the fishery at West Greenland it was selected as the end point for the analysis. A second data series was available for the Moisie River in Quebec from 1931 to 1970 (Schiefer 1971; Weeks 1971). Since there were very few grilse in the Moisie River catch, the ratio of 2SW salmon in year i to the number of 3SW salmon in year $i+1$ was used in the analysis. The yearly mean sea-surface temperature was available from Boothbay Harbour, Maine (1906 to the present; Sutcliffe et al. 1976), St. Andrews, New Brunswick (1921 to the present; Sutcliffe et al. 1976), and from Grimsey Island, Iceland (1874–1972; Stefánsson 1954). These temperature records were not necessarily from the area of interest, that is the feeding grounds for grilse, but they were correlated with such temperatures (Sutcliffe et al. 1976).

We wish to fit a linear difference model of the form:

$$(1) \quad Y_t = \delta_1 Y_{t-1} + \delta_2 Y_{t-2} + \ldots + \delta_r Y_{t-r} + \omega_0 X_{t-b} - \omega_1 X_{t-b-1} - \ldots - \omega_s X_{t-b-s} + a_t$$

where:

Y_t represents the output series, i.e. the ratio of grilse caught in year t to MSW salmon less than 25 lb caught in year $t+1$,

X_t represents the input series, i.e. the environmental index of sea temperature in year t,

a_t represents the noise model, which is assumed to be an auto-regressive moving-average process (ARMA) of the form:

$$(2) \quad a_t = \phi_1 a_{t-1} + \phi_2 a_{t-2} + \ldots + \phi_p a_{t-p} + a'_t - \theta_1 a'_{t-1} \ldots - \theta_q a'_{t-q}$$

of the order, p,q. The model (1) contains r lagged values for the output series, s lagged values for the input series, and b delay lags for the input series.

The first step in the estimation of (1) is to identify the process, i.e. to obtain some idea of the orders of r, s, and b and to derive initial guesses of the parameters δ's and ω's. We also need to identify the ARMA process generating the noise term. We begin by analyzing the input series, i.e. as univariate time series.

Box and Jenkins (1976) showed that a wide class of univariate time series could be represented by an autoregressive integrated moving average model (an ARIMA model) of the form:

$$(3) \quad (1 - \phi_1 B - \ldots - \phi_p B^p) \nabla^d X_t = \theta_0 + (1 - \theta_1 B - \ldots \theta_q B^q) a_t$$

where a_t is a random series with mean zero and variances σ_a^2 and θ_0 is a deterministic trend parameter. B is the backshift operator, i.e. $B^p X_t = X_{t-p}$. The polynomial operator:

$$\phi(B) = 1 - \phi_1 B - \ldots - \phi_p B^p$$

involving p autoregressive parameters ϕ_1, ϕ_2, ..., ϕ_p is called the autoregressive operator and the polynomial operator of degree q in B

$$\theta(B) = 1 - \theta_1 B - \ldots - \theta_q B^q$$

involving q moving average parameters θ_1, θ_2, ..., θ_q, is the moving average operator. ∇ is the difference operator applied d times. The model (3) is known as a (p,d,q) order ARIMA model.

The sea surface temperature time-series at Grimsey was identified as possibly a 4th AR process based on the auto- and partial-autocorrelations of the log-transformed data (Fig. 3a–b) and the differenced log-transformed data (Fig. 3c–d). The process was estimated as:

$$(4) \quad X_t = 0.49 X_{t-1} + 0.34 X_{t-4} + a_t$$

where X_t is temperature. The resulting mean square error (MSE) was 0.44 and the resulting residual autocorrelations had a satisfactory pattern (Fig. 3e).

Since the input has been reduced to "white noise" by the ARIMA model, this procedure is known as "prewhitening" the input. The output series, Y_t, are filtered by the ARMA model for the input series, the sea-surface temperature. The cross-correlations between the residuals of the input ARMA model and the residuals from the output and the filtered output provide the basis for identifying the transfer function model. The resulting cross-correlation (Fig. 3f) can be interpreted as the response of the output, the grilse: salmon ratio, to an "impulse" change in sea-surface temperature (Box and Jenkins 1976).

It is clear from Fig. 3f that there is no evidence of any significant effect of sea-surface temperature on the grilse: MSW salmon ratio at the appropriate time lag. Similar results were obtained for a second order MA model of the differenced temperature data.

The analysis was repeated using the sea-surface temperature data from Boothbay Harbour, Maine and St. Andrews, New Brunswick. There was a similar lack of evidence for any causal relationship. The analysis was then repeated with the data from the Moisie River for all three sea-surface temperature records with similar results.

We conclude, therefore, that there is no evidence from natural populations that sea surface temperature has any demonstrable effect on the within-population, year-to-year variation in the ratio of grilse to MSW salmon. It is worth mentioning that a standard application of linear regression of the Restigouche grilse:salmon data on the sea-surface temperature yields a "highly significant" relationship *if* one chooses to ignore the fact that both time series are obviously autocorrelated. That is, standard regression techniques give highly misleading results in this situation.

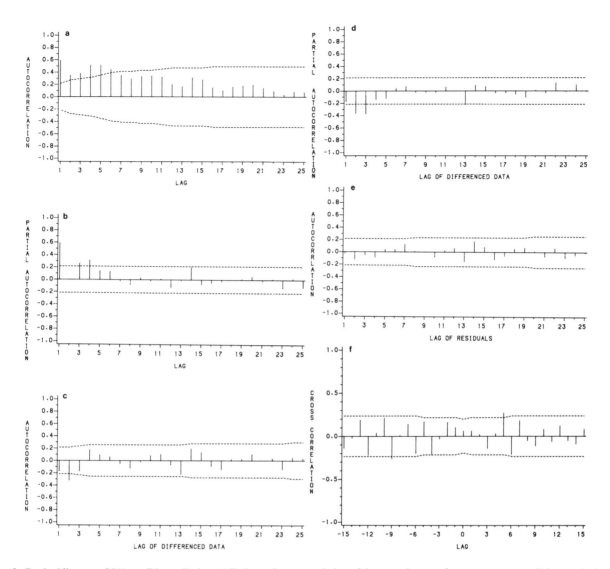

FIG. 3. Dashed lines are 95% confidence limits; (a) Estimated autocorrelation of the annual sea-surface temperature at Grimsey, Iceland, from 1880 to 1965; (b) Estimated partial autocorrelations of the Grimsey sea-surface temperature; (c) Estimated autocorrelations of the differenced Grimsey temperature data; (d) Estimated partial autocorrelations of the differenced Grimsey temperature data; (e) Auto-correlations of residuals from the Grimsey sea-surface temperature data; (f) Estimated cross-correlation function for the Restigouche grilse:salmon ratio and the Grimsey sea temperature data after pre-whitening.

Analysis of Ice Data

The annual intrusion of ice into the waters of the North-west Atlantic is one of the more obvious annual environmental events along the eastern Canadian seaboard (Markham 1980). The areas covered are those in mid-latitude on the eastern edge of North America. Ice conditions can vary considerably from year to year (Fig. 4) in volume and extent, depending on the frequency and paths of winter storms. Eastern and northern Newfoundland and Labrador coastal waters are affected by ice formed locally as well as ice floes imported from northern waters. The portion of the year affected is from December to July and sometimes August of each year.

In this section we hypothesize that heavy ice concentrations in the Northwest Atlantic alters salmon distribution and delays migration, perhaps into the next year. This would occur if age at maturity is related to growth and if salmon move to an area of low food availability because of the presence of ice. Here we are treating Newfoundland–Labrador catches as a single stock unit.

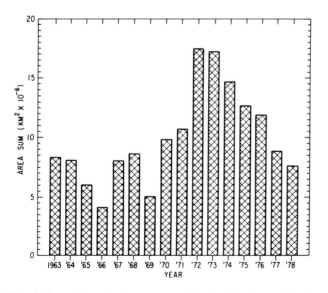

FIG. 4. Sum of yearly ice coverage for the Northwest Atlantic from Atmospheric Environmental Services.

83

TABLE 2. Summary of papers dealing with age at maturity and growth rates of different sea ages of Atlantic salmon (*Salmo salar*).

| Location | Reference | Comparison separated for | | | | Procedure | Result |
		Stock	Smolt class	Sea age	Sex		
Scotland wild	Calderwood (1925)	No	No	Yes	No	back-calculated from scales	2SW salmon grew slower than 3SW during 2nd year at sea
Scotland wild	Menzies (1927)	No	No	Yes	No	back-calculated from scales	2SW salmon grew slower than 3SW during 2nd year at sea
Scotland cage-reared	Simpson and Thorpe (1976)	Yes	No	Yes	No	see discussion	grilse grow faster than salmon
Norway cage-reared	Naevdal et al. (1976)	Yes	No	Yes	No	size at age	grilse and MSW salmon same size until onset of maturation
Norway Swedish Canadian rivers & farm fish cage-reared	Naevdal et al. (1977)	Yes	No	Yes	Yes	size at age (FL)	—sex was insignificant —stock was significant —grilse slightly but not significantly larger than MSW salmon (before maturation)
Norway cage-reared	Naevdal et al. (1981)	Yes	Yes	Yes	Yes	size at age	—stock differences —sex differences —no difference for mature vs immature —no difference attributable to age at maturity
Nevar USSR wild	Kazakov (1981)	Yes	Yes	Yes	Yes	size at age (FL, WW)	—growth differences between sexes but not consistent

The ice data were based on digitized Atmospheric Environmental Service (AES) ice charts that were available from 1963 to 1978. Mean ice cover was calculated based on the area per chart of greater than 3/10 ice cover, irrespective of the type of ice. The monthly mean was used because of the variable number of ice charts available prior to 1972. The digitization consisted of recording the type of ice and coverage within a 0.5° latitude by 1.0° longitude area from 55°N to the southerly extent of ice, excluding the Gulf of St. Lawrence. Data were provided by Petro-Canada from ice records digitized by Atmospheric Environmental Service. An ice year is defined as extending from December of year $n-1$ to July of year n.

The analysis consisted of using the Newfoundland–Labrador commercial catch statistics to calculate percentage grilse from a given smolt class. This was correlated with various combinations of ice data. The relationships tested were as follows:
1) % grilse from a given smolt class that would have been at sea during the same ice year on sum of mean monthly area of ice cover for an ice year;
2) % grilse from the smolt class at sea during the ice year on sum of mean January–February ice cover. This was done as Saunders et al. (1983) have shown that relative proportions of grilse and 2SW salmon from the same smolt class may be related to sea water temperatures;
3) % grilse from the salmon at sea as smolts in May to July of that ice year on the sum of mean monthly ice cover for May to July.
This was repeated using several series of catch statistics including (1) total Canadian catches of smolt classes, 1970–82; (2) total Newfoundland–Labrador landings, 1969–83; (3) total insular Newfoundland landings, 1969–83; (4) total Labrador landings, 1969–83; and (5)

landings by Statistical Area for Newfoundland–Labrador, 1969–83. The commercial landings were separated into grilse and MSW salmon classes based on weight categories used in fish plants (Reddin 1982). The ice cover and catch data were tested for autocorrelation using the Durbin–Watson d statistic. The ice cover data were shown to be autocorrelated but not the catch data. Owing to the limited availability of data, a more sophisticated and appropriate time-series analysis was not possible.

There were no significant correlations on a systematic basis for the relationships attempted. Therefore, it is concluded, based on this analysis, that there is no demonstrable relationship between ice cover and salmon distribution resulting in changes in age at maturity.

3. Within-Population Variation Within Smolt Classes

Sea Growth Rate

Gardner (1976), Naevdal et al. (1977), Thorpe et al. (1983), and others (Table 2) have suggested that within-population variation in age at maturity is related to growth of Atlantic salmon in the sea. There are two basic types of studies: those using sea-cages and natural enclosures for which the whole population is available for study and those that examine wild stocks returning to the river to spawn. The results from these two types of studies are dichotomous.

Much of the support for the hypothesis that faster-growing fish mature earliest has been obtained from salmon grown in sea-cages in Europe. Simpson and Thorpe (1976), Thorpe et al. (1983), Naevdal et al. (1983), Naevdal (1983), Gjerde (1984), and Gjerde and Gjedrem (1984) all indicated that the mean growth of the early-maturing fish was greater in the first sea year than for nonmaturers. They also con-

TABLE 3. Fork length at time for Atlantic salmon raised in tanks at Fisheries Research Branch laboratory, St. Andrews, New Brunswick. Data from Dr. R. L. Saunders (pers. comm.).

Stage at 16 months	n	Fork lengths (cm)		
		June 9	August 21	November 17
Mature	11	38.5	41.1	43.9
Immature	≈100	33.7	39.2	43.1

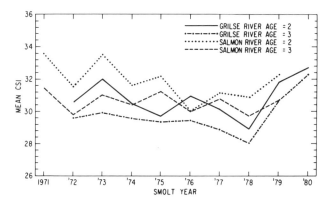

FIG. 5. Mean circuli counts of the first sea year by smolt class for 1SW and 2SW salmon from the Miramichi River, New Brunswick.

cluded that the size (growth) of the fish was the most important factor in determining the age at maturation. Data for North American salmon obtained from salmon raised in tanks at St. Andrews, New Brunswick (Table 3) (Dr. R. L. Saunders, pers. comm.), similarly showed that maturing salmon were larger in June than immature fish, yet at the time of maturity they were of similar size. Results showing that early sexual maturation is directly correlated with rapid growth have also been found within populations for *Salmo trutta, S. gairdneri,* and *Salvelinus fontinalis* raised in natural enclosures (Alm 1959).

Not all of the evidence of the influence of growth rate in wild stocks has been nearly so conclusive and in some cases contradicts the results from studies of cage-reared fish. Gardner (1976) reviewed the scale studies of the Ministry of Agriculture and Fisheries for Scotland conducted over many years on several river systems for which back-calculated growth increments were available (Gardner 1976, table VIII). In 10 out of 14 cases the growth increment during the first sea year for grilse was less than for the MSW salmon. However, for *Oncorhynchus nerka*, Foerster (1968) showed that time of maturity is correlated with growth during the first sea year, but not growth in fresh water.

We examined the hypothesis that sea growth rate influences sea age at maturity by examining scale data from salmon sampled at a fish trap on the Miramichi River, 1971–80, and from a counting fence at Sand Hill River, Labrador, 1971. Circuli counts during the first sea year (between the last freshwater annulus and the first annulus in the sea zone) were used as an index of growth. Foerster (1968), Jones (1949), and Kerr (1961) have shown that the number of circuli counts are correlated with growth. Scales were mounted on plastic slides and interpreted by standard criteria (Berg and Grimaldi 1967; Havey 1959). The circuli counts were analyzed by comparing 1SW and 2SW salmon from the same smolt class. Sex could not be examined as a factor for the Miramichi data as it was not recorded.

Comparison of mean circuli counts showed that grilse typically have fewer counts than do 2SW salmon from the same smolt class (Fig. 5), suggesting that grilse do not grow as much as 2SW salmon during the first sea year. These differences were significant at less than 5% when tested by ANOVA for the 1974, 1975, 1977, and 1978 smolt classes, but not for those of 1972, 1973, 1976, and 1979 (Table 4). These salmon were a mixture of river ages 2 and 3. Since Kazakov (1981) demonstrated that salmon of separate year-classes may have different growth characteristics, the analysis was repeated examining each sea age separately for each year-class that would have been at sea at the same time.

Four groups were available, namely, river ages 2 and 3 for grilse and the same for 2SW salmon (Table 4). Overall, the differences between circuli counts of the four groups were highly significant ($F = 24.9$, $P < 0.0001$). Com-

parison between years for each group showed significant differences in mean circuli counts for river age 2 and 3 grilse ($F = 4.06$, $P = 0.0002$; $F = 5.13$, $P < 0.0001$) and for river age 2 2SW salmon ($F = 3.01$, $P = 0.0036$) but not river age 3 2SW salmon ($F = 1.73$, $P = 0.0921$). Comparison of 2SW salmon and grilse from the same smolt class separately for each river age (e.g. 2 or 3 years) indicated that while differences in circuli counts were not always significant, grilse generally had less or the same number of circuli in the first sea year than had 2SW salmon. Similarly the mean circuli counts of the river age 3 grilse and 2SW salmon were more often less than their river age 2 counterparts (Table 4).

The following hypotheses were considered as possible factors that could bias comparisons of growth from scale interpretation studies of wild stocks.

1) Sample was biased because of the method of capture, e.g. sample was caught by gill net or in some other size-selective gear.

The samples used in the Scottish studies presented by Gardner (1976) were apparently not biased by the method of capture as nonselective gear, i.e. trap nets and net and coble, were used (Macfarlane 1932). The Miramichi samples were caught at Millbank in trap nets which are nonselective. Thus we conclude that size-selective capture gear was not responsible for differences noted in growth rates between salmon and grilse for the Scottish or Miramichi studies.

2) Sample was biased because of distant water removals prior to the sampling site, e.g. removals of fish at West Greenland.

As stated, the types of gear used in Scottish fisheries are generally not thought to be size selective (Macfarlane 1932). Furthermore, all of the Scottish studies were conducted before the Greenland fishery (Gardner 1976). The Miramichi samples, however, may have been biased by removals of salmon at Greenland as it is known that Miramichi origin MSW salmon are caught at Greenland (Saunders 1969) and because the gear used in that fishery is size selective (Doubleday and Reddin 1981). Therefore, bias of this type can only be rejected for the Scottish studies reported by Gardner (1976).

3) Results were biased by comparing grilse and 2SW salmon from different smolt or year classes.

Of the 14 examples presented in Gardner (1976) all but

TABLE 4. Circuli counts of the 1st sea zone from scale samples of Atlantic salmon caught in Millbank trap on the Miramichi River. Sample size in parentheses.

| Smolt class | Sea age 1 | | | | Sea age 2 | | | | ANOVA between smolt classes | | |
| | River age 2 | | River age 3 | | River age 2 | | River age 3 | | | | |
	Mean	SD	Mean	SD	Mean	SD	Mean	SD	df	F	P
1971	—	—	—	—	33.6 (9)	3.6	31.5 (35)	2.5	—	—	—
1972	30.5 (24)	2.1	29.6 (23)	3.0	31.5 (26)	2.2	29.8 (22)	2.8	1,98	1.67	0.1991
1973	32.0 (29)	2.2	29.9 (21)	3.4	33.5 (21)	1.7	31.0 (29)	2.5	1,98	2.99	0.0870
1974	30.5 (14)	3.2	29.6 (34)	2.6	31.6 (16)	2.5	30.4 (34)	2.0	1,98	4.91	0.0290
1975	29.7 (29)	2.0	29.3 (19)	2.4	32.1 (38)	2.3	31.2 (10)	2.5	1,98	28.06	0.0001
1976	30.9 (21)	2.6	29.4 (27)	2.7	30.0 (9)	2.9	30.0 (41)	3.0	1,98	0.12	0.7265
1977	30.1 (11)	2.0	28.9 (37)	3.4	31.1 (11)	2.7	30.7 (39)	2.4	1,98	9.65	0.0025
1978	28.9 (9)	3.0	28.0 (41)	2.4	30.8 (18)	2.7	29.7 (32)	2.8	1,98	12.87	0.0005
1979	31.8 (18)	3.3	30.6 (31)	3.2	32.2 (17)	2.7	30.7 (20)	2.5	1,84	0.27	0.6069
1980	32.7 (21)	2.6	32.2 (25)	2.2	—		—		—	—	—

TABLE 5. Circuli counts and measurements of four characters of Atlantic salmon returning to fish counting facility on Sand Hill River, Labrador.

| Smolt class | CS1S[a] | | WS1S[b] | | CS1W[c] | | WS1W[d] | | |
	Mean	SD	Mean	SD	Mean	SD	Mean	SD	n
1SW male									
1971	18.2	2.22	97.4	13.5	7.84	1.69	35.6	7.84	38
2SW male									
1971	19.0	2.38	98.1	17.9	8.43	1.90	39.4	9.98	7
1SW female									
1971	17.9	2.54	98.0	15.6	7.58	1.87	33.5	8.46	40
2SW female									
1971	19.1	2.54	104.7	15.4	7.60	1.75	34.1	8.18	30
F	1.64		1.61		0.56		1.23		
P	0.1836		0.1888		0.6445		0.3005		
df	3,111		3,111		3,111		3,111		

[a] CS1S = circuli count in summer portion of first sea zone.
[b] WS1S = width of summer portion of first sea zone.
[c] CS1W = circuli count in winter portion of first sea zone.
[d] WS1W = width of winter portion of first sea zone.

three of them compared grilse and 2SW salmon of different smolt classes. However, this source of bias was eliminated in our Miramichi study by comparing grilse and 2SW salmon from the same smolt class.

4) The differences between the field and laboratory results were due to sex-specific growth rates and ages at sea age at maturity.

Kazakov (1981) has shown growth differences between male and female salmon. We examined growth differences using salmon data obtained from a counting fence on the Sand Hill River, Labrador. Sex was determined from external characteristics. The samples, however, may still have been biased because of removals at Greenland or New-foundland prior to capture at the fence site. Comparisons were made for fish of the same sex, smolt class and year-class (river age 4). The first sea year was divided into summer and winter zones (Reddin and Burfitt 1983) to facilitate determination of time of the decision to mature. Comparison by ANOVA indicated that differences between mean circuli counts and scale length were not significant (Table 5) and we conclude, therefore, that for these data sex was not considered an important factor influencing sea

growth rate. However, in each case fish that matured during their second year had a higher growth rate, similar to the Miramichi samples and some of the Scottish studies reviewed by Gardner (1976).

5) Differences in migration routes at sea of grilse and 2SW salmon during the first year at sea cause the differences in growth of wild salmon.

Tagging studies of Miramichi River (Saunders 1969), Sand Hill River (Anderson 1985), and Scottish stocks have shown that grilse and salmon have different migration routes. Therefore, at some time during their first year at sea as postsmolts, grilse and salmon are in different environments. This being the case, there may be no contradiction between the results from the sea-cage and wild salmon studies.

There is no doubt that at time of spawning, grilse from the same stock and smolt class are smaller than those fish that remained as immatures at sea. Allen et al. (1972) sampled salmon over their life cycle and showed that these differences developed after the end of the first year. Changes in metabolic activity related to the onset of maturation are probably the cause (Gardner 1976; Simpson and Thorpe

1976).

In conclusion, the apparently contradictory results between sea-cage and wild salmon studies may be caused by invalid extrapolation of the results of sea-cage studies to the natural environment. The strongest evidence for an environmental influence on sea growth rate and age at first maturity may be that grilse and salmon have different migration routes at sea.

Discussion

Geographical Variation

Our examination of quantitative historical records suggests an increasing trend in the grilse:MSW salmon ratio on the Restigouche River since the 1930's, possibly as a result of a demographic response to changing fishing patterns. However, spectral analysis of east coast Newfoundland catch data indicates that this area was probably dominated by grilse stocks for the last 100 years.

In the marine environment, growth rate has been suggested as a contributing factor in determining age at maturity of Atlantic salmon, although it did not apply in a geographically consistent manner (Gardner 1976). Schaffer and Elson (1975) claimed that older sea age at maturation was related to higher post-grilse marine growth rate among North American populations. Reanalysis showed no relationship between sea growth and mean age at maturity among populations in North America (Myers and Hutchings 1986).

Ocean temperatures have also been suggested to have an influence on the geographical distribution and, therefore, growth rate and sea age at maturity. Huntsman (1938) hypothesized that the sea temperatures adjacent to river mouths were an important factor in determining the age at maturity and time between successive spawnings. Huntsman (1938) further stated that areas subjected to wide ranges in temperatures also had a greater within-river variation in sea age. Similarly Scarnecchia (1983) found evidence for an influence of sea temperature on age at maturity in Icelandic salmon. Saunders et al. (1983) also hypothesized that low sea temperatures during the winter act to delay the maturation process in salmon. They suggested that different stocks of salmon may have different physiological responses to low temperatures. Our analysis, however, showed no significant contribution of sea temperature to sea age at maturity. This is contrary to the conclusions of Scarnecchia (1983) for Icelandic salmon. It is quite possible, therefore, that over the wide geographic range of Atlantic salmon there may be some stocks for which sea temperature does have an influence on the sea age at maturity. We conclude that the extrapolation of data from aquaculture experiments (Saunders et al. 1983), to natural populations is best done with great caution.

Variation Within Stocks (Among and Within Smolt Classes)

Our analysis of grilse:salmon ratios and sea surface temperatures using a transfer function model indicates no evidence of any significant effect of temperature on within-stock variation in age at maturity.

Several studies using salmon enclosed in sea-cages have shown that faster-growing fish have a tendency to mature first (Thorpe et al. 1983). Studies on wild stocks, e.g.

Gardner (1976) and our results from the Miramichi River, New Brunswick, contradict the hypothesis that faster-growing fish mature earlier as 2SW salmon always had similar or higher growth than grilse over the eight-year period. However, there were no significant differences between grilse and 2SW salmon growth from Sand Hill River, Labrador, although growth indexes for grilse were less, even though the data were separated by sex and the first sea year was divided into winter and summer bands. Alm (1959) stated that studies showing higher growth for older fish in comparative years were typically flawed in some way, either through the method of back-calculation or from using mixtures of year-classes. This is not the case with most of the above studies and the contradictions with the growth hypothesis are real.

The apparent contradiction between faster-growing fish in cages maturing earlier and slower-growing fish maturing earlier in nature has a simple explanation. The cage-reared salmon, both those maturing as grilse and those maturing later, were raised in the same environment. This may not be the case for the wild fish. Saunders et al. (1983) suggested that different stocks of salmon occupy different regions during the marine phase and may have developed appropriate thermal thresholds for feeding and growth and that their locations at sea reflect these thresholds.

Conclusion

Our knowledge of the role of the marine environment on sea age at maturity of Atlantic salmon is disappointingly small. The reproductive 'decision' of when to mature may be made prior to migration to sea. This would be consistent with our lack of results for the effect of temperature on between-year variation in sea age and the contradiction between the results of sea-cage and wild salmon studies on the relationship between growth and maturation.

The cause of the geographical variation in sea age at maturity remains largely a mystery. Perhaps further studies, firmly founded in modern evolutionary theory, directed specifically at the physiology of maturation may prove worthwhile in explaining the precise mechanism of maturation and the effect of the marine environment.

Acknowledgments

We thank L. T. Marshall, Y. Côté, G. Ouellet, and R. Saunders for providing data. We also wish to thank J. Hutchings, M. F. O'Connell, J. Ritter, and G. Farmer for comments and editorial suggestions for the manuscript.

References

ALLEN, I. R. H., AND J. A. RITTER. 1977. Salmonid terminology. J. Cons. Int. Explor. Mer 37(3): 293–299.

ALLEN, K. R., R. L. SAUNDERS, AND P. F. ELSON. 1972. Marine growth of Atlantic salmon (*Salmo salar*) in the Northwest Atlantic. J. Fish. Res. Board Can. 29: 1373–1380.

ALM, G. 1959. Connection between maturity, size and age in fishes. Rep. Inst. Freshwat. Res. Drottningholm 40: 5–145.

ANDERSON, T. C. 1985. The rivers of Labrador. Can. Spec. Publ. Fish. Aquat. Sci. 81: 389 p.

ANON. 1966. Charter, by-laws, officers and members of the Restigouche Salmon Club. Club House, Matapedia, Que.
    1983. The Atlantic salmon rivers of Canada. Atlantic Salmon Association (Map).

BERG, A., AND E. GRIMALDI. 1967. A critical interpretation of the scale structures used for the determination of annuli in fish growth studies. Mem. Ist. Ital. Idrobiol. 21: 225−239.

BERG, M. 1964. Nord-Norske Lakseelver. (North Norwegian salmon rivers.) Johan Grundt Tanum Forlag, Oslo. 300 p. (In Norwegian, English summary)

BOX, G. E. P., AND G. M. JENKINS. 1976. Time series analysis, forecasting and control. Holden-Day, San Francisco, CA. 575 p.

CALDERWOOD, W. L. 1925. The relation of sea growth and spawning frequency in *Salmo salar*. Proc. R. Soc. Edinb. 45: 142−148.

CHADWICK, E. M. P. 1982. Dynamics of an Atlantic salmon stock in a small Newfoundland River. Ph.D. thesis, Memorial University of Newfoundland, St. John's, Nfld.

DALLEY, E. L., C. W. ANDREWS, AND J. M. GREEN. 1983. Precocious male Atlantic salmon parr (*Salmo salar*) in insular Newfoundland. Can. J. Fish. Aquat. Sci. 40: 647−652.

DOUBLEDAY, W. G., AND D. G. REDDIN. 1981. An analysis of the implications of alternative mesh sizes for gillnets and opening dates for the commercial salmon fishing season at West Greenland. CAFSAC Res. Doc. 81/3. 56 p.

ELSON, P. F. 1973. Genetic polymorphism in Northwest Miramichi salmon, in relation to season of river ascent and age at maturation and its implications for management of the stocks. Int. Comm. Northw. Atl. Fish. Res. Doc. 73/76. 6 p.

1974. Impact of recent economic growth and industrial development on the ecology of Northwest Miramichi Atlantic salmon (*Salmo salar*). J. Fish. Res. Board Can. 31: 521−544.

FOERSTER, R. E. 1968. The sockeye salmon, *Oncorhynchus nerka*. Bull. Fish. Res. Board Can. 162: 442 p.

GARDNER, M. L. G. 1976. A review of factors which may influence the sea age and maturation of Atlantic salmon, *Salmo salar* L. J. Fish. Biol. 9: 289−327.

GJERDE, B. 1984. Response to individual selection for age at sexual maturity in Atlantic salmon. Aquaculture 38: 229−240.

GJERDE, B., AND T. GJEDREM. 1984. Estimates of phenotypic and genetic parameters for carcass traits in Atlantic salmon and rainbow trout. Aquaculture 36: 97−110.

HAVEY, K. A. 1959. Validity of the scale method for aging hatchery-reared Atlantic salmon. Trans. Am. Fish. Soc. 88: 193−196.

HUNTSMAN, A. G. 1938. Sea movements of Canadian Atlantic salmon kelts. J. Fish. Res. Board Can. 4: 96−135.

JENKINS, G. M., AND D. G. WATTS. 1968. Spectral analysis and its applications. Holden-Day, San Francisco. 525 p.

JONES, J. W. 1949. Studies of the scales of young salmon (*Salmo salar* L.) in relation to growth, migration and spawning. Min. Agr. Fish. Fishery Investigations Ser. I, Vol. V, No. 1. 23 p.

KAZAKOV, R. V. 1981. Relation between sizes of adult Atlantic salmon (*Salmo salar* L.) and duration of river and sea-life periods. Aquaculture 24: 327−340.

KERR, R. B. 1961. Scale to length ratio, age and growth of Atlantic salmon in Miramichi fisheries. J. Fish. Res. Board Can. 18(1): 117−124.

MACFARLANE, P. R. C. 1932. Salmon of the River Tweed, 1929. Fisheries Scotland, Salmon Fish., 1932, III.

MARKHAM, W. E. 1980. Ice atlas eastern Canadian Seaboard. Canadian Government Publishing Centre, Supply and Services Canada, Ottawa, Ont. 96 p.

MENZIES, W. J. M. 1927. Some aspects of the growth of salmon in river and sea as observed from scale examination of Dee (Aberdeen) and Spey salmon, 1921 to 1923 inclusive. Fisheries Scotland, Salmon Fish. 1927 I.

MOORES, R. B., R. W. PENNEY, AND R. J. TUCKER. 1978. Atlantic salmon catch and effort data, Newfoundland and Labrador, 1953−77. Fish. Mar. Serv. Data Rep. 84: 274 p.

MYERS, R. A. 1984. Demographic consequences of precocious

maturation of Atlantic salmon (*Salmo salar*). Can. J. Fish. Aquat. Sci. 41: 1349−1353.

MYERS, R. A., AND J. A. HUTCHINGS. 1986. Tests of life history theory applied to Atlantic salmon. Ecology (in press)

MYSAK, L. A., W. W. HSIEH, AND T. R. PARSONS. 1982. On the relationship between interannual baroclinic waves and fish populations in the Northeast Pacific. Biol. Oceanogr. Vol. 2: 63−103.

NAEVDAL, G. 1983. Genetic factors in connection with age at maturation. Aquaculture 33: 97−106.

NAEVDAL, G., M. HOLM, R. LEROY, AND D. MOLLER. 1977. Individual growth rate and age at first sexual maturity in Atlantic salmon. Int. Counc. Explor. Sea C.M.1977/E:60. 15 p.

NAEVDAL, G., M. HOLM, D. MOLLER, AND O. D. OSTHUS. 1976. Variation in growth rate and age at sexual maturity in Atlantic salmon. Int. Counc. Explor. Sea C.M.1976/E:40. 10 p.

NAEVDAL, G., R. LEROY, AND D. MOLLER. 1981. Sources of variations in weight and length of Atlantic Salmon. Int. Counc. Explor. Sea C.M.1981/F:39. 13 p.

PIGGINS, D. J. 1973. The results of selective breeding from known grilse and salmon parents. Annu. Rep. Salm. Res. Trust Ireland XVIII: 35−39.

POWER, G. 1981. Stock characteristics and catches of Atlantic salmon (*Salmo salar*) in Quebec, and Newfoundland and Labrador in relation to environmental variables. Can. J. Fish. Aquat. Sci. 38: 1601−1611.

REDDIN, D. G. 1982. Reliability and corrections for size categories classifying Atlantic salmon (*Salmo salar*) to 1SW and MSW age groups in Newfoundland−Labrador catch records. ICES C.M.1982/M:18. 18 p.

REDDIN, D. G., AND R. J. BURFITT. 1983. An update: the use of scale characters and multivariate analysis to discriminate between Atlantic salmon (*Salmo salar* L.) of North American and European origin caught at West Greenland. ICES C.M.1983/M:11. 15 p.

RITTER, J. A. 1972. Preliminary observations on the influence of smolt size on tag return rate and age at first maturity of Atlantic salmon (*Salmo salar*). ICES C.M.1972/M:14.

SAUNDERS, R. L. 1969. Contributions of salmon from the Northwest Miramichi River, New Brunswick, to various fisheries. J. Fish. Res. Board Can. 26: 269−278.

SAUNDERS, R. L., E. B. HENDERSON, B. D. GLEBE, AND E. J. LOUDENSLAGER. 1983. Evidence of a major environmental component in determination of the grilse:larger salmon ratio in Atlantic salmon (*Salmo salar*). Aquaculture 33: 107−118.

SCARNECCHIA, D. L. 1983. Age at sexual maturity in Icelandic stocks of Atlantic salmon (*Salmo salar*). Can. J. Fish. Aquat. Sci. 40: 1456−1468.

SCHAFFER, W. M., AND P. F. ELSON. 1975. The adaptive significance of variations in life history among local populations of Atlantic salmon in North America. Ecology 56: 577−590.

SCHIEFER, K. 1971. Ecology of Atlantic salmon, with special reference to occurrence and abundance of grilse, in North Shore Gulf of St. Lawrence Rivers. Ph.D. thesis, Univ. Waterloo, Waterloo, Ont. 129 p.

SIMPSON, T. H., AND J. E. THORPE. 1976. Growth bimodality in the Atlantic salmon. Int. Counc. Explor. Sea C.M.1976/ M:22. 7 p.

STEFÁNSSON, U. 1954. Temperature variations in the North Icelandic coastal area. Rit. Fiskideildar 2: 27 p.

SUTCLIFFE, W. H., JR., R. H. LOUCKS, AND K. F. DRINKWATER. 1976. Coastal circulation and physical oceanography of the Scotian Shelf. J. Fish. Res. Board Can. 33: 98−115.

TAYLOR, V. R. 1985. The early Atlantic salmon fishery in Newfoundland and Labrador. Can. Spec. Publ. Fish. Aquat. Sci. 76: 71 p.

THORPE, J. E., AND K. A. MITCHELL. 1981. Stocks of Atlantic salmon (*Salmo salar*) in Britain and Ireland: discreteness, and current management. Can. J. Fish. Aquat. Sci. 38: 1576–1590.

THORPE, J. E., R. I. G. MORGAN, C. TALBOT, AND M. S. MILES. 1983. Inheritance of developmental rates in Atlantic salmon, *Salmo salar* L. Aquaculture 33: 119–128.

WEEKS, E. 1971. The Moisie salmon club. Barre Publishers, Barre, Massachusetts.

WHITE, H. C., AND A. G. HUNTSMAN. 1938. Is local behaviour in salmon heritable? J. Fish. Res. Board Can. 4: 1–18.

Biological Factors Affecting Age at Maturity in Atlantic Salmon (*Salmo salar*)

R. G. Randall

Department of Fisheries and Oceans,
Research Branch, Gulf Region, P.O. Box 5030, Moncton, N.B. E1C 9B6

J. E. Thorpe

Department of Agriculture and Fisheries for Scotland,
Freshwater Fisheries Laboratory, Pitlochry, Scotland, U.K.

and R. J. Gibson and D. G. Reddin

Department of Fisheries and Oceans,
Research Branch, Newfoundland Region, P.O. Box 5667, St. John's, Nfld. A1C 5X1

Abstract

RANDALL, R. G., J. E. THORPE, R. J. GIBSON, AND D. G. REDDIN. 1986. Biological factors affecting age at maturity in Atlantic salmon (*Salmo salar*), p. 90–96. *In* D. J. Meerburg [ed.] Salmonid age at maturity. Can. Spec. Publ. Fish. Aquat. Sci. 89.

Biological factors affecting the age when Atlantic salmon become sexually mature include intrinsic factors such as growth rate and age and size at smolting and extrinsic factors such as food supply and competition for it. Maturation is energetically costly, particularly for female salmon, and maturation cannot be initiated until sufficient energy and materials are stored. In freshwater, the age when male parr mature is directly correlated to growth, although the incidence of maturation is also under genetic control. The influence of parr maturation on subsequent maturation at sea is not well understood, and probably differs among populations. Physiological conflict between smoltification and maturation masks any direct link between growth in freshwater and final sea age at maturity. However, there does appear to be a negative correlation between size at smolting and sea age at maturity. There is insufficient evidence to conclude that growth at sea affects age at maturity. Many questions regarding biological factors affecting age at maturity in natural populations of Atlantic salmon remain unanswered. Probably the most profitable research in future will come from long-term studies on experimental rivers.

Résumé

RANDALL, R. G., J. E. THORPE, R. J. GIBSON, AND D. G. REDDIN. 1986. Biological factors affecting age at maturity in Atlantic salmon (*Salmo salar*), p. 90–96. *In* D. J. Meerburg [ed.] Salmonid age at maturity. Can. Spec. Publ. Fish. Aquat. Sci. 89.

Les facteurs biologique qui influent sur l'âge auquel le saumon de l'Atlantique devient sexuellement mature comprennent des facteurs intrinsèques comme le taux de croissance de même que l'âge et la taille au moment de la transformation en saumoneau et des facteurs extrinsèques comme la nourriture disponible et la concurrence pour cette dernière. La maturation demande énormément d'énergie, surtout pour le saumon femelle, et ne peut se déclencher tant qu'il n'y a pas suffisamment d'énergie et de matières emmagasinées. En eau douce, il y a corrélation directe entre l'âge auquel le tacon mâle devient adulte et la croissance, bien que la maturation se fasse également sous le contrôle des gènes. On ne comprend pas très bien l'effet de la maturation de tacons sur la maturation ultérieure en mer et il est probable que celui-ci diffère d'une population à l'autre. Le conflit physiologique qui existe entre la transformation en saumoneau et la maturation masque tout lien direct entre la croissance en eau douce et l'âge définitif atteint en mer à la maturité. Cependant, il semble qu'il y ait une corrélation négative entre la taille atteinte au moment de la transformation en saumoneau et l'âge en mer au moment de la maturité. Il n'y a pas suffisamment de preuves pour conclure que la croissance en mer influe sur l'âge atteint à la maturité. Un grand nombre de questions touchant les facteurs biologiques qui influent sur l'âge au moment de la maturité dans les populations naturelles de saumon de l'Atlantique demeurent sans réponse. Il est probable que les recherches les plus profitables à l'avenir seront menées dans le cadre d'études à long terme concernant des rivières expérimentales.

Intrinsic biological factors affecting the age when Atlantic salmon (*Salmo salar*) first mature include growth rate, size and age at smolting, and the status of the endocrine regulators of development. Extrinsic biological factors include external influences on these regulators, such as food supply and competition for it. Isolating biological factors is somewhat arbitrary in view of their interrelationships with other factors; however, our purpose is to identify their potential importance in the maturation process, and to discuss their implications for managing wild stocks.

Maturation

Sexual maturation in Atlantic salmon is an endogenous cyclic process which involves proliferation of gonadal tissue and subsequent release or resorption of reproductive products. It is regulated through the hypothalamo-hypophysical axis, and synchronized by environmental cues, predominantly photoperiod (Lam 1983; Lundqvist 1983). As an anabolic process, sexual maturation requires a source of energy and materials, which implies potential physiological

TABLE 1. Energy cost of spawning in anadromous fishes.

| Species | River | Energy cost of spawning: % total energy used: | | | | % weight loss | | |
| | | fat | | protein | | | | |
		female	male	female	male	female	male	both
Sockeye*								
(*Oncorhynchus nerka*)	Fraser	96	91	53	31			
American shad**								
(*Alosa sapidissima*)	Connecticut					45	48	
Atlantic salmon***								
(*Salmo salar*)	Big Salmon							64
	St. John							71
	N.W. Miramichi							85

Authorities: *Idler and Clemens 1959; in Foerster, 1968; **Leggett 1972; ***Schaffer and Elson 1975. (Loss of growth due to spawning was recalculated from Schaffer and Elson's table 8 by converting fork lengths to weights).

competition with somatic growth. Policansky (1983) suggested that under stable conditions when food is not limited, fish should grow rapidly and mature as soon as they are developmentally able to do so. Ultimately, this ability is reached when they have stored sufficient energy and materials to spawn successfully.

Atlantic salmon cease feeding when they enter freshwater to spawn (Jones 1959; Lear 1972). Therefore the energy required for completing sexual maturation, migrating upstream, physiological maintenance until the time of spawning, and for completing the spawning act must come from endogenous sources. Energy costs of spawning by anadromous fish have been estimated accurately for sockeye salmon (*Oncorhynchus nerka*; Idler and Clemens 1959) and less accurately for American shad (*Alosa sapidissima*; Leggett 1972) and Atlantic salmon (Schaffer and Elson 1975) (Table 1). The high energy demands indicated by these studies emphasise the importance of size at maturation for anadromous salmon. Consideration of life-history strategies usually focus on the trade-off between somatic growth required to achieve a minimum weight, the mortality cost of achieving that weight, and total fecundity, which is itself a function of size (Schaffer and Elson 1975; Schaffer 1979; Scarnecchia 1983; Healey and Heard 1984; Healey 1986). The values of these variables should differ between stocks, since different river environments impose different energy demands. The energetic studies mentioned also indicated that the costs for females were higher than for males, at least for sockeye salmon and shad. Higher costs for females are also probably true for Atlantic salmon. Male parr commonly mature in freshwater while females rarely do (except in wholly landlocked populations), and anadromous males usually mature earlier than females (Schaffer 1979). A smaller size at maturity suggests that energy costs for males are less than for females. Hence the dynamic processes leading to maturation must be considered for each sex separately.

Biological Factors Affecting Maturation Age

Freshwater Environment

Growth Rate

Since minimim lipid and protein stores must be acquired by salmon to support reproduction, intuitively it seems likely that maturation will be directly correlated with growth. Alm (1959) provided experimental evidence confirming this in brown trout (*Salmo trutta*), and Thorpe (1986) noted that the same relationship had been demonstrated for 11 other salmonid species, including Atlantic salmon.

Parr that do not mature in freshwater undergo smolting and further growth at sea, before maturing. The effect of freshwater growth rate on sea age at maturity must be considered indirectly by its influence on parr maturation and smolting. Both processes mask any direct link between growth in freshwater and final sea age at maturity.

Extrinsic Biological Factors Affecting Growth

The relationship between density and growth rate in juvenile Atlantic salmon was investigated under hatchery conditions by Refstie and Kittelsen (1976). Using five density regimes, mean fry weight after 247 d feeding was negatively correlated with density. In wild populations, Egglishaw and Shackley (1977) showed that over a 10-yr period in one Scottish stream the length of 0+ salmon at the end of the growing season was inversely related to their population density. In another stream, over 8 yr, they found that the weight of 0+ salmon was inversely correlated to both their population density and the biomass of 1+ salmon present (Egglishaw and Shackley 1980). Prouzet (1978) found that in a stream with a steep gradient, growth of salmon fry was density dependent, but in another stream with a lower gradient the biomass was regulated by emigration. In the Miramichi River, New Brunswick, growth of salmon fry was inversely correlated with population density but growth of parr was not (Randall 1982; Randall and Paim 1982). Here food was probably not limiting for parr, but in a northern Quebec river where it was, sizes of all age-groups were inversely related to density, although competition was not found between 1+ and 2+ parr (Gibson and Dickson 1984). Interspecific competition between underyearlings of brook trout (*Salvelinus fontinalis*) and salmon depressed the growth of salmon in a cool second order stream, but not where food was abundant in experimental stream tanks (MacCrimmon et al. 1983). In a larger river, where there was a diversity of habitat, growth of 0+ and 1+ salmon parr was not affected by brook trout, but growth of 2+ parr was negatively affected by trout (Gibson and Dickson 1984). In an experimental stream tank Symons (1976) found no competitive effects on growth of salmon parr in the presence of minnows (*Notropis cornutus, Rhinichthys atratulus*) and suckers (*Catastomus commersoni*). However, in maritime rivers salmon parr are less common in pools where these and other species co-exist (Elson and Tuomi 1975), whereas in systems with fewer species, salmon parr are common in lentic habitats (Gibson 1973; Chadwick and Green 1985).

Because growth rate of salmon parr can be affected by intra- and interspecific competition, potentially both factors can affect maturation.

Maturation of Male Parr

Male parr commonly mature in freshwater throughout the geographic range of Atlantic salmon (Jones 1959; Power 1969; Dalley et al. 1983). The proportion that mature can be high — 80% in a Newfoundland anadromous population (Myers 1984), and 100% in landlocked populations of miniature fish. Mature parr produce viable sperm, capable of fertilizing eggs (Jones 1959; Thorpe and Morgan 1980; Sutterlin and Maclean 1984; Glebe and Saunders 1986).

Under experimental conditions male parr maturation rate was positively correlated with growth rate, in agreement with the hypothesis discussed above. Murphy (1980), Bailey et al. (1980), and Thorpe et al. (1983) found that the fastest growing parr in tank experiments matured first, but incidence of maturation varied between families. Among different wild populations Dalley et al. (1983) found the same correlation, and they too noted that fast growth alone did not necessarily determine the incidence of maturation, since stock differences existed also. There are few published data on incidence of maturation within individual populations over a series of years. However, Myers (1984) and Myers et al. (1985) found that the proportion of 1+ parr that matured over a 5-yr period was positively related to growth, with a size threshold of 70−72 mm fork length below which males do not generally mature.

During maturation male parr grow faster at first and then more slowly than immatures (Lee and Power 1976; Saunders and Sreedharan 1977; Murphy 1980; Thorpe and Morgan 1980; Thorpe et al. 1983; Saunders et al. 1982; Glebe and Saunders 1986). Mortality rate in male parr that mature is higher than in immature parr (Österdahl 1969; Mitans 1973; Dalley et al. 1983; Myers 1984), possibly in part because of reduced lipid levels in mature parr (Saunders and Sreedharan 1977). The endocrine regulation of maturation also inhibits smoltification (reviewed in Thorpe 1986). Myers (1984) found that the probability of smolting in the second year for a male parr maturing at 1+ was only 13% that of an immature female. Therefore, in addition to having a higher mortality rate, mature parr are also exposed to freshwater mortality factors for a longer period than their immature counterparts.

In view of Myers' finding, it is not surprising that the effect of freshwater maturation on subsequent maturation of surviving males at sea is unclear. Schiefer (1971) hypothesised that mature parr later matured as 1-sea-winter (1SW) salmon. Data he summarised from several Quebec rivers on the North Shore of the Gulf of St. Lawrence indicated a positive correlation between the incidence of mature male parr and proportions of 1SW salmon in the adult spawning run. Results from controlled experiments (Glebe and Saunders 1986) confirmed this among specific strains of salmon from New Brunswick. At the family level no relationship was found, and Naevdal (1983) and Glebe and Saunders (1986) concluded that maturation in freshwater and seawater are probably genetically independent. However, as mature parr are the rapid developers, and if 80% of them never go to sea anyway, maturation at the parr stage could reduce rather than increase the percentage of 1SW salmon in a family. Hence the absence of correlation may be an environmental and not a genetic effect, and so the genetic independence of freshwater and seawater maturation may not exist. Bielak and Power (1986) examined other data from the Quebec North Shore and found no correlation, and others have also found no correlation between fresh and seawater maturation in other salmon rivers (Schaffer and Elson 1975; Dalley et al. 1983). So the Schiefer hypothesis remains conjectural. From present data it is likely that the relationships between maturation in freshwater and the sea differ between stocks.

Parr maturation has important demographic consequences for Atlantic salmon populations in another way. Myers (1983) argued that increases in the proportion of male parr that mature could be an evolutionary response to fishing pressure, a point made independently by Caswell et al. (1984). Because of the high mortality associated with maturation in freshwater, Myers (1984) estimated that 60% of potential sea-run male production of one Newfoundland river was lost.

Age and Size at Smolting

Smolting is the coordination of several complex physiological, morphological and behavioural changes which result in salmon migrating to and surviving in the sea (Hoar 1976; Wedemeyer et al. 1980; Bern and Mahnken 1982; Thorpe et al. 1985). Physiologically, smolting and maturation are mutually inhibitory (Thorpe 1986): smolting implies the loss of freshwater adaptations, while maturation requires their retention (see below). Age at smolting is more variable than size, and is a function of growth rate. Among different populations Symons (1979) and Power (1981) documented that smolt age and length of growing season were inversely correlated, with considerable variability in this trend. For one population studied over 9 yr, Chadwick (1981) found that mean smolt size remained relatively constant [coefficient of variation (CV) = 1], while mean smolt age varied from one year to the next (CV = 7).

The relationship between smolting age and final age at maturity is not well understood in Atlantic salmon. Hutton (1937) proposed the inverse ratio hypothesis: slow-growing parr that smolt at an older age return as younger sea-age salmon than parr which smolt earlier. Gardner (1976) noted both supporting and contradictory evidence for this hypothesis from studies of wild and hatchery stocks. Recent support comes from Bailey and Saunders (1984), and contradiction from Bielak and Power (1986). The relationship will remain obscure until the mechanisms involved are more clearly understood. One complication has already been noted: the energy costs of maturation and the rates of achieving it differ between the sexes, and so smolting−age/maturation−age relationships should be considered separately for each sex. Also, smolting age itself may not be the important variable. For wild salmon (Chadwick et al. 1986) and for hatchery salmon (Naevdal 1978, 1983; Ritter et al. 1986), positive correlations were found between size at smolting and incidence of 1SW salmon. This also applied to coho (*Oncorhynchus kisutch*) and sockeye salmon (Bilton et al. 1982; Peterman 1982). In wild Atlantic salmon populations, size at smolting increases with age (Forsythe 1967; Jessop 1975; Chadwick 1981). Such studies support the inverse ratio theory: older fish at smolting are larger and mature sooner at sea than younger smaller ones. Although the relationship between size at smolting and maturation has been shown among different populations (Chadwick et al. 1986), it has not been shown within populations over time.

The smolting process itself may delay sexual maturation. Thorpe (1982) noted that Atlantic salmon which smolted did not spawn for another 15 months, while some of their smaller male siblings matured in freshwater after only 6 months. However, Gardner (1976) and Chadwick et al. (1986) described cases where salmon matured after exceptionally short sojourns at sea; in cases where information on growth was available, these fish had smolted at an exceptionally large size.

Future research that clarifies the physiological relationships between smolting and maturation should also clarify whether or not the inverse ratio theory (or some modification of it) is applicable to most salmon populations.

Physiological State in Freshwater

Growth, maturation, and smolting, are all interrelated, as components of overall development of the individual salmon. Maturation must therefore be considered in relation to these other aspects of development. Organisms reproduce as soon as they are able to do so, but the time interval from fertilisation to reproduction is constrained both genetically and environmentally. First, the organism is the result of its own evolutionary history; its adult morphology, and the control processes involved in its production, all require energy and materials to complete its developmental programme. Secondly, the rate at which this programme can be run depends upon the opportunities provided in the organism's environment. Within any given environment, selection will have shaped the range of genotypes that can succeed there, and consequently reproductive patterns within a single species differ from one environment to the next.

The age at which a salmon will first mature becomes a question about these constraints on the developmental process. The freshwater environment is the physical context in which the greater part of this developmental differentiation takes place, whereas the bulk of growth may, but does not necessarily, occur at sea. Whether or not it does so depends on the outcome of physiological competition between the processes of smolting and sexual maturation (Thorpe 1982; Nagahama 1985; Ikuta et al. 1985; Miwa and Inui 1985; Aida et al. 1985; Langdon and Thorpe 1985; Villarreal and Thorpe 1985). Smolting represents the collective loss of freshwater adaptations, and results in the emigration of the fish to sea where it may increase its body mass by 100 times before returning to freshwater to spawn. Sexual maturation on the other hand involves the maintenance, or reassertion, of freshwater adaptations, and inhibits emigration from freshwater or promotes immigration to it. Each process is the result of complex changes under neuroendocrine control, and the hormonal regulators are themselves dependent on external and internal environmental signals (Scott and Sumpter 1983; Villarreal 1983). It has been suggested that the physiological state of the individual at times when it is susceptible to environmental triggering of each process determines which one will dominate (Thorpe 1986).

Elson (1957) argued that smolting was dependent on a size-threshold being exceeded. Bailey et al. (1980), Thorpe et al. (1980) and Bagliniere and Maisse (1985) discussed the possibility that a similar size-threshold mechanism applied to the onset of maturation, and that the relative magnitude of these thresholds and the time at which they were critical, determined which process occurred in individual fish. Such size-thresholds may be convenient indices for the observer, but how does the fish know how large it is? Present size indicates past performance: current performance is measured by instantaneous growth rate. Thorpe (1986, this workshop) has suggested that salmon are aware of the rate at which they are acquiring surplus energy, through neuro-endocrine feedback mechanisms *via* the rates of secretion and utilisation of hormones associated with its storage. Provided these rates are above genetically determined threshold levels at those seasons when the fish are sensitive to photo-periodic stimulation of the appropriate hypothalamic-releasing factors, then smolting or maturation changes will ensue. Stock differences in such threshold levels, and in the precise timing of sensitivity to environmental cues are to be expected. The growth model based on this hypothesis predicts that fry growing under very favourable conditions (as in N.W. France) may be switched in early spring to mature at 0+, whereas those not so switched may be growing fast enough in midsummer to avoid growth arrest in July, and so smolt at age 1+. At the opposite extreme, developmental conditions may be so poor that maturation as parr is never induced, and smolting does not occur until late in life (see fig. 3 in Thorpe 1986).

However, it has recently been shown (Berven and Gill 1983) that variation between populations in age and size at metamorphosis in the wood frog, *Rana sylvatica*, results from differential selection pressures in different environments. For example, in a Maryland population, size at metamorphosis was more highly correlated with survival than was time to metamorphosis, whereas in a Canadian tundra population the opposite was true. Such stock-specific evolutionary solutions to local ecological problems may well be found in age and size at maturity among Atlantic salmon stocks, leading to variation between populations in age-at-maturity response to changed environmental conditions, and consequently differential vulnerability of different stocks to exploitation.

Marine Environment

The sea age when Atlantic salmon mature is determined to a large extent before juveniles emigrate from their natal rivers. For many populations the 1SW:2SW salmon ratio remains relatively constant from one year to the next (Scarnecchia 1984; Chadwick et al. 1986), such that 2SW salmon returns can be predicted one year in advance from 1SW salmon returns of the current year (Marshall et al. 1982). A similar phenomenon is evident among coho salmon, where the adult return for the next year is predictable from the jack return of the present one, and this forms the basis of a management tool for prediction and regulation of harvests (e.g., McGie 1984). If marine influences were a major factor affecting age at maturity such predictive systems would not be usable. However, other data show long period cyclic variation in 1SW:MSW salmon ratios among

Atlantic salmon (Martin and Mitchell 1985) suggesting some marine effects. In the Pacific this may also be true (Krogius 1978), and the recent disruption of predictability of fishery patterns by the El Niño phenomenon suggest that there are episodic factors which have to be taken into account (McGie 1984).

Most somatic growth of anadromous salmon occurs at sea, and conditions for growth there fluctuate spatially and temporally. Some authors have postulated that maturation rate at sea is positively correlated with growth rate there (Schaffer and Elson 1975; but see criticism by Myers and Hutching 1985). Within two separate populations Dempson et al. (1986) were unable to find any consistent evidence of marine growth rate affecting maturation rate, but they summarised earlier studies, primarily based on cage-rearing, which did support the positive correlation. For sockeye, Peterman (1986) found that fast growth during early marine life resulted in earlier maturation, and he noted similar results from studies of other Pacific salmon species. For Atlantic salmon the evidence is still inconclusive.

Some authors have suggested that maturation at sea may be related to fluctuations of water temperature (Saunders et al. 1983; Scarnecchia 1983; Martin and Mitchell 1985), and water temperature may directly affect productivity, the location of prime feeding areas (Martin and Mitchell 1985), growth conditions, survival and migration costs (Thorpe 1984). Dempson et al. (1986) found that correlations between maturation and sea temperatures have been contradictory, and they cautioned that results from sea-cage experiments that suggest a relationship exists may not apply to wild populations.

General Discussion

Because of excessive fishing pressure, many Atlantic salmon populations are presently at low levels (Symons 1980; Chadwick 1985). On the basis of arguments presented above, the following composite predictive hypothesis is put forward for the fate of such depleted populations. At parr densities below stream carrying capacity, parr growth would be relatively high due to reduced competition. For females, fast growth would result in young small smolts, and so relatively greater proportions of females would mature as 2-sea-winter or older salmon. For males, fast growth would result in large proportions maturing in freshwater, increasing the size and age but reducing the number of parr surviving to smolting. Proportionally more of the surviving males would then mature as 1-sea-winter fish, but the absolute number would be reduced. In terms of yield to the fishery this response from the males emphasises the need to maintain spawning densities at high levels.

Several elements of this hypothesis need further testing, especially the relationships between male parr growth and maturation; juvenile density and smolting age and size; and spawning density and maturation age of the progeny.

Many questions regarding variability in age at maturity and biological factors that affect it in the wild remain unanswered. Intrinsic factors (growth, incidence of parr maturation, smolting size and age) are to some extent under genetic control. There is sufficient latitude within these genetic constraints for the environment to have a significant effect, but responses of individual stocks to increased or decreased parr growth might be quite different. Much of our knowledge of maturation in salmon is derived from hatchery or cage experiments. These have the advantage of control, and so can answer specific questions, but are these answers always applicable to stocks in the wild? Our most reliable understanding of wild populations will come from long-term observations on experimental populations (Chadwick 1982), but controlled experiments in hatcheries are needed to define the critical measurements required from populations in the wild.

The goal of salmon culture is to produce edible flesh as quickly and economically as possible. Sexual maturation of cultured fish is undesirable, since it interferes with the end product, somatic growth. The complexities of the maturation process are such that there is not yet a simple and cheap method of controlling it. Perhaps the most profitable solution will come from investigations of sterilisation techniques (Konno and Tashiro 1982; Yamazaki 1983; Villarreal and Thorpe 1985), which will eliminate problems associated with maturation altogether. Sterilisation has been used successfully for many years in other forms of animal production (cattle, poultry, and pigs) to enhance growth and improve meat quality, and should benefit salmonid culture also.

Acknowledgements

Dr. B. Glebe, E. Henderson and C. Léger contributed many helpful comments during the synthesis discussion. We thank Dr. M. F. O'Connell, Dr. R. L. Saunders, and G. Turner for reviewing the manuscript.

References

AIDA, K., T. KATO, AND M. AWAJI. 1984. Effects of castration on the smoltification of precocious male masu salmon *Oncorhynchus masou*. Bull. Jap. Soc. Sci. Fish. 50: 565–571.

ALM, G. 1959. Connection between maturity, size and age in fishes. Rep. Inst. Freshwat. Res. Drottningholm 40: 5–145.

BAGLINIERE, J. L., AND G. MAISSE. 1985. Precocious maturation and smoltification in wild Atlantic salmon in the Armorican Massif, France. Aquaculture 45: 249–263.

BAILEY, J. K., AND R. L. SAUNDERS. 1984. Returns of three year-classes of sea-ranched Atlantic salmon of various river strains and strain crosses. Aquaculture 41: 259–270.

BAILEY, J. K., R. L. SAUNDERS, AND M. I. BUZETA. 1980. Influence of parental smolt age and sea age on growth and smolting of hatchery-reared Atlantic salmon (*Salmo salar*). Can. J. Fish. Aquat. Sci. 37: 1379–1386.

BERN, H. A., AND C. V. W. MAHNKEN [ED.]. 1982. Salmonid smoltification. Aquaculture, Vol. 28 (1/2).

BERVEN, K. A., AND D. E. GILL. 1983. Interpreting geographic variation in life-history traits. Am. Zool. 23: 85–97.

BIELAK, A. T., AND G. POWER. 1986. Independence of sea age and river age in Atlantic salmon (*Salmo salar*) from Quebec North Shore rivers, p. 70–78. *In* D. J. Meerburg [ed.] Salmonid age at maturity. Can. Spec. Publ. Fish. Aquat. Sci. 89.

BILTON, H. T., D. F. ALDERDICE, AND J. T. SCHNUTE. 1982. Influence of time and size at release of juvenile coho salmon (*Oncorhynchus kisutch*) on returns at maturity. Can. J. Fish. Aquat. Sci. 39: 426–447.

CASWELL, H., R. J. NAIMAN, AND R. MORIN. 1984. Evaluating the consequences of reproduction in complex salmonid life cycles. Aquaculture 43: 123–134.

CHADWICK, E. M. P. 1981. Biological characteristics of Atlantic salmon smolts in Western Arm Brook, Newfoundland. Can. Tech. Rep. Fish. Aquat. Sci. 1024: 45 p.

1982. Stock recruitment relationship for Atlantic salmon (*Salmo salar*) in Newfoundland rivers. Can. J. Fish. Aquat.

Sci. 39: 1496−1501.

1985. The influence of spawning stock on production and yield of Atlantic salmon, *Salmo salar* L., in Canadian Rivers. Aquacult. Fish. Manage. 1: 111−119.

CHADWICK, E. M. P., R. G. RANDALL, AND C. LÉGER. 1986. Ovarian development of Atlantic salmon (*Salmo salar*) smolts and age at first maturity, p. 15−28. *In* D. J. Meerburg [ed.] Salmonid age at maturity. Can. Spec. Publ. Fish. Aquat. Sci. 89.

CHADWICK, E. M. P., AND J. M. GREEN. 1985. Atlantic salmon (*Salmo salar* L.) production in a largely lacustrine Newfoundland watershed. Verh. Int. Verein. Limnol. 22: 2509−2515.

DALLEY, E. L., C. W. ANDREWS, AND J. M. GREEN. 1983. Precocious male Atlantic salmon parr (*Salmo salar*) in insular Newfoundland. Can. J. Fish. Aquat. Sci. 40: 647−652.

DEMPSON, J. B., R. A. MYERS, AND D. G. REDDIN. 1986. Age at first maturity of Atlantic salmon (*Salmo salar*) — influences of the marine environment, p. 70−78. *In* D. J. Meerburg [ed.] Salmonid age at maturity. Can. Spec. Publ. Fish. Aquat. Sci. 89.

EGGLISHAW, H. J., AND P. E. SHACKLEY. 1977. Growth, survival and production of juvenile salmon and trout in a Scottish stream, 1966−75. J. Fish. Biol. 11: 647−672.

1980. Survival and growth of salmon, *Salmo salar* (L.), planted in a Scottish stream. J. Fish. Biol. 16: 565−584.

ELSON, P. F. 1957. The importance of size in the change from parr to smolt in Atlantic salmon. Can. Fish. Cult. 21: 1−6.

ELSON, P. F., AND A. L. W. TUOMI. 1975. The Foyle fisheries: new bases for rational management. Special Report to the Foyle Fisheries Commission, Londonderry, Northern Ireland: 1−194.

FOERSTER, R. E. 1968. The sockeye salmon, *Oncorhynchus nerka*. Bull. Fish. Res. Board Can. 162: 422 p.

FORSYTHE, M. G. 1967. Analysis of the 1965 smolt run in the Northwest Miramichi River, New Brunswick. Fish. Res. Board Can. Tech. Rep. 4: 73 p.

GARDNER, M. L. G. 1976. A review of factors which may influence the sea-age and maturation of Atlantic salmon *Salmo salar* L. J. Fish. Biol. 9: 289−327.

GIBSON, R. J. 1973. Interactions of juvenile Atlantic salmon (*Salmo salar* L.) and brook trout (*Salvelinus fontinalis* (Mitchill)). Int. Atl. Salmon Symp. 1972, Int. Atl. Salmon Found., Spec. Publ. 4: 181−202.

GIBSON, R. J., AND T. DICKSON. 1984. The effects of competition on the growth of juvenile Atlantic salmon. Naturaliste can. 111: 175−191.

GLEBE, B. D., AND R. L. SAUNDERS. 1986. Genetic factors in sexual maturity of cultured Atlantic salmon (*Salmo salar*) parr and adults reared in sea cages, p. 24−29. *In* D. J. Meerburg [ed.] Salmonid age at maturity. Can. Spec. Publ. Fish. Aquat. Sci. 89.

HEALEY, M. C. 1986. Optimum size and age at maturity in Pacific salmon and effects of size-selective fisheries, p. 39−52. *In* D. J. Meerburg [ed.] Salmonid age at maturity. Can. Spec. Publ. Fish. Aquat. Sci. 89.

HEALEY, M. C., AND W. R. HEARD. 1984. Inter- and intra-population variation in the fecundity of chinook salmon (*Oncorhynchus tsawytscha*) and its relevance to life history theory. Can. J. Fish. Aquat. Sci. 41: 476−483.

HOAR, W. S. 1976. Smolt transformation: evolution, behaviour and physiology. J. Fish. Res. Board Can. 33: 1233−1252.

HUTTON, J. A. 1937. Wye parr and smolts. The inverse ratio theory of river and sea life. Salm. Trout Mag. 87: 119−123.

IDLER, D. R., AND W. A. CLEMENS. 1959. The energy expenditures of Fraser River sockeye salmon during the spawning migration to Chilko and Stuart Lakes. Int. Pacific Salmon Fish. Comm., Prog. Rep. No. 6: 80 p.

IKUTA, K., K. AIDA, N. OKUMOTO, AND I. HANYU. 1985. Effects of thyroxine and methyltestosterone on the smoltification of masu salmon (*Oncorhynchus masou*). Aquaculture 45:

289−303.

JESSOP, B. 1975. Investigation of the salmon (*Salmo salar*) smolt migration of the Big Salmon River, New Brunswick, 1966−72. Fish. Mar. Serv. Tech. Rep. MAR/T-75-1: 57 p.

JONES, J. W. 1959. The Salmon. Collins. London. 192 p.

KONNO, K., AND F. TASHIRO. 1982. The sterility of rainbow trout (*Salmo gairdneri*) irradiated with cobalt-60 gamma rays. J. Tokyo Univ. Fish. 68: 75−80. (Transl. by M. J. Dennis, Marine Lab. Tranal. No 2185, Aberdeen 1983.)

KROGIUS, F. V. 1978. The significance of genetic and ecological factors in the population dynamics of the sockeye salmon, *Oncorhynchus nerka*, from Lake Dal'neye. J. Ichthyol. 18: 211−221.

LAM,T. J. 1983. Environmental influences on gonadal activity in fish, p. 65−116. *In* W. S. Hoar, D. J. Randall, and E. M. Donaldson [ed.] Fish physiology: reproduction. Vol. IXB. Academic Press, New York, NY.

LANGDON, J. S., AND J. E. THORPE. 1985. The ontogeny of smoltification: developmental patterns of gill Na+/Ka+−ATPase, SDH, and chloride cells in juvenile Atlantic salmon, *Salmo salar* L. Aquaculture 45: 83−95.

LEAR, W. H. 1972. Food and feeding of Atlantic salmon in coastal areas and over oceanic depths. ICNAF Res. Bull. No. 9: 27−39.

LEE, R. L. G., AND G. POWER. 1976. Atlantic salmon (*Salmo salar*) of the Leaf River, Ungava Bay. J. Fish. Res. Board Can. 33: 2616−2621.

LEGGETT, W. C. 1972. Weight loss in American shad (*Alosa sapidissima*, Wilson) during the freshwater migration. Trans. Am. Fish. Soc. 101: 549−552.

LUNDQVIST, H. 1983. Precocious sexual maturation and smolting in Baltic salmon (*Salmo salar*): photoperiodic synchronisation and adaptive significance of annual biological cycles. Ph.D. thesis, Umea University, Sweden.

MACCRIMMON, H. R., T. A. DICKSON, AND R. J. GIBSON. 1983. Implications of differences in emergent times on growth and behaviour of juvenile Atlantic salmon (*Salmo salar*) and brook charr (*Salvelinus fontinalis*) in sympatric stream populations. Naturaliste can. 110: 379−384.

MARSHALL, T. L., J. L. PEPPAR, AND E. J. SCHOFIELD. 1982. Predication of 2SW and older Atlantic salmon returning to the Millbank trap, Miramichi River, New Brunswick. Canadian Atlantic Fisheries Advisory Committee Research Document 82/51.

MARTIN, J. H. A., AND K. A. MITCHELL. 1985. Influence of sea temperature upon the numbers of grilse and multi-sea-winter Atlantic salmon (*Salmo salar*) caught in the vicinity of the River Dee (Aberdeenshire). Can. J. Fish. Aquat. Sci. 42: 1513−1521.

McGIE, A. M. 1984. Evidence for density among coho salmon stocks in the Oregon Production Index area, p. 37−49. *In* W. G. Pearcy [ed.] The influence of Ocean Conditions on the Production of Salmonids in the North Pacific. Oregon State University, Sea Grant Publication ORESU-W-83-001.

MITANS, A. R. 1973. Dwarf males and sex structure of a Baltic salmon (*Salmo salar*) population. J. Ichthyol. 13: 192−197.

MIWA, S., AND Y. INUI. 1985. Inhibitory effects of 17α-methyl-testosterone and estradiol-17β on smoltification of sterilized amago salmon (*Oncorhynchus rhodurus*). (Abstract only). Aquaculture 45: 383.

MURPHY, T. M. 1980. Studies on pecocious maturity in artificially reared 1+ Atlantic salmon *Salmo salar* L. Ph.D. thesis, Stirling University, Scotland.

MYERS, R. A. 1983. Evolutionary change in the proportion of precocious parr and its effect on yield in Atlantic salmon. I.C.E.S. CM 1983/M13: 16 p.

1984. Demographic consequences of precocious maturation of Atlantic salmon (*Salmo salar*). Can. J. Fish. Aquat. Sci. 41: 1349−1353.

MYERS, R. A., AND J. HUTCHINGS. 1985. Tests of life history

theory applied to Atlantic salmon. Ecology (In press).

MYERS, R. A., J. A. HUTCHINGS, AND R. J. GIBSON. 1985. Variation in precocious maturation within and among populations of Atlantic salmon. I.C.E.S. CM 1985/M9: 21 p.

NAEVDAL, G. 1983. Genetic factors in connection with age at maturation. Aquaculture 33: 97–106.

NAEVDAL, G., M. HOLM, O. INGEBRIGTSEN, AND D. MÖLLER. 1978. Variation in age at first spawning in Atlantic salmon (Salmo salar). J. Fish. Res. Board Can. 35: 145–147.

NAGAHAMA, Y. 1985. Involvement of endocrine systems in smoltification in amago salmon, Oncorhynchus rhodurus. (Abstract only) Aquaculture 45: 383–384.

ÖSTERDAHL, L. 1969. The smolt run of a small Swedish river, p. 205–215. In T. G. Northcote [ed.] Salmon and trout in streams. H. R. MacMillan Lectures in Fisheries, Univ. of British Columbia, Vancouver, B.C.

PETERMAN, R. M. 1982. Model of salmon age structure and its use in preseason forecasting and studies of marine survival. Can. J. Fish. Aquat. Sci. 39: 1444–1452.

PETERMAN, R. M. 1985. Patterns of interannual variation in age at maturity of sockeye salmon (Oncorhynchus nerka) in Alaska and British Columbia. Can. J. Fish. Aquat. Sci. 42: 1595–1607.

POLICANSKY, D. 1983. Size, age and demography of metamorphosis and sexual maturation in fishes. Am. Zool. 23: 57–63.

POWER, G. 1969. The salmon of Ungava Bay. Arctic Inst. N. Am. Tech. Paper 22: 72 p.

1981. Stock characteristics and catches of Atlantic salmon (Salmo salar) in Quebec, and Newfoundland and Labrador in relation to environmental variables. Can. J. Fish. Aquat. Sci. 38: 1601–1611.

PROUZET, P. 1978. Relationahip between density and growth of Atlantic salmon reared in nursery streams in natural conditions. I.C.E.S. CM 1978/M13: 14 p.

RANDALL, R. G. 1982. Emergence, population densities and growth of salmon and trout fry in two New Brunswick streams. Can. J. Zool. 60: 2239–2244.

RANDALL, R. G., AND U. PAIM. 1982. Growth, biomass and production of juvenile Atlantic salmon (Salmo salar L.) in two Miramichi River, New Brunswick, tributary streams. Can. J. Zool. 60: 1647–1659.

REFSTIE, T., AND A. KITTELSEN. 1976. Effect of density on growth and survival of artificially reared Atlantic salmon. Aquaculture 8: 319–326.

RITTER, J. A., G. J. FARMER, R. K. MISRA, T. R. GOFF, J. K. BAILEY, AND E. BAUM. 1986. Parental influences and smolt size and sex ratio effects on sea age at first maturity of Atlantic salmon (Salmo salar), p. 30–38. In D. J. Meerburg [ed.] Salmonid age at maturity. Can. Spec. Publ. Fish. Aquat. Sci. 89.

SAUNDERS, R. L., AND A. SREEDHARAN. 1977. The incidence and genetic implications of sexual maturity in male Atlantic salmon parr. I.C.E.S. CM 1977/M21: 8 p.

SAUNDERS, R. L., E. B. HENDERSON, AND B. D. GLEBE. 1982. Precocious sexual maturation and smoltification in male Atlantic salmon (Salmo salar). Aquaculture 28: 211–229.

SAUNDERS, R. L., E. B. HENDERSON, B. D. GLEBE, AND E. D. LOUDENSLAGER. 1983. Evidence of a major environmental component in determination of the grilse: larger salmon ratio in Atlantic salmon (Salmo salar). Aquaculture 33: 107–118.

SCARNECCHIA, D. L. 1983. Age at sexual maturity in Icelandic stocks of Atlantic salmon (Salmo salar). Can. J. Fish. Aquat. Sci. 40: 1456–1468.

1984. Forecasting yields of two-sea-winter Atlantic salmon (Salmo salar) from Icelandic rivers. Can. J. Fish. Aquat. Sci. 41: 1234–1240.

SCHAFFER, W. M. 1979. The theory of life-history evolution and its application to Atlantic salmon. Symp. Zool. Soc. London. 44: 307–326.

SCHAFFER, W. M., AND P. F. ELSON. 1975. The adaptive significance of variations in life history among local populations of Atlantic salmon in North America. Ecology 56: 577–590.

SCHIEFER, K. 1971. Ecology of Atlantic salmon with special reference to the occurrence and abundance of grilse in North Shore Gulf of St. Lawrence Rivers. Ph.D. thesis, University of Waterloo, Ont. 129 p.

SCOTT, A. P., AND J. P. SUMPTER. 1983. The control of trout reproduction: basic and applied research on hormones, p. 176–199. In J. C. Rankin, T. J. Pitcher and R. Duggan [ed.] Control Processes in Fish Physiology. Croom Helm, London and Canberra.

SUTTERLIN, A. M., AND D. MACLEAN. 1984. Age at first maturity and the early expression of oocyte recruitment processes in two forms of Atlantic salmon (Salmo salar) and their hybrids. Can. J. Fish. Aquat. Sci. 41: 1139–1149.

SYMONS, P. E. K. 1976. Behaviour and growth of juvenile Atlantic salmon (Salmo salar) and three competitores at two stream velocities. J. Fish. Res. Board Can. 33: 2766–2773.

1979. Estimated escapement of Atlantic salmon (Salmo salar) for maximum smolt production in rivers of different productivity. J. Fish. Res. Board Can. 36: 132–140.

1980. Comment or estimated escapement of Atlantic salmon (Salmo salar) for maximum smolt production in rivers of different productivity. Can. J. Fish. Aquat. Sci. 37: 295.

THORPE, J. E. 1982. Migration in salmonids, with special reference to juveniles in freshwater, p. 86–97. In E. L. Brannon and E. O. Salo [ed.] Proceedings of the Salmon and Trout Migratory Behaviour Symposium, Seattle, WA.

1984. An overview, p. 303–306. In W. G. Pearcy [ed.] The influence of Ocean Conditions on the Production of Salmonids in the North Pacific. Oregon State University, Sea Grant Publications, ORESU-w-83-001.

THORPE, J. E. 1986. Age at first maturity in Atlantic salmon, Salmo salar: freshwater period influences and conflicts with smolting, p. 7–14. In D. J. Meerburg [ed.] Salmonid age at maturity. Can. Spec. Publ. Fish. Aquat. Sci. 89.

THORPE, J. E., H. A. BERN, R. L. SAUNDERS, AND A. SOIVIO [ED.]. 1985. Salmonid Smoltification II. Aquaculture, Vol. 45: 403 p.

THORPE, J. E., AND R. I. G. MORGAN. 1980. Growth-rate and of progeny of male Atlantic salmon parr, Salmo salar L. J. Fish. Biol. 17: 451–460.

THORPE, J. E., R. I. G. MORGAN, E. M. OTTAWAY, AND M. S. MILES. 1980. Time of divergence of growth groups between potential 1+ and 2+ smolts among sibling Atlantic salmon. J. Fish. Biol. 17: 13–21.

THORPE, J. E., R. I. G. MORGAN, C. TALBOT AND M. S. MILES. 1983. Inheritance of developmental rates in Atlantic salmon, Salmo salar L. Aquaculture 33: 119–128.

VILLARREAL, C. A. 1983. The role of light and endocrine factors in the development of bimodality in the juvenile Atlantic salmon (Salmo salar L.) Ph.D. thesis, University of Stirling, Scotland.

VILLARREAL, C. A., AND J. E. THORPE. 1985. Gonadal growth and bimodality of length frequency distribution in juvenile Atlantic salmon (Salmo salar). Aquaculture 45: 265–288.

WEDEMEYER, G. A., R. L. SAUNDERS, AND W. C. CLARKE. 1980. Environmental factors affecting smoltification and early marine survival of anadromous salmonids. Mar. Fish. Rev. 42: 1–14.

YAMAZAKI, F. 1983. Sex control and manipulation in fish. Aquaculture 33: 329–354.

Physical Influences on Age at Maturity of Atlantic Salmon (*Salmo salar*): A Synthesis of Ideas and Questions

G. Power

Department of Biology, University of Waterloo, Waterloo, Ont. N2L 3G1

Abstract

POWER, G. 1986. Physical influences on age at maturity of Atlantic salmon (*Salmo salar*): a synthesis of ideas and questions, p. 97–101. *In* D. J. Meerburg [ed.] Salmonid age at maturity. Can. Spec. Publ. Fish. Aquat. Sci. 89.

Physical factors influencing age at maturity are difficult to modify. General trands related to latitude are known while detailed effects are more subtle and often confounded by other factors. The freshwater environment determines smolt age, sex ratios and may affect sea-age. The influences of marine conditions are less well understood. Many questions remain to be answered relating to physical effects on life cycles of Atlantic salmon.

Résumé

POWER, G. 1986. Physical influences on age at maturity of Atlantic salmon (*Salmo salar*): a synthesis of ideas and questions, p. 97–101. *In* D. J. Meerburg [ed.] Salmonid age at maturity. Can. Spec. Publ. Fish. Aquat. Sci. 89.

Les facteurs physiques qui influent sur l'âge à la maturité sont difficiles à modifier. Les tendances générales relatives à la latitude sont connues même si les effets détaillés sont plus subtils et souvent confondus avec d'autres facteurs. Le milieu d'eau douce détermine l'âge des smolts et les rapports des sexes et peut influer sur le temps d'arrivée à maturité. Les influences des conditions marines sont moins bien comprises. De nombreuses questions restent sans réponse en ce qui concerne les effets physiques sur les cycles naturels du saumon atlantique.

During the September 1984 Canadian Atlantic Fisheries Scientific Advisory Committee (CAFSAC) Workshop on age at maturity of Atlantic salmon, it became increasingly clear that we could not explain what factors determine age at first spawning or the interval between spawnings in Atlantic salmon. The value of understanding this for effective and enlightened management of this resource was emphasized by Saunders (1986) in his introduction to the workshop. Gardner (1976) reviewed the available information and concluded that the evidence was confusing and no single factor could be identified which regulated the age at which Atlantic salmon mature and return to freshwater. He felt both environmental and genetic factors played a role in the expression of this trait. This is the same conclusion arrived at by Ricker (1972) in his review of Pacific salmon. Subsequent research, discussed and reviewed by Saunders (1981) and Thorpe and Mitchell (1981), has not changed this opinion. Genetic, biological and abiotic environmental influences all operate to determine the age at which Atlantic salmon mature. This conclusion not withstanding, the synthesis workshops were asked to focus their deliberations on the role and importance of specific influences on age at maturity.

Physical influences, namely climate, geology, geomorphology and hydrology, collectively modulate the freshwater and oceanographic conditions in which the salmon's life cycle takes place. These factors, and patterns of postglacial dispersal, have determined the range and local distribution of salmon and still impose limits on the growth and movement of individuals. The thrust of this synthesis is to identify where, and to what extent, physical conditions prevail in controlling age at maturity. A second objective is to suggest avenues of research which might help clarify certain fundamental questions about life cycles and stock characteristics.

Two major frustrations are associated with any discussion of physical factors. The first is the fishery manager's inability to manipulate or change abiotic factors in the natural environment except in a few relatively minor ways. Physical obstructions are an exception. The second is that climate-related factors seldom remain constant for long; they may be selected or avoided during parts of the life cycle and responses may be similar on either side of an optimum. Thus, such influences are often obscured in natural environments. Added to this are the confounding effects of biological and genetic factors which interact with abiotic conditions to produce a response. This clearly explains why so many investigations produce conflicting results and interpretation of the results of other experiments is difficult.

Freshwater Influences

Management interests tend to emphasize sea-age at maturity, which is correlated with size and fecundity, but equally important is total age at maturity or generation time, a measure of population turnover rate.

Among the physical factors influencing the duration of freshwater life, temperature is the most obvious. Over the salmon's range, it determines growing season and mean smolt age. Within stocks, it must play a role in year-to-year differences in mean smolt age and in the proportions of different aged smolts. Its influence is probably greatest during the first summer of life and may be confounded by biological factors, eg., parr density and availability of suitable prey species. It, (and photoperiod), controls timing and synchrony of events such as spawning, incubation and emergence which may, in turn, determine mortality rates, parr densities, growth and age at smolting. Difficulties in carrying out long term studies of wild stocks mean that there are few data suitable for demonstrating these effects.

The trend towards increasing age at migration at higher latitudes has been known since Dahl (1910) first described it for Norwegian stocks and correctly identified variations in the length of growing season as a contributing factor. Duration of river life is the overriding component causing northern stocks to exhibit the longest generation times (Gardner 1976; Symons 1979; Power 1981). Symons (1979) provided the best overview of the physical determinants of length of river life and production. He concluded that a rough estimate of the growing season was the number of days annually when river temperatures equalled or exceeded 7°C and it took approximately 500 d to produce a 15 cm smolt. He stated this was an oversimplification but could provide a useful estimate of smolt age when only temperatures were available. Another often quoted and useful guideline was suggested by Elson (1957), i.e., that salmon parr must attain a threshold length of 10 cm the autumn prior to metamorphosis. Both these approximations were intended for practical purposes and were proposed before many of the recent ideas on stock specificity had been elaborated (STOCS 1981). It is not surprising that recent publications have tended to refine these guidelines.

Evans et al. (1984) in their analysis of growth and smolting in Western Arm Brook, northern Newfoundland, developed a model which implies that critical size for smoltification differs for fish of different ages, and that critical length for smolting and growth rate vary between year classes. Amongst environmental factors, temperature during the first year was most influential in changing the proportions of 3- and 4-yr old smolts. It operates through modifying growth rate and critical length for smoltification in a manner which makes its effect hard to detect. The same model did not give a satisfactory fit to data on smolts migrating from the Little Codroy River, southwest Newfoundland, possibly because density dependent effects on growth and mortality were more pronounced in this river, while they were considered minimal in Western Arm Brook (Evans et al. 1985).

Several publications by Thorpe and his co-workers have addressed the questions of what controls smoltification and parr maturation in Atlantic salmon. They first described bimodality in the length-frequency distributions of similar aged hatchery reared parr; the upper mode continued to grow and became smolts the following spring (Thorpe 1977). Separation of these groups was possible in July of the first summer for aged 1+ smolts (see Thorpe, 1985, for a fuller discussion). Bailey et al. (1980) found the same phenomena in hatchery-reared Canadian strains with clear separation of modes by November. Physical factors modifying growth play an undetermined role in this phenomenon.

Like smolting, sexual maturation of male parr is a growth-related phenomena. In the wild, the fastest growing male parr are those that mature (Dalley et al. 1983), but the price is reduced size, since energy is diverted from somatic into gonadal growth (Bailey et al. 1980; Saunders et al. 1982). In the hatchery mature male parr occur in both modes; although in November they tend to be more concentrated towards the lower mode (Bailey et al. 1980; Kristinsson et al. 1985). Stock differences exist so that the fastest growing parr do not always have the highest incidence of maturity. In their rearing experiments, Bailey et al. (1980) found differences in the proportions of male parr maturing between two year-classes which they ascribed to environmental influences − namely rearing tank densities, since identical strains and crossing procedures were used in both years. In another experiment, Glebe et al. (1980) reported only negligible differences in the proportions of precocious males amongst progeny of families reared under ambient and elevated temperatures intended to produce 1+ and 2+ smolts.

Thorpe (1986) proposed that the growth rate of parr, if it exceeds a genetically determined threshold during mid-summer when the gonadotrophic hormone system is photosensitive, triggers maturation. Previously, Thorpe and Morgan (1980) demonstrated that the progeny of male parr develop faster to the smolt stage than the progeny of sea-run males. An adaptive response can, therefore, be suggested: under reduced parr densities growth is more rapid, the incidence of male parr maturity increases and the participation of these males in reproduction reduces the generation time and speeds recovery of the stock to normal densities.

Male parr maturity can affect sea-age at maturity and sex ratios of sea-run salmon. Several authors have shown increased mortality as a result of parr maturation (Mitans 1973; Dalley et al. 1983). Post-spawning survival is likely to be affected by physical conditions during winter. Myers (1984) modelled the consequences of mortality of male parr maturity in the Little Codroy River and related this to the composition of the adult stock. Since males tend to stay at sea for a shorter interval than females, increased male parr maturity and associated mortality tend to increase the average sea-age at maturity and the proportion of females in the stock. This condition applies more to rivers in which the salmon display multi-sea-year life cycles than to grilse rivers.

Russian work reviewed by Dirin-Khalturin (1981) suggests that physical conditions play a significant role in determining age at maturity in salmon inhabiting rivers in the Kola Peninsula, White Sea region. The weight of smolts is inversely correlated with the weight of spawners; rivers producing large young smolts tend to produce small, short sea life adults. Around the Kola Peninsula, mean smolt age decreases from Zapadnaya Litsa and Ura Rivers (3.32 and 3.30 yr) in the northwest to the Kolvitsa River (2.57 yr) in the southwest. This is associated with higher water temperatures and a longer ice-free period and is accompanied by a decrease in the mean weight of adult spawners.

Water temperature is cited as the important controlling variable. In rivers where water temperature is increased by groundwater springs, incubation time is reduced; likewise, except for residual males, river life is shorter. The Soyana and Pingea rivers are cited as examples where this occurs. The annual temperature regime is more important than the accumulated degree-days; early spring warming and slow autumn cooling allow better growth. The temperature of Arctic streams is also influenced by their colour index, which affects heat absorption. Lakes, especially large northern lakes, retard the annual warming and cooling of rivers causing lower mean annual temperatures and they maintain winter flows. Dirin-Khalturn (1981) provides data for ten rivers in which the mean weight (duration of sea life) of spawners is compared to a coefficient of lake surface to drainage area. Rivers with the highest area of lake produce the largest fish, and although no statistical analysis of the data is given, simple linear regression provides an r^2 value of 0.42 ($P = 0.04$), but this relationship is mostly due to the influence of 2 out of 10 values considered.

It has been suggested that geophysical characteristics of a river may play a role in determining the life-history parameters of the salmon stock inhabiting it. Using life-history theory, Schaffer and Elson (1975) predicted that river length (distance to spawning grounds) would affect age at first maturity, viz. that longer, "harsher" rivers would select for larger salmon that might be able to survive the upstream migration, thus resulting in a delayed age at first maturity. The reasoning behind this prediction is more complex than it may appear above, and is further explained by Schaffer (1979). Regression analysis of fish weight vs. river length appear to support their prediction (Schaffer and Elson 1975). Other studies have also shown relationships between geophysical characteristics of rivers (discharge, length) and age at maturity of salmon stocks (Power 1981; Scarnecchia 1983). Any relationship that may exist, however, will certainly be more complex than a simple linear cause-effect model. The authors mentioned above used readily available physical data (eg., river length); studies involving a more detailed look at the geophysical characteristics of salmon rivers are needed before this relationship will be understood.

The work of Chadwick et al. (1985) has some intriguing implications including the possibility that ovarian development of smolts may be inversely related to the sea-age of the parents. They also found differences between stocks in smolt size and parental sea-age but there was no obvious trend as suggested in the Russian work. Significant correlations between the returns of 1 SW salmon in year y and 2 SW salmon in year $y+1$ support the hypothesis that sea-age of salmon is decided before smolts enter the sea and within stocks sea-age proportions remain fairly constant.

Marine Influences

Relatively little is known regarding the influence of the marine environment on age at maturity in Atlantic salmon. Cost and difficulty in investigating marine life is responsible for the paucity of information. There are indications that this is changing (Dutil and Verreault 1985; Dunbar 1985).

Seawater temperatures and ice distribution are the marine factors most often studied and these are influenced by climate and ocean currents (Dunbar and Thomson 1979; Power 1981; Saunders et al. 1983; Scarnecchia 1983; Reddin and Murray 1985; Dempson et al. 1986).

Dunbar and Thomson (1979) showed that the availability of salmon off West Greenland was affected by climate and could be related to the strength of the Irminger current and temperatures in the West Greenland sea area. This was supported in an analysis of West Greenland salmon catches by Reddin and Murray (1985). Dunbar (1985) has subsequently expanded these ideas in an attempt to explain periods of salmon abundance in terms of climate and a 50+ year cycle in animal populations. This broad approach is unique and may lead to new insights. Taylor (1985), for example, attributed the extraordinary abundance of salmon in the 1930's to natural causes. If these authors are correct, we may be approaching another period of salmon abundance.

Other studies address narrower issues. Power (1981), in discussing salmon movement in Ungava Bay and migration in general, related timing to sea and river temperatures. Sea surface temperatures are affected by ice distribution and there is only a short interval when smolts can leave and salmon return to the Ungava Rivers. This affects age at maturity since most males and a small proportion of females do not mature until autumn of the year following their return to freshwater (Robitaille et al. 1984).

Saunders et al. (1983) studied the effect of marine water temperature on the timing of sexual maturation in Atlantic salmon reared in sea cages. When temperature data were expressed in terms of cumulative degree-days, a striking difference was seen among years. Severe winters were followed by a lower incidence of grilse, whereas the somewhat milder winter of 1979−80 was followed by a higher incidence of grilse. The researchers hypothesized that salmon exposed to lower winter temperatures (1−3°C), particularly in December−January, may be adversely affected, resulting in delayed sexual maturation.

Scarnecchia (1983) studied several environmental factors believed to be associated with age at maturity in Atlantic salmon. Age at maturity was strongly correlated with length of river, discharge of river, latitude and ocean temperature. Variations in growth rates of Icelandic salmon stocks were seen, with smolts from the northwest growing faster than those from the northeast. Warmer Atlantic Ocean water in the west and possible increased food resources in this area were used to explain the variations. It was hypothesized that "adaptively advantageous stock-specific weights" may have evolved among salmon stocks such that those stocks in warmer waters mature earlier than stocks from colder waters. If specific weights also vary between these stocks, the strong correlation between sea temperature and percentage of grilse in the catch is easily explained. He followed this with an examination of the effects of variations in climate, weather and ocean conditions on the yield and abundance of Icelandic salmon (Scarnecchia 1984). From the early 1950's through the 1960's, a persistent high pressure system over Greenland increased the northerly air flow over Iceland and the strength of the surrounding Arctic currents. The general cooling trend was correlated with lowered primary production, low zooplankton standing crops and fewer forage fish (herring and capelin). Salmon catches in northern rivers declined with lower sea, air and river temperatures but the reasons were not always clear. Reduced smolt output, increased marine mortality or changes in marine migration routes may all have contributed to the decline. The effect of climate on salmon yield was less marked in the southern rivers where sea temperatures are higher and more stable.

Reddin and Murray (1985), in attempting to explain the poor catches of salmon off West Greenland in 1983 and 1984, examined data available on British Meteorological Office ice charts on sea-surface and air-surface temperatures. Using stepwise multiple linear regression, they concluded that 71% of the variation in abundance of salmon at West Greenland could be due to changes in the penetration of warm water into Davis Strait in August and the northward extent of warm water in the Labrador Sea in January. They suggested (on the basis of salmon returns to the Mactaquac Fish Culture Station on the St. John River, New Brunswick, and Canadian salmon landings) that cool conditions in the northwest Atlantic result in lower survival rates for Canadian stocks rather than shifts in salmon distribution. This is an interesting conclusion since it implies a possible connection between ocean circulation, marine productivity and salmon survival.

Dempson et al (1986), using a transfer function model, were unable to find a relationship between sea surface temperature and variations in the grilse:salmon ratio over time such as might be predicted from the work of Saunders et al. (1983). Their data were obtained from angling records from the Restigouche and Moisie rivers. Similarly, they were unable to show that heavy ice cover in the northwest

Atlantic, which might displace salmon and alter migration routes, had any effect on growth rates, salmon distribution or age at maturity.

Conclusions and Questions

Understanding how the physical environment relates to generation time in salmon is not easy. Perhaps it is a non-issue. The range of response available to a salmon stock is presumably that which has been selected by its environment and offers the best long-term chance of survival. What we need to be able to predict is the response, whatever its cause, to particular sets of environmental conditions.

Several major questions remain to be answered concerning the environmental effects on age at maturity. These broadly relate to whether freshwater or marine conditions have most influence on the life cycle. If rivers select the size and age of spawners, how does the selective process operate? Can we make progress by addressing several smaller questions? Suggestions that were discussed included: the effect of gravel size on the size of spawner — is there any evidence of variations in gravel size related to geology? How do the number of degree days or temperature conditions during the growing season affect male parr maturity? Is there a follow-through effect on smolt sex ratios and the mean age at maturity? Do overwintering conditions change the rates of survival of mature male parr? How does salinity affect maturation? Do extensive productive estuaries retard migration, resulting in larger smolts which mature early? Can the question of estuaries be approached experimentally by feeding smolts of similar parentage at different rates to see if immediate post-smolt growth influences the rate of maturation? Is stream order or weighted stream order correlated with smolt age over a limited latitudinal distance? To what extent do lakes and ponds influence smolt age and production? How do waterfalls and severe rapids select for different forms of fish? Are some shapes and sizes of salmon faster swimmers or better leapers than others? Does selection operate more intensively on the generally heavier, older females?

If river structure does not control the size and age of returning adults, the alternative hypothesis would seem to be that sea feeding areas or migration routes determine the sea age of the stock. The approach used by Peterman (1985) for west coast sockeye stocks offers a way of assessing which stage of the life cycle exerts most influence.

The ultimate use of knowledge of physical factors is in the prediction of the kinds of salmon stocks likely to be sustained in newly accessible waters or in the manipulation of existing rivers to change stock characteristics. With the present state of our knowledge, we are a long way from achieving such ends.

Acknowledgments

I would like to thank participants in the "Physical Factors" workshop for their ideas and contributions to this synthesis, namely: A. T. Bielak, G. Farmer, R. M. Peterman, J. A. Robitaille, and A. M. Sutterlin. Errors of interpretation or omission are my own contribution.

References

BAILEY, J. K., R. L. SAUNDERS, AND M. I. BUZETA. 1980. Influence of parental smolt age and sea age on growth and smolting of hatchery-reared Atlantic salmon (Salmo salar). Can. J. Fish. Aquat. Sci. 37: 1379–1386.

CHADWICK, E. M. P., R. G. RANDALL, AND C. LÉGER. 1986. Ovarian development of Atlantic salmon (Salmo salar) smolts and age at first maturity, p. 15–23. In D. J. Meerburg [ed.] Salmonid age at maturity. Can. Spec. Publ. Fish. Aquat. Sci. 89.

DAHL, K. 1910. The age and growth of salmon and trout in Norway as shown by their scales. London. Salmon and Trout Assoc. Fishmonger's Hall. 141 p. X plates.

DALLEY, E. L., C. W. ANDREWS, AND J. M. GREEN. 1983. Precocious male Atlantic salmon parr (Salmo salar) in insular Newfoundland. Can. J. Fish. Aquat. Sci. 40: 647–652.

DEMPSON, J. B., R. A. MYERS, AND D. G. REDDIN. 1986. Age at first maturity of Atlantic salmon (Salmo salar) — influences of the marine environment, p. 70–78. In D. J. Meerburg [ed.] Salmonid age at maturity. Can. Spec. Publ. Fish. Aquat. Sci. 89.

DIRIN-KHALTURIN, D. K. 1981. Causes of size-age differences in young salmon and spawners (Salmonidae). J. Ichthyol. 21: 64–80.

DUNBAR, M. J. 1985. Research summary — McGill University. 1985 Northeast Atlantic Salmon Workshop, Moncton, N.B., p. 92–101.

DUNBAR, M. J., AND D. H. THOMSON. 1979. West Greenland salmon and climatic change. Medd. Grønland 202(4): 19 p.

DUTIL, J.-D. 1985. Research summary — Fisheries and Oceans — Quebec Region. 1985 Northeast Atlantic Salmon Workshop, Moncton, N.B., p. 49–50.

ELSON, P. F. 1957. The importance of size in the change from parr to smolt in the Atlantic salmon. Can. Fish. Cult. 21: 1–6.

EVANS, G. T., J. C. RICE, AND E. M. P. CHADWICK. 1984. Patterns in growth and smolting of Atlantic salmon (Salmo salar) parr. Can. J. Fish. Aquat. Sci. 41: 783–797.

1985. Patterns of growth and smolting of Atlantic salmon (Salmo salar) parr in a southwestern Newfoundland river. Can. J. Fish. Aquat. Sci. 42: 539–543.

GARDNER, M. L. 1976. A review of factors which may influence the sea-age and maturation of Atlantic salmon Salmo salar L. J. Fish Biol. 9: 289–327.

GLEBE, B. D., W. EDDY, AND R. L. SAUNDERS. 1980. The influence of parental age at maturity and rearing practice on precocious maturation of hatchery-reared Atlantic salmon parr. North American Salmon Research Center NASRC Rep. 4-1980: 7 p.

KRISTINSSON, J. B., R. L. SAUNDERS, AND A. J. WIGGS. 1985. Growth dynamics during development of bimodal length–frequency distribution in juvenile Atlantic salmon (Salmo salar L.). Aquaculture 45: 1–20.

MITANS, A. R. 1973. Dwarf males and the sex structure of a Baltic salmon (Salmo salar L.) population. J. Ichthyol. 13: 192–197.

MYERS, R. A. 1984. Demographic consequences of precocious maturation of Atlantic salmon (Salmo salar). Can J. Fish. Aquat. Sci. 41: 1349–1353.

PETERMAN, R. M. 1985. Patterns of interannual variation in age at maturity of sockeye salmon (Oncorhynchus nerka) in Alaska and British Columbia. Can. J. Fish. Aquat. Sci. 42: 1595–1607.

POWER, G. 1981. Stock characteristics and catches of Atlantic salmon (Salmo salar) in Quebec, and Newfoundland and Labrador in relation to environmental variables. Can. J. Fish. Aquat. Sci. 38: 1601–1611.

REDDIN, D. G., AND J. J. MURRAY. 1985. Environmental conditions in the Northwest Atlantic in relation to salmon catches at West Greenland. Int. Cons. Explor. Mer. C.M. 1985/M: 10. 14 p.

RICKER, W. E. 1972. Hereditary and environmental factors affecting certain salmonid populations, p. 27–160. In The stock concept in Pacific salmon. H. R. MacMillan Lectures in Fisheries. Univ. of B.C., Vancouver, B.C.

ROBITAILLE, J. A., Y. CÔTÉ, G. HAYEUR, AND G. SHOONER. 1984. Particularités de la reproduction du saumon atlantique (*Salmo salar*) dans une partie du réseau Koksoak, en Ungava. Rapp. tech. can. sci. halieut. aquat. 1313: vii + 33 p.

SAUNDERS, R. L. 1981. Atlantic salmon (*Salmo salar*) stocks and management implications in the Canadian Atlantic Provinces and New England, U.S.A. Can. J. Fish. Aquat. Sci. 38: 1612−1625.

1986. The scientific and management implications of age and size at sexual maturity in Atlantic salmon (*Salmo salar*), p. 3−6. *In* D. J. Meerburg [ed.] Salmonid age at maturity. Can. Spec. Publ. Fish. Aquat. Sci. 89.

SAUNDERS, R. L., E. B. HENDERSON, AND B. D. GLEBE. 1982. Precocious sexual maturation and smoltification in male Atlantic salmon (*Salmo salar*). Aquaculture 28: 211−229.

SAUNDERS, R. L., E. B. HENDERSON, B. D. GLEBE, AND E. J. LOUDENSLAGER. 1983. Evidence of a major environmental component in determination of the grilse: larger salmon ratio in Atlantic salmon (*Salmo salar*). Aquaculture 33: 107−118.

SCHAFFER, W. M. 1979. The theory of life-history evolution and its application to Atlantic salmon. Symp. Zool. Soc. Lond. No. 44: 307−326.

SCHAFFER, W. M., AND P. F. ELSON. 1975. The adaptive significance of variations in life history among local populations of Atlantic salmon in North America. Ecology 56: 577−590.

SCARNECCHIA, D. L. 1983. Age at sexual maturity in Icelandic stocks of Atlantic salmon (*Salmo salar*). Can. J. Fish. Aquat. Sci. 40: 1456−1468.

1984. Climatic and Oceanic variations affecting yield of Icelandic stocks of Atlantic salmon (*Salmo salar*). Can. J. Fish. Aquat. Sci. 41: 917−935.

STOCS. 1981. Stock Concept International Symposium. Can. J. Fish. Aquat. Sci. 38: 1457−1921.

SYMONS, P. E. K. 1979. Estimated escapement of Atlantic salmon (*Salmo salar*) for maximum smolt production in rivers of different productivity. J. Fish. Res. Board Can. 36: 132−140.

TAYLOR, V. R. 1985. The early Atlantic salmon fishery in Newfoundland and Labrador. Can. Spec. Publ. Fish. Aquat. Sci. 76: 71 p.

THORPE, J. E. 1977. Bimodal distribution of length of juvenile Atlantic salmon (*Salmo salar* L.) under artificial rearing conditions. J. Fish. Biol. 11: 175−184.

1986. Age at first maturity in Atlantic salmon, *Salmo salar*: freshwater period influences and conflicts with smolting, p. 7−14. *In* D. J. Meerburg [ed.] Salmonid age at maturity. Can. Spec. Publ. Fish. Aquat. Sci. 89.

THORPE, J. E., AND K. A. MITCHELL. 1981. Stocks of Atlantic salmon *Salmo salar* L. in Britain and Ireland: discreteness and current management. Can. J. Fish. Aquat. Sci. 38: 1576−1590.

THORPE, J. E., AND R. I. G. MORGAN. 1980. Growth-rate and smolting-rate of progeny of male Atlantic salmon parr, *Salmo salar* L. J. Fish. Biol. 17: 451−459.

Assessment of Selective Fishing on the Age at Maturity in Atlantic Salmon (*Salmo salar*): A Genetic Pespective

B. E. Riddell

Department of Fisheries and Oceans, Fisheries Research Branch, Pacific Biological Station, Nanaimo, B.C. V9R 5K6

Abstract

RIDDELL, B. E. 1986. Assessment of selective fishing on the age at maturity in Atlantic salmon (*Salmo salar*): a genetic perspective, p. 102–109. *In* D. J. Meerburg [ed.] Salmonid age at maturity. Can. Spec. Publ. Fish. Aquat. Sci. 89.

Concerns that fisheries selectively harvesting later maturing Atlantic salmon will genetically select for younger age at maturity and reduced yields are evaluated from a genetic and evolutionary ecology perspective. Five reasons are discussed why realized response to selection would be less than predicted from models of single-trait response. The inadequacy of these models involves: their inability to account for genetic covariances; the inadequacy of the harvested portion of a population as a measure of selection intensity; and the necessity to consider the net effects of selection throughout a species life-history. Fishing mortality is numerically a minor portion of total mortality over the life-span of Atlantic salmon and is unlikely to be directionally selective enough to compensate for its relatively small numeric value. Changes in age and size at maturity of Atlantic salmon may be more associated with reduced density-dependent factors in the freshwater habitat than with fisheries. The genetic determination of age at maturity in salmon is unknown but strong evidence for negative phenotypic and genetic correlations with growth rate is accumulating.

Résumé

RIDDELL, B. E. 1986. Assessment of selective fishing on the age at maturity in Atlantic salmon (*Salmo salar*): a genetic perspective, p. 102–109. *In* D. J. Meerburg [ed.] Salmonid age at maturity. Can. Spec. Publ. Fish. Aquat. Sci. 89.

On évalue d'un point de vue génétique et évolutif les répercussions de la pêche sélective s'exerçant sur des saumons de l'Atlantique à maturation tardive, qui favoriserait sur le plan génétique des rendements réduits et un âge à la maturité plus précoce. On examine cinq raisons expliquant pourquoi la réponse obtenue par rapport à la sélection serait moins que celle prévue à partir de modèles de réponse à un seul caractère. Ces modèles sont inadéquats à cause de leur incapacité à expliquer les covariances génétiques, parce que la partie exploitée d'une population ne peut servir adéquatement de mesure de l'intensité de la sélection et parce qu'il est nécessaire d'examiner les effets nets de la sélection dans tout le cycle vital d'une espèce. La mortalité due à la pêche représente numériquement une partie peu importante de la mortalité totale au cours de la vie du saumon de l'Atlantique et il est peu probable qu'elle soit suffisamment sélective pour contrebalancer sa valeur numérique relativement faible. Les variations de l'âge et de la taille à la maturité du saumon de l'Atlantique pourraient être davantage liées à des facteurs moins importants dépendant de la densité en eau douce qu'aux pêches. On ne sait pas comment se fait la détermination génétique de l'âge à la maturité chez le saumon mais il y a de plus en plus de fortes indications qui laissent croire que les corrélations phénotypiques et génétiques avec le rythme de croissance sont négatives.

Introduction

The nearly direct association between body size and total age in Atlantic salmon stimulates an obvious concern for fishery managers responsible for maintaining yields while conserving the species. Do fisheries directed on larger, older salmon reduce long-term yield through genetic selection for younger age at maturity? This paper reviews genetic aspects of the concern and evaluates the impact of fisheries within an evolutionary ecology context.

The extensive inter-population variability of age and size at maturity in Atlantic salmon (Naevdal et al. 1978; Scarnecchia 1983; Sutterlin and MacLean 1984) has been attributed to genetic differences between populations (Gardner 1976; Naevdal 1983; Gjerde and Refstie 1984; Glebe and Saunders 1986). Sources of variation in age and size at maturity within populations are more uncertain but environmental factors are believed to be more important, as reviewed by Gardner (1976) and Randall et al. (1986). Both reviews suggest sea-age at maturity may be determined when the juveniles are in freshwater but the most obvious hypothesis that juvenile growth rate determines the age at first maturity has not been consistently supported. Thorpe (1986), however, documents evidence for a negative phenotypic correlation between these traits.

The genetic basis determining age at first maturity and the genetic component of intra-population variability have not been as thoroughly investigated as the above topics, but are more relevant to evaluating the impact of selective fishing. Consequently, genetic aspects of intra-population variability are reviewed but there is little information on genetic determination. The evaluation of selective harvests is developed through arguments based on theories of biometrical genetics and life-history evolution, and more generally from information on the salmonid genome.

The concern that fishery-induced reductions in age at maturity will result in long-term loss of yield is suggested to reflect simplistic models for genetic determination, response to selection, and demographic optimization in life-history theories. A more holistic view of selection on whole-organism phenotypes results in reduced expectations for rate of response to fishing pressure and suggests that age at maturity should not be considered as one trait in isolation of others.

The Problem

A concern regarding lost yield from populations subject to fishery-induced selection against larger, older fish at first maturity is easily developed from the literature. The simplest model to predict response in age at maturity involves heritable variation for the trait and differential breeding success of some portion of the population (Falconer 1981, p. 175). Additive genetic variance for age at maturity has been documented (Gjerde 1984; Gjerde and Refstie 1984) and supports earlier evidence for the heritability of age at maturity (references in Gardner 1976). Differential breeding success was presumed to result from the harvest of older, larger Atlantic salmon as reported by Allen et al. (1972). Further, Schaffer (1974) used Atlantic salmon as an example in his demographic model of life-history evolution in age-structured populations and suggested that increased mortality on older age classes should select for earlier age and smaller size at maturity. Consequently, the basis for predicting loss of yield have been established in the literature since the mid-1970s and more recent work has re-enforced the concern as evidence for heritable variation accumulated.

"The problem" is, however, that few data exist to substantiate the prediction. A model to predict brood year returns of multiple-sea-winter (MSW) salmon in the Miramichi River was improved by incorporating the per cent of the egg deposition in the brood year by female grilse (Ritter et al. 1986). Atlantic salmon that mature after one winter at sea are referred to as grilse. The phenotypic composition of female spawners did provide some information on the expected brood year returns; but the improvement in the forecast was modest. Further, Saunders (1986) states that there is not a clear indication in the Miramichi River that grilse are replacing MSW salmon. The proportion of male parr maturing has also been suggested as a trait responsive to fishing pressure (Randall et al. 1986). However, it is debatable whether an increased prevalence of mature parr reflects selection for an alternative life-history strategy (Caswell et al. 1984) or a phenotypic expression mediated via increased growth rate at low population densities (Myers et al. 1985).

I have considered five reasons why the predicted rate of response in age at maturity may not be observed but any one or all of the suggestions may actually be involved. The reasons proposed include: (1) limitations to data quality and/or to short a duration of monitoring to detect a response; (2) no additive variance for age at maturity; (3) a single-trait response to selection model is inappropriate or the intensity of selection is less than perceived; (4) demographic optimization models in life-history theory are inadequate to account for the realized response to selection; (5) the tetraploid ancestry in salmonids is not accounted for in quantitative genetic theory and our understanding of the linkage between genotype and phenotype is inadequate.

Data Limitations

Data limitations are probably not so problematic as to preclude observing the predicted response. However, the relatively short time-series of data in a small sample of rivers and offshore mixed-stock fisheries certainly complicate any assessment.

Information useful to this assessment begins in the 1950s but exploitation of Atlantic salmon in eastern North America has been extensive for over 200 years (Netboy 1968). Information on selectivity or intensity of these early fisheries is not available but reference to fishing with weirs or shore-to-shore gillnets suggests these fisheries could have been both selective and intense. Difficulties in information quality presently center on determining the maturity schedule of a broodyear when the stock composition by age in offshore fisheries is unknown. Proportions of grilse and MSW salmon in the escapement significantly under-represent MSW salmon in the total run (Saunders 1969), as is obviously expected since the offshore fishery is the selective pressure. The fisheries also limit our ability to partition genetic and environmental sources of variability between and within populations. Freshwater and marine environmental factors accounted for 62−72% by sex of the inter-population variation in the ratio of grilse : MSW salmon in Icelandic rivers (Scarnecchia 1983). Scarnecchia (op. cit.) reports that Icelandic salmon are not subject to ocean fisheries by Icelanders and in-river sport fisheries are not very size selective (the impact of fisheries further offshore has not been determined). Similar relationships are not evident for Atlantic salmon stocks in Canada and may simply reflect an inability to account for the impact of the mixed-stock, offshore fisheries.

Our perception of how much the age or size at maturity has changed is based on about 30 years of data and may underestimate the response over the longer exploitation history. But within these 30 years a major fishery harvesting Canadian MSW salmon off Greenland commenced and accellerated rapidly (Paloheimo and Elson 1974). If the single-trait model of response to selection, as outlined above, is an adequate description of the system, then over the past 30 years some trend to earlier maturity should have been observable.

Genetic Variation in Age at Maturity

Population specificity of maturity schedules indicates that age at maturity is modifiable in different environments, and based on heritability estimates presently available the hypothesis that there is no additive variation for this trait must be rejected. Differences between populations in maturity schedules are maintained in controlled rearing tests (Naevdal 1983) and additive genetic variance between populations has been reported (Gjerde and Refstie 1984). Additive variance is apparently also significant within Atlantic salmon populations. Animal breeding programs with Norwegian Atlantic salmon have demonstrated heritable variation for sea-age at maturity and development of mature male parr (Gjerde 1984). The observation on parr maturity is consistent with Thorpe et al. (1983) and Glebe and Saunders (1986). However, the applicability of results from animal breeding programs to natural populations is uncertain since culture practices likely inflate heritability estimates. For example, culling to reduce family size may not be random with respect to body size (Gjerde 1984), the population under selection may be a composite of several populations, and controlled environments will minimize the environmental component of the phenotypic variance. Further, how accurately mean age at maturity or its heritability can be estimated in any population is limited by the nature of the trait's expression. Mean ages may be quite sensitive to relatively small variations in growth performance among individuals during a particular time of year due to the interactions of size thresholds or growth rate and season in determining maturity (Thorpe 1986). Heritabilities are difficult to compare and can be inflated because maturity is expressed as a binomial trait. Heritability estimates for binomial traits

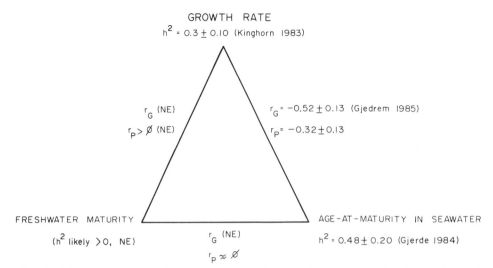

FIG. 1. Schematic summary of genetic parameters for Atlantic salmon growth rate, incidence of freshwater maturity, and age-at-maturity in seawater. Parameter estimates were derived from cultured populations and may not accurately reflect the magnitude of these parameters in natural populations. Parameters not presently estimated are signified by (NE); r_G, and r_p indicate genetic and phenotypic correlations.

are dependent upon the incidence level of the trait and can vary with estimation procedures (Van Vleck 1972). Heritabilities for any trait are specific to the population and environment within which it was estimated and recent evidence also suggests that the expression of life history traits may vary between test environments (Service and Rose 1985).

Additive variance for age at maturity is indicated, at least within the populations studied, but the relevance of heritability estimates from these studies to natural populations is uncertain. Non-additive variance apparently has little influence on age at maturity as indicated today by only one cross breeding study (Gjerde and Refstie 1984). However, the relevance of this result to studies of natural populations is also uncertain since populations that are adapted to different environments may fail to show heterosis because of epistatic interactions (Falconer 1981; Gjerde and Refstie 1984).

Early maturity of male parr has been shown to vary in incidence between populations and families within populations, to be heritable, and to have a non-additive genetic component as indicated by sire—dam interactions, maternal effects and heterosis (Thorpe et al. 1983; Gjerde 1984; Glebe and Saunders 1986). Mature parr and grilse used as sires tend to produce more progeny maturing as parr than MSW sires but all sire types produce mature parr (Glebe and Saunders 1986). Under enhanced environmental conditions, the expression of parr maturation increases but some families under the same environmental conditions didn't produce any mature parr. The relationship between development of mature parr and subsequent sea-age at maturity is also inconsistent. The incidence of mature parr and grilse within a strain is positively correlated but at the family level no relationship between incidence of mature parr and the proportion of grilse was observed (Glebe and Saunders 1986). This type of observation has led several authors to suggest that maturation in freshwater and seawater are independent genetic events (Gjerde 1984; Glebe and Saunders 1986). Naevdal (1983) supports that parr maturity is of minor importance as a grilse producing factor. At this workshop, Naevdal (G. Naevdal, Inst. Marine Res., N-5011 Nordness (Bergen), Norway; pers. comm.) reported that mature parr

that became two-year smolts showed compensatory growth in the first year at sea such that after 15 months they were similar in size to their sibs which had not matured as parr. Grilse production by previously mature parr is not necessarily contradictory to the suggested independence of freshwater and seawater maturation since growth compensation could enable grilse development without implying genetic correlation between these traits. Randall et al. (1986) cautioned that the lack of correlation between freshwater and seawater maturity may be environmental since mortalities associated with development of mature parr can be significant (supportive references in Randall et al. 1986). Individual tagging of mature male parr suggests though that the observations are not simply artifacts of mortality.

The evidence strongly supports that there is genetic variation for age at maturity in male parr and adults and that the range of expression of these traits varies between populations. Genetic parameters involved in response to selection by fisheries are summarized in Fig. 1.

The existence of heritable variation for age-at-maturity determined through biometrical genetics indicates a statistical probability that progeny will have a maturity pattern like their parents. The nature of the genetic determination of the phenotype is not specified (Kempthorne 1983). Genetic determination could range from major effects of single genes (as described by Kallman and Schreibman (1973) for Platyfish) to a phenotypic expression determined by interactions of several developmental traits. Although the means of determination is unknown, growth rate can have a major impact on age at maturity. The effect is most evident when exceptional freshwater growth has been observed. Chadwick et al. (1986) references reports of exceptionally large Atlantic salmon smolts maturing during their first summer at sea, and a similar observation was recently made for coho salmon (*Oncorhynchus kisutch*). A family of coho salmon demonstrated a remarkable freshwater growth rate and after one year in freshwater weighed 320 ± 200 g. Subsequently, 53% of the family matured after 8 mo at sea at a mean weight of only 965 ± 300 g (B. Riddell, unpubl. data). Coho salmon would normally smoltify after one year in freshwater but at only 10−20 g in most natural populations and would have matured after 17−18 mo at sea and weigh between 2−5 kg.

Heritable variation for age at maturity has been reported from some cultured populations of Atlantic salmon. The relevance of these heritability estimates to natural populations is, however, uncertain. Additivity in age at maturity is contrary to theoretical expectations for life-history traits associated with fitness but is actually consistent with recent findings in other species (Rose 1983). The demonstration of additive variance for age at maturity may not be inconsistent with the lack of response to selective fishing if correlations between traits constrain the response of age at maturity.

Response to Selection Models

The expected response of natural populations to selection against individuals at older ages at maturity is unlikely to be predictable from a single-trait response model. The model predicts response as the product of the intensity of selection, the heritability of the trait and the trait's phenotypic standard deviation. As discussed in the previous section, heritability for age at maturity in natural populations is expected to be less than in animal breeding programs and the phenotypic variation to be substantially greater. Intensity of selection is also expected to be less than occurs under truncated selection in animal breeding and selection differentials may actually be small since selective fishing will not always be equally directed or intensive. For example, gillnet selectivity can vary annually dependent upon the body size of adults (Todd and Larkin 1971).

Differential fecundity with body size is also expected to reduce response to selective harvest on MSW salmon. MSW salmon have greater fecundity than grilse and are expected to contribute more progeny per female to the next generation. The relationship between fecundity and body size varies between populations (Glebe et al. 1979) but two sea-winter salmon have at least 75% more eggs than grilse salmon (Chadwick et al. 1986) and have reduced number of eggs per kilogram body weight. Consequently the expected response to selection must be weighted by the offspring produced by the various size classes of spawners (Falconer 1981, p. 183).

Response to selection may be further countered by natural selection. For example, if grilse were at a selective disadvantage between the periods of fishing and spawning, the realized response to fishing pressures could again be reduced through differential spawning success of smaller versus larger salmon. Evidence of body size adaptations to natal rivers (Schaffer and Elson 1975; Scarnecchia 1983) and the importance of body size during spawning (Healey and Heard 1984; Van den Berghe and Gross 1984; Healey 1986) suggest that natural selection may indeed limit the realized response.

Single-trait response to selection models are clearly inadequate to predict response of age at maturity to selective fisheries and would likely overestimate the expected response. Response to selection may also be limited through genetic covariances between traits (Falconer 1981). The correlated response in a trait y is a function of the selection intensity on a trait x, the heritablities of the traits, the genetic correlation between x and y, and the phenotyic standard deviation of y. If the genetic covariance between traits is negative both traits could show additive variation but there may not be any response to selection. Genetic covariances

of age at maturity with other traits have not been studied extensively in Atlantic salmon but Gjedrem (1985) reports negative covariances between age at maturity and growth rate. Further, negative covariances between life history traits, such as age at maturity, has become a central feature of theories concerning the evolution of a species' life-history pattern.

Life History Theory

Demographic theories of life history evolution have frequently been used to estimate an "optimal" age at maturity or the age at which the overall life-time reproductive potential is maximized. The theory assumes that selection can fix the appropriate genotypes in each environment and implies that selection can act on this trait in isolation from others. It seems quite appropriate that Caswell (1983) refers to such life-history theory as genetically naive. Demographic theory has been particularly useful in providing a logical framework to generate and test hypotheses but is inadequate as a theory of life history evolution because of its inability to incorporate mating patterns (Kempthorne 1983; Healey 1986) or account for the genetic basis of the phenotypic variation observed.

Mating patterns in salmonids involve assortative and multiple matings, variations in reproductive effort with body size, and possibly alternative mating strategies. The influence of these factors on reproductive success of adults at different ages at maturity is presently poorly known. The significance of large body size on the spawning grounds does suggest that the realized response to selection may be less than expected even after compensation for relative fecundity.

Lande's (1982) dynamic theory of life history evolution provides a synthesis of population demography and a quantitative genetic basis for response to selection. The theory accounts for the influence of genetic correlations among traits and the net effect of selection episodes throughout development. Lande (1982) suggests that "negative genetic correlations among major components of fitness are often obscured phenotypically by positive environmental correlations, but commonly constitute the ultimate constraint on life history evolution." A trait's rate of change is the sum of the response to direct selection and the responses to selection on genetically correlated traits. A trait could, therefore, evolve in opposition to the direct selection if a stronger, antagonistic selection acted on genetically correlated characters. The genetic cause of correlation is chiefly pleiotropy (the property of genes having more than one phenotypic effect) and negative correlations may develop through the differential effect of pleiotropic genes on traits (Falconer 1981, p. 300). Consequently, the evolution of a life-history pattern is expected to involve trade-offs between characters that negatively covary. The central nature of trade-offs in life-history evolution has recently stimulated increased interest in testing for the existence and genetic nature of these trade-offs. Reznick's (1985) review of the literature through 1982 supports the existence of genetically mediated trade-offs or reproductive costs but the number of studies useful in evaluating the genetic basis of these trade-offs is limited. The hypothesis of negative genetic correlation or antagonistic pleiotropy as a genetic basis for life history evolution is also supported by Rose (1983). Examples of trade-offs in Atlantic salmon might include negative associations between growth rate and size or age at maturity, delayed maturity increasing body size but reducing specific fecundity (eggs per unit body weight), and possibly rapid maturation and reduced longevity in mature male parr.

A model of response to selection for life-history traits incorporating population demography and genetic covariance structure is clearly based upon selection at the level of organisms. The implications of such a level of selection has recently been discussed in detail (Toumi et al. 1983) and presents an intuitively more satisfying selection theory than selection operating on independent traits. Selection on the total phenotype emphasizes the need to associate genotype and phenotype and draws into question how traits under selection are defined. Stearns has been a recent advocate of these issues beginning with the introduction of "plastic trajectories" (Stearns 1983) as a concept to account for developmental plasticity observed in age and size-at-maturity in Mosquitofish. Stearns and Crandall (1984) present a life-history model to predict the trajectory and while the authors acknowledge that their predictions reflect their assumptions, the ability of the concept to integrate genetic and environmental variation with population demography is appealing. Ages at maturity predicted from the model for 19 populations of fish in different environments were strongly associated ($r = 0.91$, $P < 0.01$) with observed ages. Stearns and Crandall's (1984) trajectories are actually very similar to Alm's (1959) conclusions from his extensive studies of age, size, and maturity in fish. Alm (1959) suggested that fish mature along one concave age-size function and that age and size at maturity vary with growth rate. Stearns (1984) further supports studying phenotypic properties of organisms as a means of understanding genetic change and views the organism as a "coherent unit" tied together by physiology, developmental patterns and gene products (also see Saunders 1986 and Thorpe 1986 in this volume).

The basic elements of Stearns (1983, 1984) arguments can be summarized as follows. Life-history traits are assumed to be polygenic and represent the phenotypic components of fitness expressed by organisms. Fitness of genes regulating these traits is defined by the population dynamics of organisms in an environment. Variations in age and size at maturity would be viewed as life-history responses to variation in growth and demographic (juvenile and adult mortality patterns) conditions. Populations evolve a characteristic response surface or trajectory determined by average demographic conditions and variations in growth rate. Individuals maintain fitness by maturing at a position along the trajectory determined by short-term environmental effects. Stearns (1984) has not dealt with genetic mechanisms associated with the developmental plasticity required for response along a trajectory but the phenotypic response does not necessitate genetic change, as discussed by Smith-Gill (1983).

A fishery is only one of many sources of mortalities experienced throughout the salmon's life cycle. A more holoistic view of response to selection at the organism level leads to reduced expectation of response in life-history traits. In summarizing the above discussion, the reduced expectation may be attributed to genetic covariances between phenotypic traits, net effects of selection experienced over the life-span, developmental plasticity, redefining the traits actually subject to selection, and allowances for mating patterns.

Developmental Process and Tetraploidy

Response to selective harvest may be mediated by alternative developmental pathways (conversions) or alterations to the phenotype due to varying sensitivities of various traits to the environment during development (environmental modulation), neither response involving loss of genetic variation (Smith-Gill 1983). The tetraploid ancestry of salmonids may actually facilitate the persistence of these alternative pathways and allow diversification through the accumulation of mutations, as suggested by (Smith-Gill 1983). For example, an alternative explanation of the apparent heritability of maturity in male parr would be the existence of a sex-limited, alternative development path resulting in advanced ontogenetic expression of maturity. Alternative developmental pathways are also evident in dwarf and anadromous morphs of Arctic char and Atlantic salmon that mature at the same age and have common slopes to the fecundity–body size functions (Jonsson and Hindar 1982; Nordeng 1983; Sutterlin and MacLean 1984). A heritable basis for morphs in char is statistically evident but each morph produces every other morph and the expression of the morphs is suggested to depend upon juvenile growth rates, particularly for males (Nordeng 1983). Similarly, some of the suggested response of Atlantic salmon to fishery selection may simply reflect phenotypic responses to increased growth rate at reduced population densities.

Rates of response to selection in salmonids may generally be reduced compared with fully diploid species because diploidization of all chromosomes in salmonids is not complete (Allendorf and Thorgaard 1984). Tetrasomic loci respond differently to selection than disomic loci, tetrasomic loci initially having more genetic variation but responding more slowly to selection. Allendorf and Thorgaard (1984) present examples of the different rates of response in duplicate and non-duplicate loci with two alleles, but the effect of partial tetrasomy on polygenic traits can only be extrapolated.

Discussion

It is highly probable that the phenotypic variation in age at maturity observed between Atlantic salmon populations has a genetic basis as demonstrated through controlled rearing experiments. It is less probable, however, that the additive variance demonstrated for age at maturity within artificial populations is a realistic estimate of additive variance within natural populations. Genetic parameters necessary to predict response to selection are presently only available from biometrical genetic studies in cultured populations but based on these studies the hypothesis that there is no additive variation for age at maturity must be rejected. The variation may not be responsive to selection, however, if genetic covariances constrain response to selection on correlated traits. Lande (1982) and Rose (1983) present evidence from other species that covariances between life history traits are frequently negative and could, therefore, limit selection response. Further, biometrical estimates of genetic variances do not define the mechanism for genetic determination of age at maturity. The process of determination remains uncertain and merits continued research but inverse correlations with growth rate have been reported (Gjedrem

1985; Thorpe 1986) and significant developmental plasticity in expression of age at maturity has been observed for some fish (McKenzie et al. 1983; Stearns 1983). Jonsson et al. (1984) suggest that fish adjust age at maturity non-genetically to changes in growth rate and that genotypes coding for different age at maturity at the same growth rate co-exist through temporal variation in juvenile survival rates. Multiple genotypes are not inconsistent with developmental plasticity as is evident from McKenzie et al. (1983) where the range of expression for age and size at maturity for two genotypes was highly plastic but non-overlapping. In Stearns' trajectory model genotypic variation could be maintained through variation in development rates within and between tissues; different tissues are reported to have intrinsic rates of development (Bryant and Simpson 1984).

Heritable variation in age at maturity in Atlantic salmon is consistent with additive variation in individual life-history traits in other species (references in Rose 1983) and may be maintained as a consequence of joint optimizations between life-history traits comprising the organism. Heritability for age at maturity is expected to be less in natural populations than in controlled but its magnitude may not even be the critical issue in determining response to selection. Selection on life-history traits logically occurs at the level of organisms, and response to selection is then dependent upon the genetic covariances, associations between genotype and phenotype, intensity of selection, and fecundity of spawners. Consideration of these factors, plus incomplete diploidization in salmonids, strongly suggests that the response of age at maturity to fishing pressure would be substantially less than expected from single-trait selection models. Data available to assess response to selective fishing must be qualified as only evaluating the recent period of a much longer exploitation history but unequivocal evidence of a progressive trend to early maturity in North American Atlantic salmon does not appear to be available. The apparent absence of response to selective fishing is more consistent with an organismic theory of selection (Toumi et al. 1983) than single-trait selection on age at maturity.

Evaluating the impact of selective fisheries is essentially the same as studying the evolution of life-histories but over a shorter time period. Fishing is only an additional adult mortality. Long-term environmental changes or new sources of mortality may impose directional selection on a population and any response would be mediated through the demography of the population. The evaluation of a fishery as a source of directional selection within a population should consider the incremental selection imposed relative to the mortality schedule experienced throughout the life span and how directed the selection is. Most of the mortality during the life-span of Atlantic salmon occurs during freshwater phases (Symons 1979) and early sea-life (Chadwick et al. 1986). Fishing mortality must, therefore, be a numerically small portion of the total mortality and could only cause a selection response if fishing was very efficient and directional.

The difficulty in determining the genetic selectivity of fisheries is part of the background for this workshop. An assessment of genetic selection on juveniles in freshwater is an alternative approach to this question. If there is no evidence of adaptation to freshwater environments then fishing may be a stronger selection pressure than juvenile mortalities. However, adaptation of salmonid juveniles to freshwater environments has frequently been documented (Ricker 1972; Saunders 1981). If populations were assumed to be evolutionarily stable then present juvenile mortalities may not be selective and fishing could still be important. Such an hypothesis is untestable since past pressure can not be estimated and is an unlikely scenario for several reasons. Notable reasons would include that the freshwater environment, both biotic and abiotic factors, is not temporally stable; that natural selection is not perfect (Gould and Lewontin 1979) and increased genetic variances will follow reproduction; and that fishery induced changes in the breeding population may be counter-balanced by natural selection on the progeny. Arguments previously presented, concluded that fisheries on Atlantic salmon are not likely to represent a strong directional pressure. Given that freshwater mortality is selective and numerically dominates, I suggest that the fishery represents a minor increment in total selection on age at maturity. It is noteworthy that life-history models developed to predict age at maturity are far more sensitive to juvenile mortality variation than to adults (Jonsson et al. 1984; Stearns and Crandall 1984). Impacts of fisheries more likely involve reduced density-dependent factors on juveniles and traits less associated with fitness than age at maturity. The former was discussed by Randall et al. (1986) as an extrinsic factor influencing the incidence of mature parr and the latter has been hypothesized by Ricker (1981) to account for changes in size at maturity of Pacific salmon. Healey (1986), however, extends Ricker's analyses through 1982 and suggests that the environment may have been more influential than previously suggested, and that countervalent forces may also exist to reduce the impact of size-selective fisheries on body size at maturity.

These arguments do not preclude genetic effects of fisheries but predict that their effects on life-history traits will be small so long as exploitation does not become extreme. These effects may reduce yield, however, so it seems reasonable to consider the consequences of reduced exploitation. The only fishery situation where a directional selection has been eliminated, that I am aware of, concerns migration timing of pink salmon in S.E. Alaska. The date by which 50% of the spawners arrived at a monitored stream returned to pre-selection dates in five generations following elimination of the selection pressure (Alexanderdotter and Mathisen 1982). Response in Atlantic salmon would depend on whether the long period of exploitation has eliminated some genetic variation but response would be anticipated and may actually be a very useful method of studying the genetic cost of fishing. A series of stepped reductions in fishing mortality and monitoring of juvenile and adult yields in a few populations is suggested as a practical method for estimating optimal biological utilization of Atlantic salmon.

The basic premise of this discussion has been that, given the intensity of fisheries on Atlantic salmon and the heritability reported for age at maturity, the observed response to selective harvest of MSW salmon is less than expected. Other researchers or managers, particularly those more closely associated with these stocks, may have a different perception. If so, they should evaluate alternative causes for the change before simply attributing it to direct selection of fisheries since several plausible reasons have been presented why a life-history trait, such as age at maturity, may not respond rapidly to selective fishing. The impact of intensive fisheries is likely mediated by reductions in juvenile population densities. Further, it has been suggested that the freshwater environment for juveniles directly affects age at maturity and fecundity in Atlantic (Thorpe et al. 1984) and Pacific salmon (Ivankov 1983). Excessive fishing obviously can reduce future yields through reduced spawning abundances (Chadwick 1985) and/or changes in parr maturity patterns (Caswell et al. 1984; Myers 1984) but these responses may not involve genetic change in the populations. I submit that a fishery is unlikely to exert selection pressures strongly, directionally, and consistently enough to impose permanent loss of yield by selection for early maturity. Life-history evolution and production in anadromous salmonids with periods of prolonged freshwater residence are hypothesized to be most strongly determined by environmental influences during the juvenile phase in freshwater. Given the consequences of the alternative hypotheses on conservation of Atlantic salmon, however, studies to evaluate environmental and genetic determinants of age at maturity in natural populations should be strongly encouraged.

Acknowledgments

This paper follows from a workshop synthesis session on genetic aspects of size and age at maturity of Atlantic salmon; R. Myers, G. Naevdal, and J. Bailey contributed to this session and to ideas developed in this paper. Reviews by R. L. Saunders, W. K. Hershberger, and J. Bailey assisted in revising an earlier draft, their help is gratefully acknowledged.

References

ALEXANDERSDOTTER, M., AND O. A. MATHISEN. 1982. Changes in SE Alaska pink salmon (*Oncorhynchus gorbuscha*) populations. 1914–1960. FRI-UW-8212: 55 p. School of Fisheries, University of Washington, Seattle, WA.

ALLEN, K. R., R. L. SAUNDERS, AND P. F. ELSON. 1972. Marine growth of Atlantic salmon (*Salmo salar*) in the northwest Atlantic. J. Fish. Res. Board Can. 29: 1373–1380.

ALLENDORF, F. W., AND G. H. THORGAARD. 1984. Tetraploidy and the evolution of Salmonid fishes, p. 1–53. *In* B. J. Turner [ed.] Evolutionary genetics of fishes. Plenum Press, New York, NY.

ALM, G. 1959. Connection between maturity, size and age in fishes. Rep. Inst. Freshwater Res., Drottningholm 40: 1–145.

BRYANT, P. J., AND P. SIMPSON. 1984. Intrinsic and extrinsic control of growth in developing organs. Quart. Rev. Biol. 59: 387–415.

CASWELL, H. 1983. Phenotypic plasticity in life-history traits: demographic effects and evolutionary consequences. Am. Zool. 23: 35–46.

CASWELL, H., R. J. NAIMAN, AND R. MORIN. 1984. Evaluating the consequences of reproduction in complex salmonid life cycles. Aquaculture 43: 123–134.

CHADWICK, E. M. P. 1985. The influence of spawning stock on production and yield of Atlantic salmon, *Salmon salar* L., in Canadian rivers. Aquaculture and Fish. Man. 1: 111–119.

CHADWICK, E. M., R. G. RANDALL, AND C. E. LÉGER. 1986. Ovarian development of Atlantic salmon smolts (*Salmo salar*) and age at first maturity, p. 15–23. *In* D. J. Meerburg [ed.] Salmonid age at maturity. Can. Spec. Publ. Fish. Aquat. Sci. 89.

FALCONER, D. S. 1981. Introduction to quantitative genetics. 2nd ed., Longman Group Ltd, Essex, U.K. 340 p.

GARDNER, M. L. G. 1976. A review of factors which may influence the sea-age and maturation of Atlantic salmon *Salmo salar* L. J. Fish Biol. 9: 289–327.

GJEDREM, T. 1985. Genetic variation in age at maturity and its relation to growth rate, p. 52–61. *In* R. N. Iwamoto and S. Sower [ed.] Salmonid reproduction. Washington Sea Grant Program, University of Washington, Seattle, WA.

GJERDE, B. 1984. Response to individual selection for age at sexual maturity in Atlantic salmon. Aquaculture 38: 229–240.

GJERDE, B., AND T. REFSTIE. 1984. Complete diallel cross between five strains of Atlantic salmon. Livestock Prod. Sci. 11: 207–226.

GLEBE, B. D., AND R. L. SAUNDERS. 1986. Genetic factors in sexual maturity of cultured Atlantic salmon (*Salmo salar*) parr and adults reared in sea cages, p. 24–29. *In* D. J. Meerburg [ed.] Salmonid age at maturity. Can. Spec. Publ. Fish. Aquat. Sci. 89.

GLEBE, B. D., T. D. APPY, AND R. L. SAUNDERS. 1979. Variation in Atlantic salmon (*Salmo salar*) reproductive traits and their implications in breeding programs. I.C.E.S. C.M.1979/M: 23. 11 p.

GOULD, S. J., AND R. C. LEWONTIN. 1979. The spandrels of San Marco and the Panglossian paradigm: a critique of the adaptationist programme. Proc. R. Soc. London B 205: 581–598.

HEALEY, M. C. 1986. Optimum size and age at maturity in Pacific salmon and effects of size-selective fisheries, p. 39–52. *In* D. J. Meerburg [ed.] Salmonid age at maturity. Can. Spec. Publ. Fish. Aquat. Sci. 89.

HEALEY, M. C., AND W. R. HEARD. 1984. Inter- and intrapopulation variations in the fecundity of chinook salmon (*Oncorhynchus tshawytscha*) and its relevance to life history theory. Can. J. Fish. Aquat. Sci. 41: 476–483.

IVANKOV, V. N. 1983. Causes of variation in fecundity and age at sexual maturation in monocylcic fishes with examples from salmon, Genus *Oncorhynchus*. J. Ichthyol. 23: 84–92.

JONSSON, B., AND K. HINDAR. 1982. Reproductive strategy of dwarf and normal Arctic char (*Salvelinus alpinus*) from Vangsvatnet Lake, western Norway. Can. J. Fish. Aquat. Sci. 39: 1404–1413.

JONSSON, B., K. HINDAR, AND T. G. NORTHCOTE. 1984. Optimal age at maturity of sympatric and experimentally allopatric cutthroat trout and Dolly Varden charr. Oecologia (Berlin) 61: 319–325.

KALLMAN, K. G., AND M. P. SCHREIBMAN. 1973. A sex-linked gene controlling gonadotrop differentiation and its significance in determining the age-at-maturation and size of the Platyfish, *Xiphophorus maculatus*. Gen. Comp. Endo crinol. 21:287–304.

KEMPTHORNE, O. 1983. Evaluation of current population genetics theory. Am. Zool. 23: 111–121.

KINGHORN, B. P. 1983. A review of quantitative genetics in fish breeding. Aquaculture 31: 283–304.

LANDE, R. 1982. A quantitative genetic theory of life history evolution. Ecology 63: 607–615.

MCKENZIE, W. D. JR., D. CREWS, K. D. KALLMAN, D. POLICANSKY, AND J. J. SOHN. 1983. Age, weight and the genetics of sexual maturation in the Platyfish, *Xiphophorus maculatus*. Copeia 1983: 770–774.

MYERS, R. A. 1984. Demographic consequences of precocious maturation of Atlantic salmon (*Salmo salar*). Can. J. Fish. Aquat. Sci. 41: 1349–1353.

MYERS, R. A., J. A. HUTCHINGS, AND R. J. GIBSON. 1985. Variation in precocious maturation within and among populations of Atlantic salmon. I.C.E.S. C.M. 1985/M:9. 20 p.

NAEVDAL, G. 1983. Genetic factors in connection with age at maturation. Aquaculture 33: 97–106.

NAEVDAL, G., M. HOLM, O. INGEBRIGTSEN, AND D. MOLLER. 1978. Variation in age at first spawning in Atlantic salmon (*Salmo salar*). J. Fish. Res. Board Can. 35: 145–147.

NETBOY, A. 1968. The Atlantic Salmon, a vanishing species? p. 345–378. Houghton Mufflin Co, Boston, MA.

NORDENG, H. 1983. Solution to the 'char problem' based on Arctic char (*Salvelinus aplinus*) in Norway. Can. J. Fish. Aquat. Sci. 40: 1372–1387.

PALOHEIMO, J. E., AND P. F. ELSON. 1974. Reduction of Atlantic salmon (*Salmo salar*) catches in Canada attributed to the Greenland fishery. J. Fish. Res. Board Can. 31: 1467−1480.

RANDALL, R. G., J. E. THORPE, R. J. GIBSON, AND D. REDDIN. 1986. Biological factors affecting age at maturity in Atlantic salmon (*Salmo salar*), p. 90−96. *In* D. J. Meerburg [ed.] Salmonid age at maturity. Can. Spec. Publ. Fish. Aquat. Sci. 89.

REZNICK, D. 1985. Costs of reproduction: an evaluation of the empirical evidence. Oikos 44: 257−267.

RICKER, W. E. 1972. Hereditary and environmental factors affecting certain salmonid populations, p. 19−169. *In* R. C. Simon and P. A. Larkin [ed.] The stock concept in Pacific salmon. H. R. MacMillan Lectures in Fisheries, University of British Columbia, Vancouver, B.C.

1981 Changes in the average size and average age of Pacific salmon. Can. J. Fish. Aquat. Sci. 38: 1636−1656.

RITTER, J. A., G. J. FARMER, R. K. MISRA, T. R. GOFF, J. K. BAILEY, AND E. T. BAUM. 1986. Parental influences and smolt size and sex ratio effects on sea age at first maturity of Atlantic salmon (*Salmo salar*), p. 30−38. *In* D. J. Meerburg [ed.] Can. Spec. Publ. Fish. Aquat. Sci. 89.

ROSE, M. R. 1983. Theories of life-history evolution. Am. Zool. 23: 15−23.

SAUNDERS, R. L. 1969. Contributions of salmon from the Northwest Miramichi River, New Brunswick, to various fisheries. J. Fish. Res. Board Can. 26: 269−278.

1981. Atlantic salmon (*Salmo salar*) stocks and management implications in Canadian Atlantic provinces and New England, U.S.A. Can. J. Fish. Aquat. Sci. 38: 1612−1625.

1986. The scientific and management implications of age and size at maturity in Atlantic salmon (*Salmo salar*), p. 3−6. *In* D. J. Meerburg [ed.] Salmonid age at maturity. Can. Spec. Publ. Fish. Aquat. Sci. 89.

SCARNECCHIA, D. L. 1983. Age of sexual maturity in Icelandic stocks of Atlantic salmon (Salmo salar). Can. J. Fish. Aquat. Sci. 40: 1456−1468.

SCHAFFER, W. M. 1974. Selection for optimum life histories: the effects of age structure. Ecology 55: 291−303.

SCHAFFER, W. M., AND P. F. ELSON . 1975. The adaptive significance of variations in life history among local populations of Atlantic salmon in North America. Ecology 56: 577−590.

SERVICE, P. M., AND M. R. ROSE. 1985. Genetic covariance among life-history components: the effect of novel environments. Evolution 39: 943−945.

SMITH-GILL, S. J. 1983. Developmental plasticity: developmental conversions versus phenotypic modulation. Am. Zool. 23: 47−55.

STEARNS, S. C. 1983. The evolution of life-history traits in Mosquitofish since their introduction to Hawaii in 1905: rates of evolution, heritabilities, and developmental plasticity. Am. Zool. 23: 65−75.

1984. How much of the phenotype is necessary to understand evolution at the level of the gene?, p. 33−45. *In* K. Wohrmann and V. Loeschcke [ed.] Population biology and evolution. Springer-Verlag, Berlin Heidelburg.

STEARNS, S. C., AND R. E. CRANDALL. 1984. Plasticity for age and size at sexual maturity: a life-history response to unavoidable stress, p. 13−33. *In* G. W. Potts and R. J. Wootton [ed.] Fish reproduction: strategies and tactics. Academic Press Inc. Lond. Ltd, London, U.K.

SUTTERLIN, A. M., AND D. MACLEAN. 1984. Age at first maturity and the early expression of oocyte recruitment processes in two forms of Atlantic salmon (*Salmo salar*) and their hybrids. Can. J. Fish. Aquat. Sci. 41: 1139−1149.

SYMONS, P. E. K. 1979. Estimated escapement of Atlantic salmon (*Salmo salar*) for maximum smolt production in rivers of different productivity. J. Fish. Res. Board Can. 36: 132−140.

THORPE, J. E. 1986. Age at first maturity in Atlantic salmon, *Salmo salar*: freshwater period influences and conflicts with smolting, p. 7−14. *In* D. J. Meerburg [ed.] Salmonid age at maturity. Can. Spec. Publ. Fish. Aquat. Sci. 89.

THORPE, J. E., M. S. MILES, AND D. S. KEAY. 1984. Developmental rate, fecundity and egg size in Atlantic salmon, *Salmo salar* L. Aquaculture 43: 289−305.

THORPE, J. E., R. I. G. MORGAN, C. TALBOT, AND M. S. MILES. 1983. Inheritance of developmental rates in Atlantic salmon, *Salmo salar* L. Aquaculture 33: 119−128.

TODD, I. ST. P., AND P. A. LARKIN. 1971. Gillnet selectivity on sockeye (*Oncorhynchus nerka*) and pink salmon (*O. gorbuscha*) of the Skeena River system, British Columbia. J. Fish. Res. Board Can. 28: 821−842.

TUOMI, J., T. HAKALA, AND E. HAUKIOJA. 1983. Alternative concepts of reproductive effort, costs of reproduction, and selection in life-history evolution. Am. Zool. 23: 25−34.

VAN DEN BERGHE, E. P., AND M. R. GROSS. 1984. Female size and nest depth in coho salmon (*Oncorhynchus kisutch*). Can. J. Fish. Aquat. Sci. 41: 204−206.

VAN VLECK, L. D. 1972. Estimation of heritability of threshold characters. J. Dairy Sci. 55: 218−225.

Implications of Varying the Sea Age at Maturity of Atlantic Salmon (*Salmo salar*) on Yield to the Fisheries

T. R. Porter

Fisheries Research Branch, Department of Fisheries and Oceans
P.O. Box 5667, St. John's Nfld. A1C 5X1

M. C. Healey

Fisheries Research Branch, Department of Fisheries and Oceans, Pacific Biological Station
P.O. Drawer 100, Nanaimo, B.C. V9R 5K6

M. F. O'Connell

Fisheries Research Branch, Department of Fisheries and Oceans
P.O. Box 5667, St. John's Nfld. A1C 5X1

with E. T. Baum

Atlantic Sea Run Salmon Commission
P.O. Box 1298, Bangor, ME, USA 04401

A. T. Bielak

Atlantic Salmon Federation
1435 Rue Saint Alexandre, Suite 1030, Montreal, Que. H3A 2GH

Y. Côté

Ministère du Loisir, de la Chasse et de la Pêche, Direction générale de la faune,
Direction de la faune aquatique, Service des espéces d'eau froide
150, boul. St.Cyrille est, 6e étage, Québec, Qué. G1R 4Y1

Abstract

PORTER, T. R., M. C. HEALEY, AND M. F. O'CONNELL (WITH E. T. BAUM, A. T. BIELAK, AND Y. CÔTÉ). 1986. Implications of varying the sea age at maturity of Atlantic salmon (*Salmo salar*) on yield to the fisheries, p. 110–117. *In* D. J. Meerburg [ed.] Salmonid age at maturity. Can. Spec. Publ. Fish. Aquat. Sci. 89.

Many spawning populations of Atlantic salmon (*Salmo salar*) have declined in size in recent years. Concurrent with this decline there have been marked decreases in mean sea age and body size at maturity. Users and fisheries managers are concerned about the possible impacts of younger age and smaller size at maturity on yield to the fisheries. A fixed-recruitment model was used to compare the yield in numbers and weight of salmon to the fisheries of spawning stocks of different sea ages. The projections indicate a substantial decrease in potential yield (kg) to the commercial fisheries with decrease in sea age, but only a small change in numbers of fish. In the recreational fishery a decrease in sea age would result in an increase in yield in numbers of fish, but a decline in weight. Recommendations for management and future research are presented.

Résumé

PORTER, T. R., M. C. HEALEY, AND M. F. O'CONNELL (WITH E. T. BAUM, A. T. BIELAK, AND Y. CÔTÉ). 1986. Implications of varying the sea age at maturity of Atlantic salmon (*Salmo salar*) on yield to the fisheries, p. 110–117. *In* D. J. Meerburg [ed.] Salmonid age at maturity. Can. Spec. Publ. Fish. Aquat. Sci. 89.

Un grand nombre de populations reproductrices de saumon de l'Atlantique (*Salmo salar*) ont connu une baisse au cours des dernières années. En même temps que cette diminution, il y a eu une baisse sensible de l'âge moyen en mer et de la taille du corps à la maturité. Les utilisateurs et les gestionnaires des pêches sont préoccupés des répercussions que peuvent avoir un âge plus jeune et une taille plus petite à la maturité sur le rendement des pêches. On s'est servi d'un modèle de recrutement fixe afin de comparer le rendement (nombre et poids) pour la pêche des stocks reproducteurs ayant des âges différents en mer. Les prévisions indiquent une diminution importante du rendement potentiel (kg) des pêches commerciales de même qu'une diminution de l'âge en mer, mais seulement un faible changement dans le nombre de poissons. En ce qui concerne la pêche sportive, une diminution de l'âge en mer amènerait une augmentation du rendement pour ce qui est du nombre de poissons, mais une baisse de poids. On présente les recommandations concernant la gestion et les recherches futures.

Introduction

Self-sustaining populations of Atlantic salmon (*Salmo salar*) in the northwest Atlantic Ocean are distributed from Maine northward to northern Quebec (Fig. 1). Throughout the species range there is considerable between-river variation in the proportion of the adult population which matures after one, two, or three years at sea. Generally, stocks can be categorized into three types. Type I stocks consist of individuals that mature after one-sea-winter (1SW) as grilse.

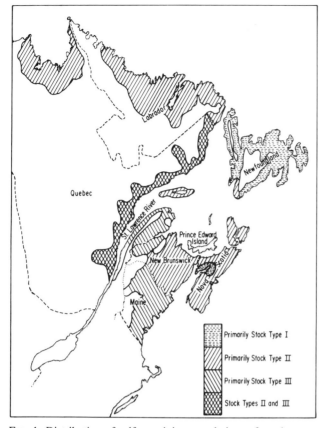

FIG. 1. Distribution of self-sustaining populations of anadromous Atlantic salmon in the Northwest Atlantic showing a generalized grouping of stock Types. Stock Type 1 is comprised of stocks in which the spawning populations are 1SW salmon (grilse). Stock Type II represents stocks in which the spawning populations consist of 1SW and 2SW salmon. In stock Type III the spawning population consists of 1SW, 2SW, and 3SW salmon. It should be noted that within each stock type area shown on the map, there may be a few stocks which belong to another stock type.

(The terminology we use to describe life stages is that recommended by Allan and Ritter (1977)). The proportion of female grilse in Type I stocks is usually greater than 0.60. Type II stocks have some individuals maturing as grilse and others that mature after two-sea-winters (2SW). Type III stocks have some individuals that mature at each of the three sea ages: grilse, 2SW, and three-sea-winter (3SW). Grilse in stock Types II and III generally have a low proportion of females (<0.30); whereas 2SW and 3SW salmon are predominantly females (>0.50). Previous spawners generally occur in all stock Types and sea ages. The proportion of previous spawners varies among stocks and annually; however, it is usually a low percentage (<10%) of the total spawning population. Each of the stock types tends to dominate in a particular geographical area (Fig. 1). Stock Type I predominates in Newfoundland; stock Type II in Nova Scotia, most of New Brunswick, and Labrador and northern Quebec; and stock Type III in Maine, Gaspé and Restigouche area. The Quebec north shore of the St. Lawrence is a mixture of stock Types II and III.

The Atlantic salmon makes an important contribution to the commercial, recreational, and native food fisheries in the northwest Atlantic (Anon. 1982). The importance of each type of fishery varies between areas. The average harvest by the commercial fisheries in Canada, 1980–84, was 518 700 Atlantic salmon (1654 t). During the same period

TABLE 1. Parameter values used in calculation of potential yield per 10 000 smolts for Atlantic salmon populations of different sea age structures. These are representative natural stock compositions.

Parameter inputs	Sea age	Stock Type		
		I	II	III
Proportion of spawners	1	1.0[a]	0.74[f]	0.39[b]
	2	0.0	0.26[f]	0.45[b]
	3	0.0	0.0	0.16[b]
Proportion female	1	0.74[a]	0.24[f]	0.02[b]
	2	—	0.86[f]	0.54[b]
	3	—	—	0.76[b]
$\bar{x}$ Weight (kg)	1	1.6[a]	1.6[f]	1.5[g]
	2	—	4.5[f]	4.8[g]
	3	—	—	9.2[g]
Eggs/kg	1	2106[b]	1764[f]	2246[h]
	2	—	1764[f]	1638[h]
	3	—	—	1341[h]
Natural mortality rate[c,j]	1	0.78	0.78	0.78
	2	—	0.12	0.12
	3	—	—	0.12
Commercial fishing mortality rate[c,j]	1	0.857[d]	0.421[d]	0.520[d]
	2	—	0.90	0.69
	3	—	—	0.90
Angling mortality rate[e,j]	1	0.25	0.25	0.25
	2	—	0.25	0.25
	3	—	—	0.25
Egg-to-smolt survival		0.017[a]	0.017[a]	0.032[i]

[a]Chadwick (1982a, 1982b) based on mean smolt age 3.9 for Atlantic salmon from Western Arm Brook, Nfld.
[b]Randall (1984) data for Atlantic salmon from Restigouche River.
[c]See Methods section.
[d]Adjusted to balance model.
[e]Assumed value.
[f]Randall and Chadwick (1983) data for Atlantic salmon from Miramichi River.
[g]Peppar (1983) for Atlantic salmon from Restigouche River.
[h]Calculated from eggs/female in Randall (1984) and mean weights from Peppar (1983) for Atlantic salmon from Restigouche River.
[i]Symons (1979) for smolt age 3+.
[j]Natural and fishing mortality rates proceed in sequence.

about 412 t of North American origin Atlantic salmon were caught annually at West Greenland (Anon. 1985). There was no commercial Atlantic salmon fishery in the United States of America. Although both multi-sea-winter (MSW) and 1SW salmon are harvested in the Canadian commercial fisheries, the MSW salmon are more highly sought because these receive a higher price per kg and the yield in weight is greater than for 1SW salmon (Gardner 1976).

The average annual recreational catch of Atlantic salmon (1980–84) was 93 700 fish (237 t). Size of the Atlantic salmon is not as economically important in the recreational fishery as in the commercial fishery; but anglers tend to prefer the larger Atlantic salmon. The larger fish are the main attraction for some commercial sport fishing camps.

Food fisheries for Atlantic salmon are pursued by some Natives (Indian or Inuit) in New Brunswick, Nova Scotia,

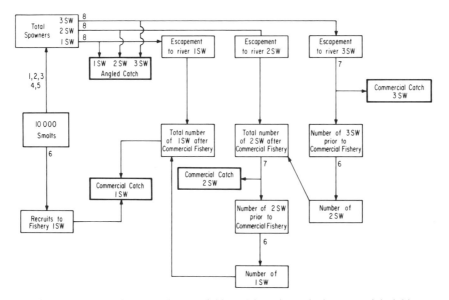

FIG. 2. Schematic of fixed-recruitment yield model used to calculate potential yield per 10 000 smolts for Atlantic salmon populations of different sea age structures. The direction of the arrows show the pathway followed during the execution of the model which is generally in the opposite direction to production flow. Parameter values are in Tables 1 and 3. The numbers on the arrows refer to the location of entry of the following input parameters: (1) Proportion of the spawning population at each sea age; (2) Proportion of females at each sea age; (3) Average weight of females at each sea age; (4) Eggs per kg of females at each sea age; (5) Egg-to-smolt survival; (6) Natural mortality rate during each year at sea; (7) Commercial fishing mortality rate at each sea age; (8) Angling mortality rate; (9) Egg-to-smolt survival at each sea age.

and Québec. Catch records for the food fisheries are incomplete. Although the total harvest by the food fisheries is small in relation to the commercial and sport fisheries, it represents a significant proportion of the escapement to some rivers.

Since the late 1950s, many spawning populations of MSW salmon have been observed to decline in abundance, particularly those in the Restigouche River (Chadwick and Randall 1983), the Miramichi River (Ruggles and Turner 1973; Randall and Chadwick 1983), the Gaspé rivers (Côté, unpublished data), the Matamek River (Gibson 1978), and the rivers on the west coast of Newfoundland (Chadwick et al. 1978). Concurrent with these declines in abundance, there has been an increase in the proportion of grilse in the spawning populations in some rivers as evident from the enumeration of Atlantic salmon at the Millbank trap on the Miramichi River (Ruggles and Turner 1973; Randall et al. 1985) and angling data for rivers on the southwest coast of Newfoundland (Chadwick et al. 1978).

The present trend in Atlantic salmon fisheries management is toward more intensive management of stocks or stock complexes in individual rivers, with effort directed to restoring stock abundance and increasing the proportion of MSW salmon. Size-selective fisheries may affect the size and age composition of Atlantic salmon stocks systematically similar to the observed changes in age of Pacific salmon (Ricker 1981). Of particular interest are the implications of varying the sea age at maturity of Atlantic salmon in the spawning population on yield to the fisheries. However, very little information on this subject is available in the published literature. In this paper, we compare, by a fixed-recruitment model, the yield in numbers and weight of Atlantic salmon to the fisheries for the three stock types identified above, and evaluate the effects of systematically

changing the sea age composition of a spawning population. We discuss the results as they pertain to yields to the recreational and commercial fisheries; and we provide recommendations for further fisheries management and research.

Methods

We used a fixed-recruitment model to calculate potential yields in numbers and weight (kg) per 10 000 smolts for each stock type (defined above). Input parameters include (1) the proportion of the spawning population at each sea age; (2) the proportion of the spawning population at each sea age which is female; (3) the average weight of individuals at each sea age; (4) the number of eggs per kg of body weight produced by females at each sea age; (5) the natural mortality rate from one sea age to the next; (6) the commercial fishing mortality rate at sea ages 2 and 3; (7) the angling mortality rate at each sea age; (8) the average egg-to-smolt survival rate. Typical population parameter values which have previously been observed for each stock type were used in the analysis (Table 1). Where possible, parameter values from published data were used. Natural mortality rate for 1SW salmon (smolt to 12.5 months) was developed using tagging data for Sand Hill River, 1969–71 (Pratt et al. 1974), and applying a non-catch fishing mortality rate of 0.10 for all fisheries, a tag reporting rate of 0.84, and an instantaneous mortality (M) rate of 0.01 per month for salmon older than 12.5 months. The non-catch fishing mortality rate of 0.10 is the low value of the range 0.10–0.3 adopted by the ICES Working Group on North Atlantic Salmon to describe the fishery at West Greenland (Anon. 1980). The tag reporting rate of 0.84 is the same as the rate used by Jensen (1980) to describe the reporting rate at West Greenland during the 1972 fishery. $M = 0.01$ is the upper rate of the range 0.005−0.01 by Doubleday et al. (1979) for salmon with sea age 14−24 months. Fishing mortality rate for maturing 2SW salmon was calculated using tagging data from Pratt et al. (1974) and natural mortality rates described above. The fishing mortality rate on maturing 3SW salmon was assumed to be the same as the rate on 2SW salmon. The fishing mortality rate for non-maturing 2SW and 3SW salmon was assumed to be 0.40. In this model the commercial fishing mortality on 1SW salmon is used to balance the stock and recruitment equation. Thus the parameter value for fishing mortality rate on 1SW salmon is calculated in the model. Sources of other parameter values are given in the footnotes to Table 1. Previous spawners were excluded because they represent only a small component of most populations and there is uncertainty as the their population dynamics. The angling catch and escapement to the river is predetermined by the spawning requirements. Once the population parameters are entered, the model proceeds with the following calculations:

1 From the proportion of each sea age in the spawning population, the proportion of females at each sea age, the average weight of females, the number of eggs per kg at each sea age, and the egg-to-smolt survival, the model calculates the total number of spawners of each sea age class required to produce 10 000 smolts.

2 Beginning with the oldest age in the spawning population, the model uses the number of spawners in this sea age class and the angling mortality rate to calculate the escapement of fish of that sea age to the river and the number captured by anglers. The model then uses the escapement of this sea age class and the commercial fishing mortality rate to calculate the numbers at this sea age prior to commercial fishing and the commercial catch of this sea age class. Finally the model uses the natural mortality rate to calculate the numbers which entered this sea age class from the next youngest sea age class.

3 The model then moves to the spawning population of the next youngest sea age class and repeats these calculations, except that the recruits to the next older sea age class as calculated in (2) are added to the escapement of this sea age class before commercial catch and natural mortality calculations are made.

4 The model proceeds back through the sea age classes in this way until the youngest sea age class is reached. Calculations for the youngest sea age class in the population are essentially the same as for other sea age classes except that commercial catch is calculated as the difference between (smolts × first ocean-year survival) and (escapement plus recruits to second sea winter). The 1SW fishing mortality rate is then calculated as: (catch at 1SW)/(smolts × first ocean-year survival) and thus providing a balanced model.

5 Catch in weight is calculated as catch in numbers times mean weight at age. A schematic of the model is presented in Fig. 2. Note that the model is a fixed-recruitment model (10 000 smolts); also it is assumed that natural and fishing mortalities are sequential rather than concurrent.

To explore the effects on yield of systematic changes in sea age composition of the spawning populations, yield in numbers and weight were calculated for seven hypothet-

TABLE 2. Predicted yields per 10 000 smolts and spawning populations required to produce 10 000 smolts based on parameter values in Table 1.

Output value	Sea age	Stock Type		
		I	II	III
Total spawners	1	236	191	35
	2	0	67	41
	3	0	0	15
	All	236	258	91
Commercial catch (no.)	1	1885	927	1145
	2	0	806	612
	3	0	0	175
	All	1885	1733	1932
Commercial catch (kg)	1	3016	1483	1717
	2	0	3628	2938
	3	0	0	1606
	All	3016	5111	6261
Angling catch (no.)	1	79	64	12
	2	0	22	14
	3	0	0	5
	All	79	86	31
Angling catch (kg)	1	126	102	18
	2	0	101	65
	3	0	0	45
	All	126	203	128
Total production (no.)	All	1964	1819	1963
(kg)	All	3142	5314	6389
$\bar{x}$ Sea age of spawners		1	1.26	1.77
$\bar{x}$ Sea age of female spawners		1	1.56	2.29

ical stocks which differ in age composition of spawners (Table 3). The results were used for qualitative comparisons of yield from each stock type. Strict quantitative comparisons were not possible because of the static nature of our model, uncertainties in parameter values, and uncertainty as to the effect that changing the sea age composition in the spawning population would have on the sea age composition of progeny and subsequent recruitment to the fisheries.

Results and Discussion

The projected yields per 10 000 smolts and number of spawners required to produce 10 000 smolts for each of the three stock types are shown in Table 2. The numbers of Atlantic salmon projected to be caught in the commercial fishery do not vary a great deal among stock types. This is due to the low natural mortality during the salmon's second and third year at sea. However, the yields in weight in the commercial catch increased by about twice from stock Type I to stock Type III. Angling yields varied in both numbers and weight by nearly 2×. Angling yield in weight showed no trend with increasing sea age in the spawning population, but yield in numbers declined.

The yield projections (Table 4), from the assumed parameter values (Table 3) for the seven hypothetical stocks, show similar results to the output for the "real" stocks (Table 2). The commercial catch in numbers does not vary much, but the yield in weight increases as the sea age at maturity increases. Angling catch in numbers decreases dramatically

TABLE 3. Parameter values used in calculating potential yield per 10 000 smolts for Atlantic salmon populations of different hypothetical sea age stuctures. The sea age structures are chosen to permit exploration of effects of changing $\bar{x}$ age at maturity on yield.

Parameter inputs	Sea age	Hypothetical stocks						
		1	2	3	4	5	6	7
Proportion of spawners	1	1.0	0.0	0.0	0.6	0.5	0.2	0.0
	2	0.0	1.0	0.0	0.4	0.3	0.6	0.6
	3	0.0	0.0	1.0	0.0	0.2	0.2	0.4
Proportion female	1	0.60	—	—	0.2	0.2	0.2	—
	2	—	0.60	—	0.8	0.6	0.6	0.6
	3	—	—	0.60	—	0.8	0.8	0.8
$\bar{x}$ Weight (kg)	1	1.5	1.5	1.5	1.5	1.5	1.5	—
	2	—	4.5	4.5	4.5	4.5	4.5	4.5
	3	—	—	8.5	—	8.5	8.5	8.5
Eggs/kg	1	2000	—	—	2000	2000	2000	—
	2	—	1700	—	1700	1700	1700	1700
	3	—	—	1400	—	1400	1400	1400
Natural mortality rate	1	0.78	0.78	0.78	0.78	0.78	0.78	0.78
	2	—	0.12	0.12	0.12	0.12	0.12	0.12
	3	—	—	0.12	—	0.12	0.12	0.12
Commercial fishing mortality rate	1	0.832	0.75	0.09	0.77	0.50	0.57	0.50
	2	—	0.70	0.70	0.70	0.70	0.70	0.70
	3	—	—	0.80	—	0.80	0.80	0.80
Angling mortality rate	1	0.25	—	—	0.25	0.25	0.25	0.25
	2	—	0.25	—	0.25	0.25	0.25	0.25
	3	—	—	0.25	—	0.25	0.25	0.25
Egg−smolt survival		0.020	0.020	0.020	0.020	0.020	0.020	0.020

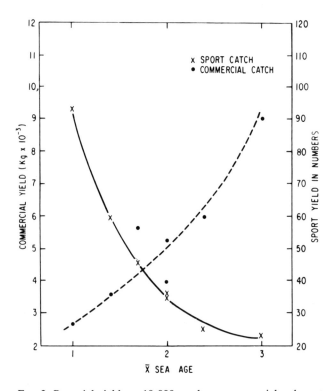

FIG. 3. Potential yield per 10 000 smolts to commercial and sport fisheries in relation to sea age of spawners.

as sea age at maturity increases while yield in weight increases a small amount.

It is apparent from the above yield projections (Tables 2 and 4) that the model is sensitive to the sea age and sex composition of the spawning population. The trends of increasing commercial yield in kg and decrease in angling yield with sea age are illustrated by plots of yield against mean sea age in the spawning population (Fig. 3).

The conclusion apparent from these estimates is that any reduction in sea age at maturity, whether fishery induced or otherwise, could have rather serious consequences for potential commercial yield in weight. This result is because biomass accumulated as a result of rapid growth of nonmaturing salmon far exceeds that lost through natural mortality during second and third years at sea.

The implications of varying the sea age at maturity on the recreational fishery are more complex and whether or not it is a negative or positive influence will depend largely on the preferences of anglers on specific rivers and federal-provincial regulations put in place to harvest these fish. Assuming no change in the exploitation by the commercial fishery, a reduction in the sea age at maturation will increase the numbers, but decrease the size of fish available to the anglers. This may be beneficial for some anglers, but for other anglers and sport fishing camp operators reductions in size of fish may be undesirable. It should be pointed out that this model is developed around a no-surplus/wastage management strategy, where all surplus salmon are harvested by

TABLE 4. Predicted yields per 10 000 smolts and spawning populations required to produce 10 000 smolts from parameter values in Table 3.

Output value	Sea age	Hypothetical stocks						
		1	2	3	4	5	6	7
Total spawners	1	278	0	0	107	70	21	0
	2	0	109	0	71	42	63	46
	3	0	0	70	0	28	21	30
	All	278	109	70	178	140	105	76
Commercial catch (no.)	1	1830	1650	190	1698	1094	1254	1094
	2	0	339	1238	222	624	565	681
	3	0	0	373	0	149	112	163
	All	1830	1989	1801	1920	1867	1931	1938
Commercial catch (kg)	1	2744	2474	285	2546	1641	1881	1641
	2	0	1525	5570	997	2808	2544	3064
	3	0	0	3175	0	1266	949	1382
	All	2744	3999	9030	3543	5715	5374	6087
Angling catch (no.)	1	93	0	0	36	23	7	0
	2	0	36	0	24	14	21	15
	3	0	0	23	0	9	7	10
	All	93	36	23	60	46	35	25
Angling catch (kg)	1	139	0	0	53	35	10	0
	2	0	163	0	107	63	94	69
	3	0	0	198	0	79	59	86
	All	139	163	198	160	177	163	155
Total production (no.)		1923	2025	1824	1980	1913	1966	1963
(kg)	All	2883	4162	9228	3703	5892	5537	6242
$\bar{x}$ Sea age of spawners		1.0	2.0	3.0	1.4	1.7	2.0	2.4
$\bar{x}$ Sea age of female spawners		1.0	2.0	3.0	1.7	2.1	2.2	2.5

the commercial fisheries prior to the angling fishery. Alternate management strategies which provide higher yields in the conventional angling fisheries would probably result in surplus spawning escapements since the conventional angling fishery is a relatively ineffieicnt method of harvesting salmon. Under this scenario the combined total yield to all fisheries would be lower than if the surplus was harvested in a commercial fishery either at sea or in the river.

Changing the sea age at maturity may induce other changes in population parameters not considered in the above simulations, which might affect potential yield; e.g., changes in maturation as parr, age at smoltification, egg-to-smolt survival, early ocean survival, and sex composition of spawning populations. An increase in the proportion of grilse could result in an increase in early maturation of male parr (Glebe and Saunders 1986) with subsequent increase in mortality of male parr and decrease in yield (Myers 1983). In a scenario where a reduction in sea age of the spawning population is accompanied by an insufficient number of spawners to seed the river fully, there will be a subsequent reduction in parr densities. Since parr tend to grow faster at low densities and emigrate as younger smolts (Gibson 1983), there will be an overall increase in egg-to-smolt survival (Symons 1979) and subsequent increase in yield per unit of spawners. There is also evidence from hatchery sea-ranching experience that smaller younger smolts produce more MSW salmon than larger older smolts (Ritter and Newbould 1977; Bailey and Saunders 1984). To add to the complexity of understanding the implications of changing sea age at maturity, Paloheimo and Elson (1974) provide evidence that MSW salmon eggs, which are larger than

grilse eggs, have a higher survival. This impact would tend towards increasing yield in MSW populations. Available data are insufficient to include the dynamics of all these parameter values in the model.

To the knowledge of the authors, there is insufficient empirical evidence to demonstrate that the sea age composition of any wild Atlantic salmon stock (spawners plus harvest) has changed or will be changed by a fishing induced change in sea age of spawners. It has been well documented with hatchery-reared salmon that hereditary factors influence the sea age and freshwater age at maturity (Elson 1973; Piggins 1969, 1974; Gardner 1976; Sutterlin and MacLean 1984; Naevdal, unpublished data) and that the environment can influence the expression of these traits (White and Huntsman 1938; Piggins 1969, 1974; Gardner 1976; Saunders et al. 1983). Gee and Radford (1982) simulated the effects of a fishery selecting for older sea age groups on sea age at maturity for a hypothetical Atlantic salmon population with variable recruitment. It was assumed that sea age at maturity had a genetic basis (adults of a given sea age were produced in the same proportions as the fraction of the total eggs which were contributed by that sea age) and also that spawners of one sea age produced some progeny of a different sea age. The simulation was run for a period of years with zero exploitation followed by a 20-yr exploitation phase (in fresh water) then another 20 yr with no exploitation. The simulation showed that compared to the stabilized pre-exploitation population, during the exploitation phase the numbers of grilse entering the river increased, there was no significant change in numbers of 2SW salmon and numbers of 3SW salmon decreased. In the spawning escapement, the ratio of grilse to MSW salmon increased nearly six-fold over that of the pre-exploitation period. After exploitation ceased, the population returned to the pre-exploitation equilibrium. With respect to the finding that selective removal of MSW salmon resulted in an increase in the relative proportion and absolute abundance of grilse but still maintained moderate runs of MSW fish, Gee and Radford (1982) stated that the degree of differential exploitation that can be sustained without drastically reducing the MSW stock component depends on the ability of salmon of one sea age to produce progeny of another sea age. The sea age of Atlantic salmon stocks appears to be an evolutionary adaptation to freshwater and marine environmental conditions (Schaffer and Elson 1975; Power 1981; Scarnecchia 1983; Robitaille et al. 1986). Thus, it is entirely possible, as suggested by Healey (1986), that strong selective influences in the natural environment may be sufficient to counteract any selection for size or age-at-maturity imposed by selective fisheries. Atlantic salmon, which have strong homing tendencies, can be considered to have near isolated stocks and, as such, are most susceptible to loss of genetic diversity (Thorpe et al. 1981).

Management and Research Recommendations

Management

Sea age at maturation is only one of many life-history characteristics of Atlantic salmon stocks that have gone through a process of natural selection and adaptation to their freshwater and marine environments (Saunders 1981). The stability of populations and possibly their continued existence, could depnd on how fisheries are designed to maintain stock structure. It has been demonstrated above that a decrease in sea age of Atlantic salmon in the spawning population will result in a decrease in yield in weight to the commercial fisheries, and an increase in numbers of fish to the sport fishery. However, the mean weight of individual fish in the sport fishery will be reduced. The evidence available is not clear as to the effect that perturbations, such as size-selective fisheries, will have on changing the age at maturity and subsequent yield. Managers should be cognizant of stock-specific characteristics such as sea age at maturity, and ensure that these are represented in the spawning population. With respect to sea age at maturity we recommend that:

1 a target egg deposition by each sea age be established for each stock. The proportional contribution should be determined based on historical sea age composition of the spawning stock. The fisheries should be managed to ensure that these target egg depositions are met each year;

2 where stocks are to be restored, spawning populations that have stock structure similar to the original population should be used as donor stock. This would ensure greatest probability of restoration success within the shortest time frame and will safeguard against introgression.

Research

It was evident at the workshop that there is a serious lack of time series of information on characteristics of individual wild stocks. The sea age at maturation has obviously changed in some spawning populations, but there are cur-

rently no data sufficient to determine possible changes in the sea age composition of the progeny and yield to the fisheries. We recommended that:

1 monitoring occur on index rivers where biological characteristics of the exploited and spawning populations are able to be measured annually, as well as smolt production and yield to the fisheries;

2 stock manipulation studies be undertaken to determine if change in sea age of parents will affect sea age at maturity of progeny. The opportunity to do this may occur in enhancement programs where a pre-determined sea age composition can be stocked in areas of rivers previously without Atlantic salmon. Subsequent monitoring of sea age composition of progeny would identify any change in sea age at maturity.

3 government agencies should compile existing data sets in a common format such that these data are comparable and ensure that they are readily accessible.

Acknowledgments

We thank Mr. R. Cutting, Dr. R. Randall, and Mr. J. Ritter for reviewing the manuscript; Mrs. K. Harding and Ms. M. Bursey for typing; and Mr. H. Mullett for drafting the figures. Special thanks is given to J. Ritter for his suggestions on calculating natural and fishing mortality rates.

References

ALLAN, I. R. H., AND J. A. RITTER. 1977. Salmonid terminology. J. Cons. Int. Explor. Mer 37: 293–299.

ANON. 1980. Report of the Working Group on North Atlantic Salmon. Int. Counc. Explor. Sea C.M.1980/M:10. 52 p.

　　　 1982. Management of the Atlantic salmon in the 1980's: A discussion paper. Department of Fisheries and Oceans, Government of Canada. 21 p.

　　　 1985. Report of meeting of Working Group on North Atlantic salmon. Int. Counc. Explor. Sea C.M.1985/Assess:11. 67 p.

BAILEY, J. K., AND R. L. SAUNDERS. 1984. Returns of three year-classes of sea-ranched Atlantic salmon of various river and strain crosses. Aquaculture 41: 259–270.

CHADWICK, E. M. P. 1982a. Dynamics of an Atlantic salmon stock (Salmo salar) in a small Newfoundland river. Ph.D. thesis, Memorial Univ. Newfoundland, St. John's, Nfld. 267 p.

　　　 1982b. Stock-recruitment relationship for Atlantic salmon (Salmo salar) in Newfoundland rivers. Can. J. Fish. Aquat. Sci. 39: 1496–1501.

CHADWICK, M., R. PORTER, AND D. REDDIN. 1978. Atlantic salmon management program, Newfoundland and Labrador, 1978. Atl. Salmon J. 1: 9–15.

CHADWICK, E. M. P., AND R. G. RANDALL. 1983. Assessment of the Restigouche River salmon stock in 1982. Canadian Atlantic Fisheries Scientific Advisory Committee Res. Doc. 83/30.

DOUBLEDAY, W. G., J. A. RITTER, AND K. U. VICKERS. 1979. Natural mortality rate estimates for North Atlantic salmon in the sea. Int. Counc. Explor. Sea C.M.1979/M:26.

ELSON, P. F. 1973. Genetic polymorphism in Northwest Miramichi salmon in relation to season of river ascent and age at maturation and its implications for management of stocks. Int. Comm. Northwest Atl. Fish. Res. Doc. 73/76. 6 p.

GARDNER, M. L. G. 1976. A review of factors which may influence the sea-age and maturation of Atlantic salmon, Salmo salar L. J. Fish. Biol. 9: 289–327.

GEE, A. S., AND P. J. RADFORD. 1982. The regulation of stock characteristics in a simulated Atlantic salmon population. Fish. res. 1: 105−116.

GIBSON, R. J. 1978. Recent changes in the population of juvenile Atlantic salmon in the Matamek River, Quebec, Canada. J. Cons. Int. Explor. Mer 38(2): 201−207.

1983. Large Atlantic salmon parr (*Salmo salar*) of a boreal river in Québec. Nat. Can. (Que.) 110: 135−141.

GLEBE, B. D., AND R. L. SAUNDERS. 1986. Genetic factors in sexual maturity of cultured Atlantic salmon (*Salmo salar*) parr and adults reared in sea cages, p. 24−29. *In* D. J. Meerburg [ed.] Salmonid age at maturity. Can. Spec. Publ. Fish. Aquat. Sci. 89.

HEALEY, M. C. 1986. Optimum size and age at maturity in Pacific salmon and effects of size-selective fisheries, p. 39−52. *In* D. J. Meerburg [ed.] Salmonid age at maturity. Can. Spec. Publ. Fish. Aquat. Sci. 89.

JENSEN, J. M. 1980. Recaptures of salmon a West Greenland tagged as smolts outside Greenland waters, p. 114−121. *In* B. B. Parrish and Sv. AA. Horsted [ed.] ICES/ICNAF Joint Investigations on North Atlantic Salmon. Rapp. P.-V. Reun. Cons. Int. Explor. Mer 176.

MYERS, R. A. 1983. Evolutionary change in the proportion of precocious parr and its effect on yield in Atlantic salmon. Int. Counc. Explor. Sea C.M.1983/M:13. 16 p.

PALOHEIMO, J. E., AND P. F. ELSON. 1974. Reduction of Atlantic salmon (*Salmo salar*) catches in Canada attributed to the Greenland fishery. J. Fish. Res. Board Can. 31: 1467−1480.

PEPPAR, J. L. 1983. Adult Atlantic salmon (*Salmo salar*) investigations, Restigouche River system, New Brunswick, 1972−80. Can. MS Rep. Fish. Aquat. Sci. 1695: 33 p.

PIGGINS, D. J. 1969. Talking points in salmonid research. Salmon Trout Mag. 185: 51−68.

1974. The results of selective breeding from known grilse and salmon parents. Annu. Rep. Salm. Res. Trust Ireland XVIII: 35−39.

POWER, G. 1981. Stock characteristics and catches of Atlantic salmon (*Salmo salar*) in Quebec, and Newfoundland and Labrador in relation to environmental variables. Can. J. Fish. Aquat. Sci. 38: 1601−1611.

PRATT, J. D., G. M. HARE, AND H. P. MURPHY. 1974. Investigations on production and harvest of an Atlantic salmon population, Sandhill River, Labrador. Resource Development Branch, St. John's, Nfld., Tech. Rep. Series No. NEW/T-74-1: 27 p.

RANDALL, R. G. 1984. Number of salmon required for spawning in the Restigouche River, N.B. Canadian Atlantic Fisheries Scientific Advisory Committee Res. Doc. 84/16: 15 p.

RANDALL, R. G., AND E. M. P. CHADWICK. 1983. Assessment of the Miramichi River salmon stock in 1982. Canadian Atlantic Fisheries Scientific Advisory Committee Res. Doc. 83/21: 24 p.

RANDALL, R. G., E. M. P. CHADWICK, AND F. J. SCHOFIELD. 1985. Status of Atlantic salmon in the Miramichi River, 1984. Canadian Atlantic Fisheries Scientific Advisory Committee Res. Doc. 85/2: 21 p.

RICKER, W. E. 1981. Changes in the average age and average size of Pacific salmon. Can. J. Fish. Aquat. Sci. 38: 1636−1656.

RITTER, J. A., AND K. NEWBOULD. 1977. Relationships of parent age and smolt age to age at first maturity of Atlantic salmon (*Salmo salar*). Int. Counc. Explor. Sea C.M.1977/M:32. 5 p.

ROBITAILLE, J. A., Y. CÔTÉ, G. SHOONER, AND G. HAYEUR. 1986. Growth and maturation patterns of Atlantic salmon, *Salmo salar*, in the Koksoak River, Ungava, Quebec, p. 62−69. *In* D. J. Meerburg [ed.] Salmonid age at maturity. Can. Spec. Publ. Fish. Aquat. Sci. 89.

RUGGLES, C. P., AND G. E. TURNER. 1973. Recent changes in stock composition of Atlantic salmon (*Salmo salar*) in the Miramichi River, New Brunswick. J. Fish. Res. Board Can. 30: 779−786.

SAUNDERS, R. L. 1981. Atlantic salmon (*Salmo salar*) stocks and management implications in the Canadian Atlantic Provinces and New England, U.S.A. Can. J. Fish. Aquat. Sci. 38: 1612−1625.

SAUNDERS, R. L., E. B. HENDERSON, B. D. GLEBE, AND E. J. LOUDENSLAGER. 1983. Evidence of a major environmental component in determination of the grilse: large salmon ratio in Atlantic salmon (*Salmo salar*). Aquaculture 33: 107−118.

SCARNECCHIA, D. L. 1983. Age at sexual maturity in Icelandic stocks of Atlantic salmon (*Salmo salar*). Can. J. Fish. Aquat. Sci. 40: 1456−1468.

SCHAFFER, W. M., AND P. F. ELSON. 1975. The adaptive significance of variations in life-history among local populations of Atlantic salmon in North America. Ecology 56: 577−590.

SUTTERLIN, A. M., AND D. MACLEAN. 1984. Age at first maturity and the early expression of oocyte reuitement processes in two forms of Atlantic salmon (*Salmo salar*) and their hybrids. Can. J. Fish. Aquat. Sci. 41: 1139−1149.

SYMONS, P. E. K. 1979. Estimated escapement of Atlantic salmon (*Salmo salar*) for maximum smolt productin in rivers of different productivity. J. Fish. Res. Board Can. 36: 132−140.

THORPE, J. E., AND J. F. KOONCE (WITH D. BORGESON, B. HENDERSON, A. LAMSA, P. S. MAITLAND, M. A. ROSS, R. C. SIMON, AND C. WALTERS). 1981. Assessing and managing man's impact on fish genetic resources. Can. J. Fish. Aquat. Sci. 38: 1899−1907.

WHITE, H. C., AND A. G. HUNTSMAN. 1938. Is local behavior in salmon heritable? J. Fish. Res. Board Can. 4: 1−18.

Appendix
List of Participants

Bailey, J. K.
North American Salmon Research Institute
St. Andrews, New Brunswick
E0G 2X0

Baum, E. T.
Atlantic Sea Run Salmon Commission
P.O. Box 1298
Bangor, MAine 04401
USA

Beacham, T.
Department of Fisheries and Oceans
Pacific Biological Station
Nanaimo, British Columbia
V9R 5K6

Bielak, A. T.
Atlantic Salmon Federation
1435, rue Saint Alexandre
Suite 1030
Montreal, Quebec
H3A 2C

Chadwick, E. M. P.
Department of Fisheries and Oceans
Gulf Region
P.O. Box 5030
Moncton, New Brunswick
E1C 9B6

Côté, Y.
Ministère des Loisirs, de la Chasse et
   de la Pêche
150, boul. St. Cyrville
Québec (Québec)
G1R 4Y1

Cutting, R.
Department of Fisheries and Oceans
Scotia-Fundy Region
P.O. Box 550
Halifax, Nova Scotia
B3J 2S7

Dempson, J. B.
Department of Fisheries and Oceans
Newfoundland Region
Northwest Atlantic Fisheries Centre
P.O. Box 5667
St. John's, Newfoundland
A1C 5X1

Farmer, G. J.
Department of Fisheries and Oceans
Scotia−Fundy Region
P.O. Box 550
Halifax, Nova Scotia
B3J 2S7

Gibson, R. J.
Department of Fisheries and Oceans
Newfoundland Region
Northwest Atlantic Fisheries Centre
P.O. Box 5667
St. John's, Newfoundland
A1C 5X1

Glebe, B. D.
The Huntsman Marine Laboratory and
Salmon Genetics Research Program
St. Andrews, New Brunswick
E0G 2X0

Healey, M. C.
Department of Fisheries and Oceans
Pacific Biological Station
Nanaimo, British Columbia
V9R 5K6

Henderson, E. B.
Department of Fisheries and Oceans
Biological Station
St. Andrews, New Brunswick
E0G 2X0

Léger, C.
Department of Fisheries and Oceans
Gulf Region
P.O. Box 5030
Moncton, New Brunswick
E1C 9B6

Meerburg, D. J.
Department of Fisheries and Oceans
200 Kent Street
Ottawa, Ontario
K1A 0E6

Myers, R. A.
Department of Fisheries and Oceans
Newfoundland Region
Northwest Atlantic Fisheries Centre
P.O. Box 5667
St. John's, Newfoundland
A1C 5X1

Naevdal, G.
Institute of Marine Research
N-5000 Bergen
Norway

O'Connell, M. F.
Department of Fisheries and Oceans
Newfoundland Region
Northwest Atlantic Fisheries Centre
P.O. Box 5667
St. John's, Newfoundland
A1C 5X1

Peterman, R.
Simon Fraser University
Burnaby, British Columbia
V5A 1S6

Porter, T. R.
Department of Fisheries and Oceans
Newfoundland Region
Northwest Atlantic Fisheries Centre
P.O. Box 5667
St. John's, Newfoundland
A1C 5X1

Power, G.
University of Waterloo
Department of Biology
Waterloo, Ontario
N2L 3G1

Randall, R. G.
Department of Fisheries and Oceans
Gulf Region
P.O. Box 5030
Moncton, New Brunswick
E1C 9B6

Reddin, D. G.
Department of Fisheries and Oceans
Newfoundland Region
Northwest Atlantic Fisheries Centre
P.O. Box 5667
St. John's, Newfoundland
A1C 5X1

Riddell, B. E.
Department of Fisheries and Oceans
Pacific Biological Station
Nanaimo, British Columbia
V9R 5K6

Ritter, J. A.
Department of Fisheries and Oceans
Scotia−Fundy Region
P.O. Box 550
Halifax, Nova Scotia
B3J 2S7

Robitaille, J. A.
Department of Fisheries and Oceans
Québec Region
901 Cap Diamant, P.O. Box 1550
Québec, Québec
G1K 7Y7

Saunders, R. L.
Department of Fisheries and Oceans
Biological Station
St. Andrews, New Brunswick
E0G 2X0

Sutterlin, A.
21 Avenue Road
Nepean, Ontario
K2G 0J4

Thorpe, J. E.
Department of Agriculture &
   Fisheries Scotland
Freshwater Fisheries Laboratory
Pitlochry, Scotland
PH165 LB